Dr Ambedkar and Democracy

Dr Ambedkar and Democracy

An Anthology

edited by

CHRISTOPHE JAFFRELOT

and

NARENDER KUMAR

OXFORD

UNIVERSITY PRESS

OXFORD

UNIVERSITY PRESS

Oxford University Press is a department of the University of Oxford.
It furthers the University's objective of excellence in research, scholarship,
and education by publishing worldwide. Oxford is a registered trademark of
Oxford University Press in the UK and in certain other countries.

Published in India by
Oxford University Press
22 Workspace, 2nd Floor, 1/22 Asaf Ali Road, New Delhi 110002, India

© Oxford University Press 2018

The moral rights of the authors have been asserted.

First Edition published in 2018
Seventh impression 2023

ISBN-13: 978-0-19-948316-7
ISBN-10: 0-19-948316-7

Typeset in Arno Pro 10.5/13
by Tranistics Data Technologies, New Delhi 110 044
Printed in India by Manipal Technologies Limited, Manipal

Contents

Foreword

The Indian Institute of Dalit Studies, New Delhi, has set up a research programme on Dr B.R. Ambedkar. Under the aegis of this programme, the Institute has brought out a few books on Dr Ambedkar; some of them have been co-published with Oxford University Press. Out of them, *B.R. Ambedkar: Perspectives on Social Exclusion and Inclusive Policies* (2009, eds, Sukhadeo Thorat and Narender Kumar) is unique in that it includes the original text of Dr Ambedkar's writings on themes of national importance and its analysis.

This volume focuses on Dr Ambedkar's thinking on democracy. The second part of the book presents the original writings of Dr Ambedkar on democracy and related issues, some of which the authors have brought together from his writings and speeches. Therefore, this compilation is useful for the readers. In the first part, the readers would find the interpretation of Dr Ambedkar's views on various aspects of democracy by two very distinguished scholars of Dr Ambedkar—Christopher Jaffrelot, and Narender Kumar. I am thankful to both of them for undertaking this exercise for the Indian Institute of Dalit Studies and Oxford University Press. I also thank Oxford University Press for undertaking the printing of this volume, and their cooperation in the publication of earlier volumes.

The book covers a number of aspects on Dr Ambedkar's views on democracy. The authors have provided a great deal of insight, particularly on four themes—the way Dr Ambedkar conceived or defined democracy, conditions for successful working of political democracy or conditions which make political democracy function better, the concept of minority or the need of minority representation, and methods of political representation for minorities.

While studying the views of Dr Ambedkar, one generally has to draw a distinction between his views on a particular theme, and the modification in the original views in the process of policy framing. Dr Ambedkar was not only a scholar but also a man of action who pursued policies with government on many issues, some of which took the shape of policy. In this process, Dr Ambedkar was required to make accommodation, as a result of which we often see a deviation from his original position.[1] However, when it comes to placing Dr Ambedkar's view on a specific issue, we need to refer to his original position. Therefore, I will follow the former in summarizing the content of the book.

On definition of democracy: Among other themes, the authors have looked at Dr Ambedkar's notion of democracy, which according to them, is different from the traditional view. In Dr Ambedkar's view, a democracy is not confined just to a form of government and state apparatus; rather it is more than a system of political governance—it embraces social governance. For Dr Ambedkar, democracy is primarily a mode of associated living with an attitude of respect and reverence towards fellowmen. Therefore, the roots of political democracy are located in social relationship among the people in a society. Political democracy thus, lives in society extending to the economic and social domain. Political democracy will be more effective if the social relations are governed by fraternity and brotherhood. It is in this context that Dr Ambedkar looked at democracy as a form and method of government whereby revolutionary changes in the economic and social life of people are brought about without bloodshed. *The ultimate principle in his view is that the democracy is self-government and that means that final decision on all matters must be made by popularly elected persons.*

On Conditions for success of Democracy: Dr Ambedkar was concerned about the successful working of political democracy, and therefore, he devoted much of his academic energy on highlighting the conditions which are essential for the success of political democracy—what makes democracy successful in practice in the Indian social situation?

The essence of democracy, according to Dr Ambedkar, is the doctrine of 'one man, one value'. Political democracy attempts to give effect to this doctrine by adopting the rule of one man one vote, and by securing political liberty for all (civil liberty—liberty of movement, of speech, thought, reading, writings, discussion, and of action, and political liberty in the right of the individual in the framing of laws and in making and unmaking of governments).

Given that Dr Ambedkar saw the roots of political democracy in economic and social structure, to secure political liberty for everyone, both structures should be such that they enable people to use liberty and fundamental rights. This means that political democracy would succeed in securing liberty and fundamental rights provided there is social and economic liberty and equality at the base of the political system. The authors quote Dr Ambedkar: 'Social and economic democracy are the tissues and fibre of a Political Democracy. The tougher the tissue and the fibre, the greater the strength of the body. Thus Democracy is another name for equality.'

Economic democracy: The line of argument related to linkage between political democracy and the shape and form of economic structure of society was more systematically developed by Dr Ambedkar in a memorandum, 'State and Minorities' in 1947 (Ambedkar 1947). Dr Ambedkar pointed out the limitation of the Constitutions of democratic countries that only provide political structure with adult suffrage and fundamental rights leaving the economic structure to be decided by legislature. In his view, they never realized that it was equally essential to prescribe the shape and form of economic structure if a democracy was to live up to its principle of one man, one value. At best, what most democratic countries did was to invoke the ordinary power of legislative to restrain the more powerful individual from imposing arbitrary restraints on the less powerful in the economic field, observed Dr Ambedkar. In his view this method had serious limitation:

> The inadequacy and the futility of the plan has been well established. Therefore, the successful invocation by less powerful of the authority of legislature is a doubtful proposition. Having regard to the fact that even under adult suffrage all legislatures and government are controlled by the more powerful, an appeal to the legislature to intervene in economic spheres is a very precarious safeguard against invasion on liberty of less powerful. (Ambedkar 1947: 410)

Dr Ambedkar argued that some economic structures are supportive of political democracy while some are not. He maintained that an economy based on private enterprise and in pursuit of personal gain, made people relinquish their fundamental constitutional rights in order to gain their livelihood, as the system delegated powers to private (non-state) persons to govern others. Therefore, Dr Ambedkar proposed an alternative economic framework in the form of a particular type of socialism in which he suggested State ownership in agriculture, and key and basic industries, leaving other activities to the private sector. He also suggested that insurance, health and education be under state domain. The unique feature of this proposal was that it did not leave it to the will of the legislature the establishment of what he called state socialism. Dr Ambedkar's proposed alternative economic framework, thus established state socialism by the law of the constitution, making it unalterable by any act of the legislature and the executive. In order to provide stability to socialism under parliamentary democracy, it suggested establishment of state socialism by constitutional law, without abrogating parliamentary democracy. Dr Ambedkar believed that only in this way one can achieve triple objectives: to establish socialism (i.e., to have economic equality), retain parliamentary democracy (i.e., to have liberty), and avoid dictatorship.

Indeed, while responding to the resolution related to 'Aims and Objectives' of the future Constitution of India moved by Jawaharlal Nehru on 13 December 1946, Dr Ambedkar argued for a socialistic economic framework for Indian society.

Dr Ambedkar responded:

> I find that this part of the resolution, although, it enunciates certain rights, does not speak of remedies. I find complete absence of remedies....I must confess that... this resolution is to my mind very disappointing--there are certain provisions which speak of justice, economic, social and political. I should have expected some provision whereby it would have been possible for the state to make economic, social and political justice a reality and I should have from that view expected the resolution to state in most explicit terms that in order that there may be social and economic justice in the country, that there would be nationalization of industry and nationalization of land. I do not understand how it could be possible for any future government which believes in doing justice, socially, economically and politically, unless its economy is a socialistic economy. (Ambedkar 1947: 9)

Prescribing economic framework along with political structure in the constitution was not an old conception of constitutional law of democracy.

It was a new initiative that Dr Ambedkar undertook by suggesting an innovation in constitutional jurisprudence. He justified this initiative: 'They never realized that it was equally essential to prescribe the shape and form of the economic structure of society, if democracy is to live up to its principles of one man one value. Time has come to take a bold step and define both economic structure as well as political structure of society by the law of the Constitution. All countries like India which are latecomers in the field of constitution making should not copy the faults of other countries. They should profit by the experience.' (Ambedkar 1947: 412)

Thus, socialist solution advocated by Dr Ambedkar for meaningful political democracy was persisting and unequivocal. Only social and economic reforms would take India on the path of a truly democratic trajectory.

However, Dr Ambedkar, did not receive support for his proposal of constitutional socialism by the Constituent Assembly. As an accommodation, Dr Ambedkar brought the provision for social and economic justice through Directive Principles of State Policy, which place responsibility on the state to follow the principles to pursue the goal of social and economic equality through laws and policies. As we know from the later interpretation by learned judges of Directive Principles, they emphasised its significance for social and economic transformation. It is stated that the Fundamental Rights primarily aim at assuring political freedom to citizens, while the Directive principles aim at securing social and economic freedoms by appropriate state action. It expects the state to secure social order for promotion of welfare of the people. In particular, the state is expected to strive to 'minimise the inequalities in income, and eliminate inequalities in status, facilities and opportunities, amongst individuals and amongst groups of people'. The state is obliged to secure for the common man an adequate means of livelihood. The ownership of the material resources of the community are to be distributed in a manner such that it best serves the common good of the people. Further, the operation of the economic system should not result in concentration of wealth and means of production in the hands of a few people to the detriment to public interest. One can see how the goal of economic and social equality are brought forth through Directive Principles as a substitute to the socialist system suggested by Dr Ambedkar. It was a weak alternative not enforceable in court of law, yet it emphasized the need of social and economic equality for real political democracy. This was one such accommodation that Dr Ambedkar had to be contented with.

Social Democracy: In addition to economic democracy, Dr Ambedkar viewed social democracy as a necessary condition for success of political democracy, and the authors bring out this aspect emphatically. Dr Ambedkar argued that social democracy primarily involves the idea of social justice. According to him, the principle of social justice includes most other principles which have become the foundation of moral order. Justice has always evoked ideas of equality. Rules and regulations, rights and righteousness are concerned with equality in value. If all men are equal, all men are of same essence therefore, common essence entitled them to the same civic and political rights (Ambedkar 1987).

Equality has a central place in Dr Ambedkar's notion of justice. He believed that fraternity, liberty, and freedom are derivative notions. The basic and fundamental conceptions are equality and respect for human personality. Fraternity and liberty take roots in these two fundamental conceptions. Digging further down, it may be said that equality is the original notion, and respect for human personality is a reflection of it so that where equality is denied, everything else may be taken to be denied... (Ambedkar 1987: 66).

However, the Indian caste system which is based on graded inequality, denies liberty and freedom. The most devastating feature of the Hindu social order is isolation, exclusion and anti-social sprit, particularly towards untouchables. It does not permit the sharing of joys and sorrows pertaining to vital facts of life. Everything is separate and exclusive. The Hindus have been separate and exclusive all through. For the untouchable, it means forced physical and social isolation.

Thus, in Dr Ambedkar's view, from the point of view of justice, it is blatant that the Hindu social order is inimical to equality, antagonistic to liberty and freedom, and opposed to fraternity. Therefore, for political democracy to be effective, equality in social rights of citizens is necessary for political freedom and liberty. If liberty is to take its appointed end, it is important that there should be social equality. For healthy political and economic democracy social equality is a must. Without it liberty and freedom have no meaning.

Dr Ambedkar brought equality to the centre of the political governance in the Constitution. The equality in status, facilities and opportunities and principle of non-discrimination irrespective of caste, ethnicity, religion, gender, or race are made the core of Fundamental Rights. He did not stop there and brought in prohibition on the practice of untouchability in Fundamental Rights making it punishable by law. Later in 1955, the Untouchability Offence Act was enacted. It was renamed Protection of Civil Rights Act, 1979. Thus, Dr Ambedkar recognized the need to overturn Manu's law based on graded inequalities, and secure civil rights for the discriminated group of untouchables. Also, similar safeguards were provided against discrimination in employment, education, and legislature through the Reservation Policy.

Although Dr Ambedkar emphasized the need for legal safeguards against discrimination, he clearly recognized, more than anybody else, the limitation of the law in securing equal rights to the untouchables. In his famous lecture 'Ranade, Gandhi and Jinnah,' delivered in 1943 in Gokhale Institute, Pune, Dr Ambedkar observed:

> The idea of making gift of fundamental rights to every individual, no doubt, is laudable. The question is how to make them effective? The prevalent view is that once rights are enacted in a law, then they are safeguarded. This again is an unwarranted assumption. An experience proves that rights are not protected by law but the social and moral conscience of society. If social conscience is such that it is to recognize the rights which law chooses to enact, rights will be safe and secure. But the fundamental rights are opposed by the community. No Parliament, no judiciary can guarantee them in the real sense of the word. Dr Ambedkar quoted Burke who said, 'There is no method found for punishing the multitude. Law can punish a single solitary recalcitrant criminal. It can never operate against a whole body of people who are determined to defy it. Social conscience –is the only safeguard of all rights fundamental or non-fundamental.' (Ambedkar 1943)

He further added that:

> [T]here are no rights in the Hindu society (based on system of caste) which the moral sense of man could recognize. There are privileges and disabilities and the privileges for a few and disabilities for vast majority. (Ambedkar 1943)

Thus, in the Hindu social order social conscience supportive of equal rights and equal status to all is nearly absent, its foundation is in the principles of graded inequality. The continuation of denial of equal rights to untouchables is thus the outcome of the absence or limited presence of social conscience in favour of equality.

It means that the laws help to prevent the diseases but do not cure the diseases, when the community as a whole is opposed to giving equal rights to others. What then is the cure? Economic democracy is one, but it needs to be supplemented by social democracy— hence in the 'State and Minorities' memorandum, Dr Ambedkar proposed dual remedy— safeguards against economic exploitation and safeguards against social discrimination.

This also means purposeful efforts for change in the norms of behaviour that would support equal rights and equal status to all. The development of a social conscience supportive of equal rights is the ultimate guarantee of equality. In 'Annihilation of Caste', Dr Ambedkar argued:

> People are not wrong in observing caste. In my opinion, what is wrong is their religion, which has inculcated this notion of caste. If this is correct, then obviously the enemy, you must grapple with, is not the people who observed caste, but the Shastras which teach them this religion of caste. The real remedy is to destroy the belief (of people) in the sanctity of the Shastras, because Shastras continue to mold the belief and opinion of the people. We should realize that the acts of the people are merely the results of their belief inculcated in their mind by the Shastras and that people will not change their conduct until they cease to believe in the sanctity of the Shastras on which their conduct is founded. (Ambedkar 1936: 68)

Buddhism as the crucible of social democracy: In this context, the authors rightly bring forth the views of Dr Ambedkar on the relevance of Buddhism in promoting social democracy, that is, social relations based on equality and fraternity. In the context of Indian tradition, equality could be achieved in the Buddhist religion. The authors point out that Dr Ambedkar's reading of Buddhism does not only have social implications but it also has political implications. Considering that the 'religion of the Buddha gives freedom of thought and freedom of self-development to all', Dr Ambedkar observed that 'the rise of Buddhism in India was as significant as the French Revolution'—a political event in the first place. In that sense, Buddhism is a democratic religion and Ambedkar, eventually found in this religion the societal values he had tried to promote through political democracy. The authors observe that in his historic speech of 25 November 1949 when Dr Ambedkar presented the final draft of the Indian Constitution to the Constituent Assembly, which was to pass on 26 January 1950, he pointed out that by becoming a parliamentary constituency 'again', India is back to its Buddhist roots. Such an 'invention of the tradition' shows that even in his interpretation of the historical impact of Buddhism over India, Dr Ambedkar remained deeply interested in political ideas, the authors observed.

On the question of representation: The discussion on the issue of representation of social minorities is very elaborate and insightful. The authors have lucidly discussed the contribution of Dr Ambedkar on three aspects of minorities—the definition of minority, principles justifying minority representation, the electoral method for minority representation, and general safeguards against communal legislative majority.

For the purpose of political representation, minorities were conventionally identified on the basis of the population of a religious group. Dr Ambedkar however, took a different view and argued that 'separation in religion is not the only test of a minority. Nor is it a good and efficient test. Social discrimination constitutes the real test for determining whether a social group is or is not a minority.' So, he recognized discrimination as the main criterion for identifying a community for the purpose of protection through policies.

Dr Ambedkar further went on to justify that by this criterion, untouchables are not only in minority in the demographic sense but in so far as they face isolation, exclusion, and intense discrimination, they deserved to be recognized as minority for the purpose of constitutional safeguards.

Having built up the case of minority status for untouchables or *dalits*, Dr Ambedkar had to provide justification for their representation in legislature. He did so by invoking the limits to real representation by others on behalf of untouchables. Dr Ambedkar believed that a popular government should not only be a government for the people but also by the people. Government by the people means representation of the people. Representation, however, can be of 'interest or persons'. In case of untouchables he preferred representation of persons to represent their own interests as a minority. Thus, the representation of persons means that social groups should be able to send some of their own members in the elected assemblies to represent their interests because others could not represent them truly. In Dr Ambedkar's views, the social attitude of a candidate towards the mass of men whom he/she wishes to represent matters. The real line of cleavage, among the Hindus being between the 'touchable' and 'untouchable'—the 'touchable' could not represent 'untouchables'. The personal representation of untouchable, therefore, is the only alternative, as they understand their problems and would represent them better than others (Ambedkar 1947: 422).

What electoral method needed to be followed for giving representation is the third issue with respect to minorities that kept Dr Ambedkar engaged. And we see a tension brewing within him about the effectiveness of the alternative methods of representation. This tension remained till the end, up to 1956. The criteria he suggested to judge the relative effectiveness of the alternative electoral method of minority representation is independent of minority representative in raising the issue of minorities. These need to be real and not normal (conventional) and be true truly representative of their people. The alternative method of election of minority candidate has to be judged by this these criteria with in the overall unity of the nation. There are the two methods which Dr Ambedkar considered in early 1930, namely to reserve seats and consequently of communal representation. The latter is popularly known as separate electorates. He also talked about 'community electorate' for the untouchables with some hesitations, as the authors observed. In early 1930, he preferred separate electorate with duel voting rights—untouchables having the right to elect their own person and an additional vote for the non-untouchable candidate in a dual-member constituency. He preferred separate electorate because it enabled the untouchables to elect their own candidate who would be independent, and not be dependent on high-caste vote. On the one hand, the reserve seat method, namely single-member constituency, on the other, since the election of untouchables would be dependent on high caste vote who are in majority, the elected candidate would not be independent. Later in 1995, he also spoke about plural member constituencies (of two or three or four members) with cumulative voting, in place of single-member constituency (Ambedkar 1945: 170). All this shows that Dr Ambedkar was looking for a personal representation of the Scheduled Caste as a social minority through an appropriate method which would enable them to elect independent representatives, real and not nominal representatives to legislatures.

Dr Ambedkar also applied his mind to the issue of minority in a more general way and suggested some innovative proposals containing safeguards for minorities from communal majority in legislature in a memorandum 'Communal Dead lock and Way to Solve it', submitted to the government in 1945. He was immensely concerned about the political consequences of the communal character of Indian polity. He firmly believed that in India the majority is not a political majority. It is communal majority. He drew a useful distinction between the two, 'The communal majority is born, it is not made. The political majority is not fixed or it is not a permanent majority. It is majority which is always, unmade and remade. A communal majority on the other hand is permanent, and that majority is fixed in its attitude' (Ambedkar 1945).

Therefore, he suggested specific safeguards against communal majority in legislature. He suggested the concept of *relative majority* to overcome the dominance of communal majority vis-à-vis minority and suggested a method to give relatively high weightage to minorities in representation in legislature in terms of number of seats. Between the minorities, however, he suggested high priority to those minorities that were educationally and economically more backward compared to others. In other words, he suggested a scheme which moderated the majority power and ensured *balanced representation.*

To reduce the dominance of communal majority in legislature, Dr Ambedkar preferred the principle of *unanimity* for decision-making wherein the minority would also have an equal say.

In 1945, he proposed the principle of faith by minorities in the elected members of the majority community who would occupy Executive positions. He recommended that the Prime Minister and the Ministers from the majority party should have the faith of the whole House. Following this principle of faith, he proposed the election of Prime Minister, and the member of the Cabinets from among the majority party by the whole House. Similarly, the minority Cabinet ministers from the majority party would be elected by members of each minority community in the legislature. All this creative thinking shows that Dr Ambedkar was looking for a suitable check on the communal majority in representation in Legislature and in Executive to give space to the minority in political governance.

Before I conclude this long forward, I must share the implication of communal political majority for the nation and nationalism. In this context Dr Ambedkar commented on a particular trend that he had observed in mid-1940s. He stated:

> Unfortunately, for the minorities in India, Indian nationalism has developed a new doctrine which may be called the Divine Right of the Majority to rule the minorities to the wishes of majority. Any claim for the sharing of power by the minority is called communalism while the monopolizing of the whole power by the majority is called nationalism. (Ambedkar 1947: 427)

Dr Ambedkar was, in a way, prophetic in his articulate prediction. What he saw in mid-1940s is fairly obvious from the experience after independence

of caste and religious base of electoral democracy. This tendency of caste
and religion forming the base of political democracy has implications for
nationalism and nation-building. In fact it undermines the very process
of nation building. It is quite clear the way Dr Ambedkar defined and
conceived nation and nationalism. He stated:

> A nation is not a country in the physical sense, whatever degree of
> geographical unity it may possess. A nation is not a people synthesized by
> a common culture derived from common language, common religion or
> common race .... Nationality is a subjective psychological feeling. It is feel-
> ing of corporate sentiment of oneness which makes those who are charged
> with it feel that they are kith and kin .... It is a feeling of 'consciousness
> of kind' 'which binds together those who are within the limits of kindred.
> It is longing (a strong feeling of wanting added) to belong to one's own
> group....This is the essence of what is called a nationality and national feel-
> ing. (Ambedkar 1943: 223)

Dr Ambedkar went on to argue:

> The point is that nationality is not primarily a matter of geography, culture or
> language... The nation is not a physical thing in which certain objective char-
> acteristics, such as commonality of language, race, territory, persists etc. Nation
> on the contrary, is a spiritual reality binding people into a deep comradeship.

And added that:

> Nationality is social feeling of a corporate sentiment of oneness. It is a feeling
> of consciousness of kind, like mindedness, possessing things in common
> in life of communication, participation and of sharing with all those who
> constitute one nation. In this sense nation is a society where there is an
> unlimited scope for 'social endosmosis'. Nation is a democracy, a mode of
> associated living, of conjoined communicated. (Ambedkar 1946)

Thus, the inter communication, participation, and sharing with all those
who constitute one nation is a key thing for nationhood. The relevant message from Dr Ambedkar is that economic and social equality, and above
all fraternity is a necessary condition for making a political democracy
function successfully and for a nation to become strong and all inclusive.
Fraternity and brotherhood makes this possible. Fraternity encourages a
mental attitude of fair play and equality towards the co-nationalists. The
lack of equality in social and economic life and of fraternity in our social
relations undermine the efforts towards strengthening democracy and the

nation. With persistence of economic and social inequalities and lack of fraternity, we remain a nation in the making. We remain a democracy in the making. The message from Dr Ambedkar is loud and clear: That there is an unfinished agenda; therefore, lot more efforts are necessary to make the Indian nation inclusive of all, enabling all to enjoy liberty and fundamental rights, which political democracy promise.

SUKHADEO THORAT

Professor Emeritus,
Jawaharlal Nehru University, New Delhi;
Distinguished Professor in Social Science,
Savitribai Phule University, Pune, Maharashtra, and
K.R. Narayanan Chair for Human Rights and
Social Justice, Mahatma Gandhi University of Kottayam, Kerala

Note

1. There are few occasions and issues when Dr Ambedkar had to deviate from his original position under compelling circumstances. For instance he favoured separate electorate, but had to settle down on reservation of seats in assemblies (under the threat of Gandhi's fast unto death). He wanted reservation in both government and private sector, but agreed for jobs in government to begin with. He formed the Independent Labour Party in 1937, but renamed it as Scheduled Caste Federation due to some consideration (finally changed it in to Republican Party), he advocated state socialism as a part of law of Constitution but settled for an alternative in the form of Directive Principles of State policy to achieve social and economic equality and justice, following opposition to his views in the Constituent Assembly. Similar situation prevailed with regard to his position on inclusion of socialism in the Constitution and a provision on right to private property.

References

Ambedkar, B.R. 1936. 'Annihilation of Caste', in *Dr Babasheb Ambedkar Writings and Speeches, Vol. I.* New Delhi: Dr Ambedkar Foundation, Ministry of Social Justice and Empowerment, Government of India.

————— 1943. 'Ranade, Gandhi and Jinnah, Reprint', in *Dr Babasaheb Ambedkar Writings and Speeches. Vol I.* New Delhi: Ministry of Social Justice and Empowerment, Government of India.

————— 1987. 'Philosophy of Hinduism', in *Dr Babasaheb Ambedkar Writings and Speeches. Vol 3.* New Delhi: Dr Ambedkar Foundation, Ministry of Social Justice and Empowerment, Government of India.

————— 1946. 'Pakistan or Partition of India, Reprint', in *Dr Babasaheb Ambedkar Writings and Speeches. Vol 8.* New Delhi: Dr Ambedkar Foundation, Ministry of Social Justice and Empowerment, Government of India.

————— 1947. 'State and Minorities: What Are Their Rights and How to Secure Them in the Constitution of Free India', Reprint in *Dr Babasaheb Ambedkar Writings and Speeches. Vol I.* New Delhi: Dr Ambedkar Foundation, Ministry of Social Justice and Empowerment, Government of India.

————— 1945. 'Communal Deadlock and Way to Solve it', in *Dr Babasaheb Ambedkar Writings and Speeches. Vol I.* New Delhi: Dr Ambedkar Foundation, Ministry of Social Justice and Empowerment, Government of India.

————— 1955. 'Thoughts on Linguistic States', in *Dr Babasaheb Ambedkar Writings and Speeches. Vol I.* New Delhi: Dr Ambedkar Foundation, Ministry of Social Justice and Empowerment, Government of India.

————— 1946. *Pakistan or Partition of India.* New Delhi: Ambedkar Foundation, Ministry of Social Justice and Empowerment, Government of India.

Thorat, Sukhadeo and Narender Kumar. 2010. *B. R. Ambedkar: Perspectives on Social Exclusion and Inclusive Policy.* Delhi: Oxford University Press.

Thorat, Sukhadeo and Katherine Newmen. 2010. *Block by Caste: Economic Discrimination in Modern India.* Delhi: Oxford University Press.

Acknowledgements

The compilation of various writings for the present anthology has been an onerous and arduous task. The whole process took almost five years. This volume was conceived while working on another volume (*B.R. Ambedkar: Perspectives on Social Exclusion and Inclusive Policy*, 2009) when one of the editors, Narender Kumar, chanced upon some writings on democracy by Dr Ambedkar. He found these interesting in many ways. The idea crystallized when Professor Sukhadeo Thorat had a long conversation with him to publish the lesser known contribution made by Dr Ambedkar on democracy and its relevance in contemporary times. This ignited the whole process of bringing out the present volume. In this light, Director, Indian Institute of Dalit Studies (IIDS), encouraged the publication by supporting the logistics required for selection of writings. We express our deep gratitude to Dr Babasaheb Ambedkar Source Material Publication Committee, Government of Maharashtra, and especially to Professor Avinash Dolas, its Member Secretary, for permitting us to reproduce Dr Ambedkar's writings on democracy in this anthology. Thanks are also due to Professor Thorat for writing the

Foreword on the contextual importance of this work. Thanks to Arvind, Neha, and Deepjyoti for their assistance at various stages, especially during proof-reading. Finally we express our appreciation and thanks to Narendra Kumar of IIDS for scanning the material and Oxford University Press for understanding the theme to be publishable.

CHRISTOPHE JAFFRELOT

NARENDER KUMAR

Introduction

CHRISTOPHE JAFFRELOT

NARENDER KUMAR

B himrao Ambedkar was born on 14 April 1891 in Mhow, a garrison town close to Indore. His family came, however, from Maharashtra. His native village, in Konkan, in the coastal region of Maratha country was called Ambavade, and Ambedkar's real name, Ambavadekar comes from there. He changed it to that of Ambedkar, in 1900, when his Brahmin school teacher, impressed by the qualities of the child, decided to give him his own.

Ambedkar was, for a long time, protected from the discriminations afflicting the Dalits because of the particular conditions of life in the garrison where his father, a soldier in the British Indian army, worked.[1] However, little by little he had an experience of it. As a child, he wondered as to why no barber was ready to cut his hair. Especially, he underwent a humiliating experience which he was never able to forget—one day he got ready, along with his brother and sister, to meet up with his father by the train. On reaching their destination, the three children were questioned by the station master who, after learning their caste, 'retreated five steps back.'[2] Except the *tonga* drivers, none of them was ready to take them to their father's village. One of them accepted that they ride, provided they drive it themselves. During a halt, this *tongawala* took a snack in an inn whereas the children were forced to stay outside and were reduced to drinking the muddy water of a stream. Ambedkar's realization then was all the more harsh as the child was gifted with a sharp mind.

In 1907, these intellectual qualities permitted him to get his matriculation certificate at the Elphinstone High School of Bombay, where his father had just settled down. He then enrolled with the university, at the prestigious Elphinstone College, thanks to a scholarship, and qualified there, in 1912, for a degree in Bachelor of Arts (B.A.). Then he secured a scholarship for pursuing higher studies in the United States, a chance which no person from his social milieu had till then had. He received an M.A. and a Ph.D. from Columbia University in New York and then left in 1916 for London where he was admitted at Gray's Inn to pursue his law studies, and later he went to the London School of Economics where he wanted to continue his studies in economics. However, soon after, he had to return to India—where he arrived in August 1917—because his scholarship came to expire.

The success that he knew in the pursuit of his studies drew the attention of the British who saw in him a powerful representative of the Depressed Classes (as they said). He was consulted in 1919 by the Southborough Committee that the British government had set up to revise the franchise and thus enable a larger number of Indians to vote to designate the assemblies that had been established in the provinces and in Delhi. The issue was all the more significant as the reform of 1919 was to give greater power to the governments and to the legislative councils.

In 1920, Ambedkar launched a new journal, *Mook Nayak* ('leader of those with no voice') with the financial support of the Maharajah of Kolhapur, Shahu Maharaj, who was none other than the descendant of Shivaji. He did not however hesitate to resume his studies when this ruler offered him the necessary funds to go back to England. On his return to London, he obtained a master of science degree in 1921, then next year he presented his thesis entitled 'The Problem of the Rupee'.

On his return to India, he tried to settle down as a lawyer in Bombay but his caste pushed away the clients. Deeply hurt, he decided to devote his life to fight against the caste system. So he created in July 1924, the *Bahishkrit Hitakarini Sabha* (Association of the Victims of Ostracism) which he will lead until 1928. The previous year, he had been nominated by the British to the Legislative Council of the Bombay Presidency. Ambedkar tried hard to secure an access of the Dalits to wells (it was to become the target of a mobilization at Mahad, on the Konkan coast, in 1927), and entry into temples. The agitation that Ambedkar led on the latter issue was to continue in a sporadic way until 1935.

The 1930s marked, however, Ambedkar's transition to political activity. He demanded from the British a separate electorate for the Dalits, who, in this way, could have constituted themselves into a real political force. The British government sided partly in favour of his arguments in the arbitration (the Communal Award) which it announced on 14 August 1932. Gandhi, who considered that such a measure would threaten the unity of the Hindus, immediately began a hunger strike in the Yerwada jail at Poona (in Bombay Presidency) where he was imprisoned. This step forced Ambedkar to give up the demand for separate electorates and to sign the 'Poona Pact' on 24 September 1932. He felt an immense bitterness of it, even if Gandhi, being magnanimous, recognized the right of the Dalits to a substantial reserved quota of seats.

Ambedkar created his first political formation in 1936, the Independent Labour Party (ILP), in view of the 1937 election, which took place within the framework of *Government of India Act* of 1935, a law giving to provincial governments and assemblies still increased powers as compared to the reform of 1919. The ILP presented candidates only in the Bombay Presidency and in the Central Provinces, where it gained a notable success, Ambedkar was elected together with nine other leaders of the party.

The Second World War appreciably modified the political scene from 1939 onwards. The British having involved India in the conflict without consulting the Congress, its representatives resigned from the eight provincial governments which they controlled. Concerned about associating other Indians to their war effort, the British authorities co-opted leaders of less important political formations, such as the Muslim League, the Hindu Mahasabha and the ILP. This is how Ambedkar entered the Defence Advisory Committee in 1941 before being appointed as Minister of Labor in 1942.

Ambedkar combined this ministerial activity with a revival of his partisan strategy, as he created a new organization in 1942, the Scheduled Castes Federation (SCF). The expression 'Scheduled Castes' designates 'the listed castes', that is the untouchable castes, whose list was established by the government so that they could benefit from a quota in the administration. After having tried to broaden his political base to all the 'labourers',

Ambedkar therefore concentrated his efforts only on the Dalits. Faced with an all powerful Congress, the SCF recorded, however, a crushing defeat during the provincial assemblies' elections in March 1946. Ambedkar himself was defeated.

He arose nevertheless as the incontestable representative of the Dalits. Jawaharlal Nehru appointed him, on 3 August 1947, as Minister of Law in his government. On 29 August he was made the head of the committee charged with the drafting of the Constitution (the Drafting Committee) which took away the main part of his energy from 1947 to 1950.

If the Constitution outlined then a favourable framework for social reform, particularly by abolishing untouchability and by prohibiting all discrimination based on caste, race, and sex, Ambedkar wanted to attack the ills of the Indian society in a more concrete way. That is why he launched from January 1950 a campaign for the revision of the Hindu Code Bill. This text, which concerned the matrimonial relations (the law of marriage and divorce), inheritance, adoption, etc., had to be, according to him, the instrument of a far reaching reform of the Hindu society. But Nehru, anxious not to alienate the most conservative elements of the Congress, distanced himself from these proposals and Ambedkar left the government in September 1951. On returning to the opposition, he got closer to the Socialists but this alliance suffered a severe setback during the elections of 1951–2.

He then turned towards Buddhism, to which he dedicated his last work, *The Buddha and His Dhamma*, which was to be published posthumously in 1957. The previous year, he had chosen the day of the important Hindu festival of *Dasahara*, on 14 October, to convert to Buddhism at Nagpur, during a big ceremony where thousands of Dalits followed his example. Returning to Delhi on 30 November, he died there on 6 December 1956.

Dr Ambedkar came down in history as a scholar as much as a man of action, and even a statesman. He studied the caste system as a sociologist and anthropologist in order to identify the nature of untouchability before fighting inequality. He was also a man of religion who declared that he would not die a Hindu in the mid-1930s and converted to Buddhism in October 1956 after applying his mind to many other creeds.

This volume focuses on the way Dr Ambedkar related to politics and in particular to democracy. He considered this regime as the only one, which could contribute to the emancipation of the Dalits—his life-long cause. He tried to systematically promote it, opting—as a lawyer by training—for a constitutionalist approach against any form of political violence. For Dr Ambedkar, democracy offered a framework for solving problems through deliberations. He looked at democracy as a transformative government to change the lives of citizens and opined that democracy is 'a form and method of government whereby revolutionary changes in the economic and social life of the people are brought about without bloodshed' (p. 219, this volume). In that sense, he was a pure product of the philosophy of Enlightenment. As a result, parliamentary democracy was his favourite variant of this political system—and not a presidential regime, which implies a concentration of power in the hands of one man and conveys a plebiscitary dimension. In democracy the government needs to be more of the people and by the people than being for the people as in the latter case the prominence is taken by the government and in this light he argued that 'the principle of self-government expresses the desire of the people to rule itself rather than be ruled by others whether the rulers be absolute monarchs, dictators or privileged classes. It is called democracy' (BAWS, Vol. 10, 1991: 39).

As a believer in democracy, Dr Ambedkar created a political party as early as the mid-1930s and contested elections from 1937 onwards. But he had already realized that democracy in India could only succeed if it was adapted to the social conditions of the country. Economic and social equality were, for him, the pre-conditions of the democratic functioning of parliamentary institutions. Poverty and hierarchy—including the caste system—would undermine democracy, since the political mechanisms were over determined by social realities. This assumption persuaded him that social and economic reforms should go on a par with political democratization.

But he also thought that political democratization could contribute to social change if it was followed by some rules in terms of positive discrimination. In fact, as early as the 1920s, Ambedkar advocated such a policy in order to ensure a meaningful representation of the Dalits in the assemblies of the Raj. After independence, he gave up his previous objective—the creation of a dalit separate electorates—and resigned himself to the reserved seats formula, probably because he believed that the Constitution he was writing as the chairman of the Drafting Committee would open a new chapter of India's history where democracy would promote a sense of fraternity between Indians. He realized very soon that such developments were illusory, that politics would not be sufficient to take Dalits on the road to equality and therefore, to convert to Buddhism was a better strategy.

The Question of Representation

As a public figure with dalit origins, the first democracy-related question that Dr Ambedkar has had to consider was that of the political representation of the minorities. He had an opportunity to do it as early as 1919 when he was consulted by the Southborough Committee, the body which had been entrusted with redefining electoral franchise within the framework of the constitutional reform—that was to be called 'Montford', after the names of Montagu and Chelmsford.

In his testimony, Dr Ambedkar referred straightaway to theories of democracy in which he was initiated in the US—where he had just completed his MA in economics but had followed classes in philosophy by John Dewey and political economy by Robert Anderson Seligman (Jaffrelot 2005: 28). Criticizing the definition of 'popular government' that he had learnt from the American historian, Albert Bushnell Hart, he pointed out that popular government should not be 'only Government for the people but by the people' (p. 2, this volume). This assumption had a clear implication in terms of representation. Indeed, Dr Ambedkar argued that democracy should ensure 'representation of opinions and representation of persons' (p. 2, this volume). By saying that, he was articulating a theory of 'mirror representation' that would reach its highest degree of sophistication many years later in the book of Hanna Pitkin (1972). 'Representation of the persons' here means that social groups should be able to send some of their own members in the elected assemblies to 'mirror' their interests because others could not represent them truly.

Dr Ambedkar will make this point very clear few years later in his memorandum to the Simon Commission when he will argue in favour of the 'restriction upon the right of the upper classes to represent the lower classes' (p. 44, this volume):

> For aptitude and experience are not more important than the social attitude of a candidate towards the mass of men whom he wishes to represent. Indeed, mere aptitude and experience will be the cause of ruination if they are not accompanied and regulated by the right sort of social attitude. There is no doubt that the social attitude of the higher classes towards the lower classes is not of the right sort. It is no doubt always said to the credit of these communities that they are intellectually the most powerful communities in India. But it can with equal truth be said that they have never utilized their intellectual powers to the services of the lower classes. On the other hand,

they have always despised, disregarded and disowned the masses in belonging to a different strata, if not to a different race than themselves. No class has a right to rule another class, much less a class like the higher classes in India. By their code of conduct, they have behaved as the most exclusive class steeped in its own prejudices and never sharing the aspirations of the masses, with whom they have nothing to do and whose interests are opposed to theirs. It is not, therefore, unjust to demand that a candidate who is standing to represent others shall be such as shares the aims, purposes and motives of those whom he desires to represent.

What is true of classes is even more true of castes. In his 1919 testimony, Ambedkar told his British interlocutors that the real line of cleavage, among the Hindus was between the 'touchables' and 'untouchables'. He made it clear that 'touchables' could not represent 'untouchables' for quasi-cognitive and cybernetic reasons (p. 4, this volume):

The touchables have enough communication between them to enable us to say that the conflict of like-mindedness so far as they are concerned is not much to be dreaded. But there is a real difference and consequent conflict between the like-mindedness of the touchables and the untouchables.

How should political representation be organized if 'touchables' and 'untouchables' cannot represent each other? Not by any electoral system which would be based on territorial constituencies, because the latter would then be in a minority and therefore deprived of representation. In 1919, Ambedkar considered that there are 'two possible methods of meeting the situation: either to reserve seats in plural constituencies for those minorities that cannot otherwise secure personal representation or grant communal representation' (p. 7, this volume) a formula also known under the label of 'separate electorates' and already enjoyed by the Muslims since 1909. It was only in an appended document that Ambedkar emphasized the need for a 'community electorate' for the untouchables, a sign of his hesitations.

Things will change. Ten years later, when he submitted a memorandum on behalf of the Bahishkrit Hitakarini Sabha before the Simon Commission, he argued in favour of a quota of seats for the untouchables. He asked for 22 seats in the Bombay Assembly which counted for 140 (15 seats only would have been granted on the basis of their demographic weight) and the right to vote to every untouchable adult. He explained, during his speech before a delegation of the Simon Commission at Poona, that in case universal suffrage was not being granted for the dalits, then he would campaign for separate electorates. He justified this position on the basis of new arguments, which are clear indications that he still nurtured great hopes towards the upper castes, and that he still had nationalist scruples, which prevented him from severing his links with social and political, mainstreams (pp. 46–7, this volume):

> At any rate, this must be said with certainty that a minority gets a larger advantage under joint electorates than it does under a system of separate electorates. With separate electorates the minority gets its own quota of representation and no more. The rest of the house owes no allegiance to it and is therefore not influenced by the desire to meet the wishes of the minority. The minority is thus thrown on its own resources and as no system of representation can convert a minority into a majority, it is bound to be overwhelmed. The reserved seats being single member-constituencies would make Untouchables' representatives dependent on general caste due to their majority in numbers. For, every member of the majority who has partly succeeded on the strength of the votes of the minority if not a member of the minority will certainly be a member for the minority.

Dr Ambedkar's reservations about the separate electorates stem from his fears that such a reform could create divide if continued for a long period. This state of mind is reconfirmed by his justification of the reserved seats not in the name of the interests of the Dalits, but in the name of the general interest. Responding to those who claim that the entry of untouchables in the assemblies in larger numbers would affect their efficiency, he replies— drawing his inspiration from another western scholar, Professor Dicey—that not only parliaments are not supposed to be 'far superior in intelligence to the mass of the nation' (p. 44, this volume) but that the intellectual 'loss will be more than amply recompensed by the natural idealism of the backward communities' (pp. 44–5, this volume):

> There is no doubt that the representatives of the higher orders are occupied with the pettiest cares and are more frequently concerned with the affairs of their own class than with the affairs of the nation. Their life is too busy or too prosperous and the individual too much self-contained and self-satisfied for the conception of the social progress to be more than a passing thought of a rare moment. But the lower orders are constantly reminded of their adversity, which can be got over only by a social change. The consciousness of mutual dependence resulting from the necessities of a combined action makes for generosity, while the sense of untrained powers and of undeveloped faculties gives them aspirations. It is to the lower classes that we must look for

the motive power for progress. The reservation of seats to the backward Hindu communities makes available for the national service such powerful social forces, in the absence of which any Parliamentary government may be deemed to be poorer.

In other words, reservations are not only good for their beneficiaries, but also for the general public, a clear indication that Ambedkar was hopeful to make the Dalits parts and parcels of the national, political body.

This very objective also explains his craze for universal franchise which, according to him, would make separate electorates redundant. In 1929 he declared (p. 31, this volume):

> The majority has proceeded as though communal electorates were a good to be preserved and have treated adult suffrage as though it was an evil, to be kept within bonds. My view of them is just the reverse. I hold communal electorates to be an evil and adult suffrage to be a good. Those who agree with me will admit that adult suffrage should be introduced not only because of its inherent good but also because it can enable us to get rid of the evil of communal electorates.

The reason why universal franchise would make separate electorate unnecessary remains somewhat unclear,[3] but his defense of such a granting of the right to vote 'to all adults, males and females, above the age of 21' (BAWS, Vol 2, 1982: 338) reflects his desire to create a body politics transcending social divisions—including those based on education. He argues, in that regard, that illiteracy should not bar those who do not know how to read and write to join the political society in the making (p. 34, this volume):

> Those who insist on literacy as a test and insist upon making it a condition precedent to enfranchisement in my opinion, commit two mistakes. Their first mistake consists in their belief that an illiterate person is necessarily an unintelligent person. (...) Their second mistake lies in supposing that literacy necessarily imports a higher level of intelligence or knowledge than what the illiterate possesses.

These objections went on a par with Dr Ambedkar's assumption that 'in a democracy, the ultimate principle is after all self-government and that means that final decision on all matters must be made by popularly elected persons and not by experts' (p. 41, this volume).

Dr Ambedkar changed his mind about reserved seats in the early 1930s. During the Second Round Table Conference he got closer, within the Minorities Committee, to other dalit leaders as well as Muslim, Anglo-Indian, and European Christian representatives. They drafted a memorandum together. Ambedkar and Rao Bahadur Rettamalle Srinivasan, a dalit member of the Legislative Council of the Madras Presidency, put down on it the demand for a separate electorate with reserved seats for the untouchables, a scheme that they planned to subject to referendum within twenty years or which would come to an end before if the suffrage became universal.

The arbitration given by the British following the Second Round Table Conference as regards the status of various communities in the Constitution to come, the Communal Award, was announced in August, 1932. This award recognized the right of the untouchables to have separate electorates. Henceforth, they were given the right to vote at the same moment within the framework of general constituencies and within 71 separate constituencies, which could only be filled up by dalit candidates. Immediately, Gandhi, who was then imprisoned at Poona for having revived the Civil Disobedience movement, went on fast against the separate electorates granted to the Scheduled Castes.

His fast arose an enormous emotion all over India. Madan Mohan Malaviya, a leader of the Hindu Mahasabha, who was recognized inside the Congress as the representative of the upper caste Hindus because of his strict Brahminical orthodoxy, took the initiative of convening a meeting in Bombay. It was held on 19 September 1932, the morning of the day when Gandhi went on fast. Ambedkar was invited to it to renegotiate the terms of the Communal Award.[4]

The preliminary draft compromises, which were successively elaborated by these leaders, were submitted to Gandhi, whose condition deteriorated day by day.

The final phase of bargaining took place when Ambedkar came to meet Gandhi at the Yerwada prison. The Mahatma then proposed him that the Dalits should benefit from a number of reserved seats larger than the one that would have come to them within the framework of the separate electorate, in exchange for the renunciation by Ambedkar of this system. 'The Poona Pact' finally established a system of reserved seats, in which 148 seats (instead of 71 as put forward by the Communal Award) were granted to the Scheduled Castes in the Legislative Council. But it excluded the principle of separate electorates: in 148 constituencies— those where the untouchables were the most numerous—the members of the Depressed Classes (the official phrase) would designate by themselves the four Dalit Leaders who would be the candidates among whom all the voters of the constituency, mixed of all castes, would then have to elect their representative. This scheme, as a matter of fact, was close to the one advocated by the Rajah-Moonje pact (Jaffrelot 2005: 58–9). For Gandhi, the Poona Pact was much more than an exercise in political engineering: it had societal implications, as evident from what he said to Dr Ambedkar one day in 1933: 'In accepting the Poona Pact you accept the position that you are Hindus'(Jaffrelot 2005: 67).

While Ambedkar had to resign himself to reserved seats, he remained passionate with the question of the representation of the Dalits in power centres other than the assemblies. In 1933 he argued in favour of a 'special representation for the depressed classes' (p. 58, this volume) in the village Panchayats (councils). In a speech he made in the Bombay Legislative Council he argued that 'the judiciary has abused and prostituted its position' (BAWS, Vol 2, 1981: 119) because of its upper caste bias, in such a manner that caste-based reservations may also be legitimate in this institution.

The 1937 elections strengthened Ambedkar's opposition to the reserved seats. In the Bombay Presidency, the ILP presented 17 candidates, 13 in the constituencies reserved for the Scheduled Castes where they recorded 11 victories, and 4 upper castes people—in the general constituencies where it gained 3 seats. Dr Ambedkar, who had acquired a national stature since the Round Table Conferences and his conflict with Gandhi, wished also to implant his party outside the Bombay Presidency. However, in the Central Provinces and in Berar, the party gained only 3 out of 20 seats reserved for the Scheduled Castes.

Dr Ambedkar became more radical in his demand in favour of the dalits to such an extent, that he asked for separate Dalit settlements. In 1942, the Scheduled Castes Federation (SCF), a party Dr Ambedkar had created to replace the ILP in 1942, passed a resolution and envisaged the creation of 'separate Scheduled Caste villages away from and independent of Hindu villages' (BAWS, Vol. 9, 1991: 405). But he did not lose interest in the question of their representation in the power centres of the Indian state. In fact, during the same meeting, the SCF passed another resolution asking for a representation of the Scheduled Castes not only in the Assemblies, but also in all the central and state governments as well as in the state machinery, including the bureaucracy and the judiciary, and, on the top of it 'in accordance with their numbers, their needs and their importance'. This stood in stark contrast with Dr Ambedkar's previous opposition to 'communal representation in the executive of the country' (BAWS, Vol. 2, 1982: 332) something which, he thought in 1929, would have a debilitating effect on 'a most vital organ of the governmental machinery'.

In March 1947, he presented to the Constituent Assembly, on its own initiative, a project of the Constitution. Therein he asked for separate electorates for the Dalits as well as a quota proportional to their demographic weight in the Central government and in the state governments; and also in the local, regional, and national administrations. Secondly, he claimed that the Constitution should establish a Commission charged with the redistribution of land belonging to the State for settling the untouchables in 'separate villages'. In this document, one could read:

> One of the issues, which have embittered the relations between the Hindus and the Scheduled Castes in the political field, is the issue of electorate. The Scheduled Castes are insisting upon separate electorates. The Hindus are equally insistent on opposing the demand. To arrive at a settlement on this issue—without which there can be no peace and amity between the Hindus and the Scheduled Castes—it is necessary to determine who is right and who is wrong and whether the opposition is based on rational grounds or is based on mere prejudice.

> The grounds, which are generally urged against the demand of the Scheduled Castes for separate electorates, are:

> (i) that the Scheduled Castes are not a minority;
> (ii) that the Scheduled Castes are Hindus and therefore they cannot have separate electorates;
> (iii) that separate electorates will perpetuate untouchability;
> (iv) that separate electorates are anti-national; and
> (v) that separate electorates enables British Imperialism to influence the communities having separate electorates to act against the interests of the country.

> Are these arguments valid?

> (i) To say that the Scheduled Castes are not a minority is to misunderstand the meaning of the word 'minority'. Separation in religion is not the only test of a minority. Nor is it a good and efficient test. Social discrimination constitutes the real test for determining whether a social group is or is not a minority. Even Mr Gandhi thought it logical and practical to adopt this test in preference to that of religious separation. Following this test, Mr Gandhi in an editorial under the

heading. 'The Fiction of Majority' in the *Harijan* dated 21 October 1939 has given his opinion that the Scheduled Castes are the only real minority in India.

(ii) To argue that the Scheduled Castes are Hindus and therefore cannot demand separate electorates is to put the same argument in a different form. To make religious affiliation the determining factor for constitutional safeguards is to overlook the fact that the religious affiliation may be accompanied by an intense degree of social separation and discrimination. The belief that separate electorates go with separation in religion arises from the fact that those minorities who have been given separate electorates happen to be religious minorities. This, however, is not correct. Muslims are given separate electorates not because they are different from Hindus in point of religion. They are given separate electorates because—and this is the fundamental fact—the social relations between the Hindus and the Musalmans are marked by social discrimination. To put the point in a somewhat different manner, the nature of the electorates is determined not by reference to religion but by reference to social considerations. (pp. 165-6, this volume)

Dr Ambedkar seems to have returned to a more moderate approach of this issue after joining Nehru's government and the Drafting Committee of the Constituent Assembly. The Minorities Committee had rejected the very idea of separate electorates for the Dalits where Dr Ambedkar had argued—in vain—that the candidate of a minority (including a Dalit) should be declared elected only if a large proportion of the members of his community had voted for him. When this issue came in discussion in a plenary session in August 1947, one of the lieutenants of Ambedkar, S. Nagappa, proposed that, in the constituencies reserved for the Scheduled Castes, only the candidates who obtained at least 35 per cent of the dalit votes could be returned. This provision avoided the presence, in the assemblies, of dalit representatives mainly elected by the upper castes. This amendment was welcomed but with a cruel irony by Sardar Patel who had obtained, in advance, the promise of its withdrawal from Nagappa. He declared, seriously in the midst of laughers, that the former was 'moving it only to make a speech and then withdraw it.'[5] He went on and on in the same vein, '... Mr Nagappa was allowed to move the amendment on condition that he will withdraw it. There is no use in carrying on the debate. He only wanted to show to his community that he has not sold himself away. If you take it seriously and give importance to this business, then it would show that there is some substance in it'.[6] Concluding this debate, Patel called on the untouchables to 'forget what Dr Ambedkar or his group have done' and added, '...I feel that the vast majority of the Hindu population wish you well. Without them where will you be? Therefore, secure their confidence and forget that you are a Scheduled Caste'.[7] Nagappa withdrew his amendment, which had been signed by four representatives, including Ambedkar who was, strangely enough, absent on this day.

Dr Ambedkar had been transformed by his appointment as Law Minister and more so by his elevation to the post of Chairman of the Drafting Constitution on 29 August 1947. As he was to write later, 'I came into the Constituent Assembly with no greater aspiration than to safeguard the interests of the Scheduled Castes. I had not the remotest idea that I would be called upon to undertake more responsible functions' (BAWS, Vol. 13, 1994: 1208). These more responsible functions meant that he had to go back to some of his previous stands instead of sticking to the dissenting views he was cultivating since the early 1940s. He remained committed to the defense of the minorities. And to those who, within the Constituent Assembly, argued that India should wait and see what Pakistan would do with its minorities before legislating on the subject, he objected that, 'Rights of minorities should be absolute rights (...) no matters what others do ...' (BAWS, Vol 13, 1994: 20). But he finally rallied around the scheme of temporary reserved seats and the Indian Constitution eventually contented itself with establishing a quota of reserved seats for the untouchables, for ten renewable years, and proportional to their number.

Though, he was concerned with the rights of minorities but desired to transcend the old divide between majorities and minorities. On 4 November 1948, while he was presenting to the Assembly the first draft of the Indian Constitution, he declared in this connection (p. 180, this volume):

> In this country, both the minorities and the majorities have followed a wrong path. It is wrong for the majority to deny the existence of minorities. It is equally wrong for the minorities to perpetuate themselves. A solution must be found which will reserve a double purpose. It must recognise the existence of the minorities to start with. It must also be such that it will enable majorities and minorities to merge some day into one.

Ambedkar had expressed this idea—this hope!—many times earlier, always in connection with his definition of democracy. In fact, Ambedkar looked at the political system that was democracy, the instrument of a social transformation. However, looking at the ground realities, he was immensely apprehensive about the consequences of communal character of Indian polity. For him, in India the majority is not a political majority but communal majority. The communal majority is born, not made, whereas the political majority is not fixed or is not permanent majority. Political majority is always, made, unmade, and remade under various circumstance. A communal majority on the other hand is permanent and a majority fixed in its attitude not only towards others but also in itself.

Solution to Minority Issue

The minority question is something to which Dr Ambedkar had applied his mind right from early 1920s and provided workable solution. His contributions, therefore are more fundamental and relevant even today.

From the very beginning of special safeguards for the minorities, the population and religion had been the main criterion to identify the community as minority. And by the criterion of religion and population, Anglo-Indians, Sikhs, Muslims, etc. were identified as minorities and got representation in legislative bodies during colonial rule. While presenting the case of untouchables for special representation, Ambedkar argued during Southborough Committee in 1919, that Hindu society was divided between touchables and untouchables, so the latter required minority status as a separate social group.

During the 1940s, he came out with two important documents on the issue of minorities—(i) Communal Deadlock and a Way to Solve it; and (ii) States and Minorities. He was critical of the way the minorities' question had been looked at and the attempts to resolve the issue. He believed that there was utter lack of principles to deal with the problem of minorities. In his view emphasis was more on methods rather than principles. The solution to minorities question has been dwindling from one method to another as one failed another was employed. 'There being no principle there is no guide to tell why a particular method has failed. There being no principle there is no assurance that the new method will succeed.' (p.170, this volume).

While addressing the minorities' concerns, Ambedkar refers to three components and one could consider this to be his significant contribution on the issue of minorities: (1) Definition of minorities; (2) Principles of Representation of minorities; and (3) Methods for minorities' representation. Minorities, for him, did not mean minorities based on population and religious categories, but minorities were to be determined with their social, economic, and educational standing. Thus religion cannot be the only basis for determining the status of minority; rather social discrimination, for him, constitutes the real test for such determination. In his view, Muslims were given separate electorates not because that they were different from Hindus but because the relation between the two are marked by social discrimination. And that is why social minorities like Depressed Classes/Scheduled Castes were also minorities in his scheme of things as discrimination marked the difference between the castes—Hindus and the Scheduled Castes.

The second contribution is related to principles to deal with minorities' issues. Elaborating about the principles for the minorities' question, he underlined the following:

1. Majority Rule is untenable in theory and unjustifiable in practice. A majority community may be conceded a relative majority of representation but it can never claim an absolute majority.
2. The relative majority of representation given to a majority community in the legislature should not be so large so as to enable the majority to establish its rule with the help of the smallest minorities.
3. The distribution of seats should be so made that a combination of the majority and one of the major minorities should not give the combine such a majority as to make them impervious to the interest of the [other] minorities.
4. The distribution should be so made that if all the minorities combine, they could, without depending on the majority, form a government of their own.
5. The weightage taken from the majority should be distributed among the minorities in inverse proportion to their social standing, economic position, and educational condition so that a minority which is large and which has a better social, educational, and economic standing gets a lesser amount of weightage than a minority whose numbers are less and whose educational, economic and social position is inferior to that of the others. (p. 116, this volume)

Thus Ambedkar suggested larger safeguards against communal majority and innovated the concept of *relative majority*. This was to overcome the dominance of communal majority vis-vis minority that would make the absolute majority a relative majority. In this scheme of things, he suggested a method to give relatively high weightage to minorities in legislature in number of seats so that majority community could be checked for any kind of undue impositions on the minorities in democracy. He was not only concerned with the absolute majority of the majority community but about a bigger minority within the minority communities that might become a majority among the minorities. And to address this he suggested high priority to be given to those minorities who are educationally and economically more backward. This would pave the way to moderate the majority power and ensure steady representation.

Thus, the most significant contribution of his relates to principles of political representation of minorities. After proposing the broader principles for the representation in the legislatures he proposed a method that might elect real and not nominal representatives of the minority. He proposed the following method for the minorities' representation in the legislatures:

1. Joint electorate or separate electorate is a matter of machinery for achieving a given purpose. It is not a matter of principle.
2. The purpose is to enable a minority to select candidates to the Legislature who will be real and not nominal representatives of the minority.
3. While separate electorate gives an absolute guarantee to the minority, that its representatives will be no others except those who enjoy its confidence, a system of joint electorates, which will give equal protection to the minorities, should not be overlooked.
4. A four-member constituency, with a right to the minorities to have a double vote and requiring a minimum percentage of minority votes, may be considered as a possible substitute. (p. 117, this volume)

Thus Ambedkar was continuously engaged with the ideas of real and effective representation of minorities. Though, he clearly took the position that separate electorates gave absolute guarantee to have representatives which are independent and of their confidence by the minorities including dalits but under the changed circumstances he was not averse to an alternative method and finally suggested that joint electorates with four-member constituencies should not be overlooked where the minorities will have a dual vote requiring a minimum percentage of minority votes as a possible alternative.

After underlining the principles for solving the minorities' question and suggesting a method for the representation in legislatures, he discussed safeguards with regard to the *nature of electorates and protection against communal Executive.* This he addressed through three components: (1) Quantum of representation in the Executive; (2) Nature of the Executive; and, (3) Method of filling the places in the Executive. Regarding the quantum, for three major groups, that is, the Hindus, Muslims, and Scheduled Castes, he wanted it to be as per their proportion in the legislature and for smaller minorities, one or two members compulsorily as proportionately they being too small, their representation in Executive may not be possible. Secondly, on the nature of Executive, he wanted it to be non-parliamentary so that it will not be removable before the end of the term of the legislature and it would be parliamentary in the sense that the members of the Executive shall be chosen from the members of the Legislature and shall have the right to sit in the House, speak, vote, and answer questions. Thirdly, to reduce the dominance of communal majority, he preferred principle of *unanimity* for decision making where the minority will also have an equal say and suggested: (1) that the prime minister needs to be elected by the whole House by single transferable vote; and (2) the representatives of the minorities in the Executive must be selected by members of each minority community in the Legislature by single transferable vote (p. 142, this volume).

Thus, he proposed that the whole House should elect the Prime Minister and his colleagues in the Cabinet belonging to the majority community by a single transferable vote. Secondly, different minorities' representatives in the Cabinet should be elected by a single transferable vote of the members of each minority community in the legislature. This shows that Ambedkar brought new and meaningful insights and workable solutions to the minority issue in working democracy, and one could consider this to be an original and creative solution.

Parliamentary Democracy for Fraternity—and against Autocracy

As early as 1919, Dr Ambedkar offered an anthropological definition of democracy, which implied that this political system had the power to dissolve the hierarchical dimension of the caste system. Democracy for Ambedkar was not only confined in the State and its apparatus but extended to the societal sphere where the people revere fraternity despite differences. For him, 'Democracy is not merely a form of Government. It is primarily a mode of associated living of conjoint communicated experience. It is essentially an attitude of respect and reverence towards fellowmen' (BAWS, Vol 1, 1979: 57). In his testimony before the Southborough Committee he declared (pp. 3–4, this volume):

> Participation in a group is the only way of being like-minded with the group. Each group tends to create its own distinctive type of like-mindedness, but where there are more groups than one to be brought into political union, there would be conflict among the differently like-minded. And so long as the groups remain isolated the conflict is bound to continue and prevent the harmony of action.

In other words, a political body can only be formed when barriers between groups are abolished to some extent—and communication made possible. To achieve this goal, is even more difficult in a caste-based society where the groups are not only 'exclusive and isolated' but also organized according to a strict scale of 'graded inequality'. [8]

For Ambedkar, democracy has the power to dissolve these social barriers, even in the context of separate electorate because of the very presence of members of the minorities and the majority that this system permitted. He made that point very clear in his testimony 1919 statement before the Southborough Committee (pp. 18–19, this volume):

> Communal Representation is a device to ward off the evil effects of the divisions. To those who, while agreeing to this particular benefit of communal representation, object to it on the score that it perpetuates the divisions it can be shown that there is another perspective from which it can be said that communal representation instead of perpetuating the social divisions is one of the ways of dissolving them. While communal electorates will be co-terminous with social divisions their chief effect will be to bring together men from diverse castes who would not otherwise mix together into the Legislative Council.

Not only parliamentary democracy with some form of representation of the minorities (including the Dalits) makes groups which are socially poles apart to meet, but it also makes them debate. In a speech he gave in 1938, Dr Ambedkar points out—in a grammatically incorrect manner—that 'democracy must learn that its safety lies in having more than one opinion regarding the solution of any particular problem, and in order that people may be ready to advice with their opinions, democracy must learn to give a respectful hearing to all who are worth listening' (Keer 1954: 298–9).'

But Ambedkar does not attribute this social virtue to parliamentary democracy without qualifications. In fact, he saw the defects of this system in the historical trajectories of many European countries, which made him suspicious. In a speech he delivered in 1943 at the All India Trade Union Workers' Study Camp held in Delhi, he showed his perplexity:

The Government of human society has undergone some very significant changes. There was a time when the government of human society had taken the form of autocracy by Despotic Sovereigns. This was replaced after a long and bloody struggle by a system of government known as Parliamentary Democracy. It was felt that this was the last word in the frame work of government. It was believed to bring about the millennium in which every human being will have the right to liberty, property and pursuit of happiness. And there were good grounds for such high hopes. In Parliamentary Democracy there is the Legislature to express the voice of the people; there is the Executive which is subordinate to the Legislature and bound to obey the Legislature. Over and above the Legislature and the Executive there is the Judiciary to control both and keep them both within prescribed bounds. Parliamentary Democracy has all the marks of a popular Government, a government of the people, by the people and for the people. It is therefore a matter of some surprise that there has been a revolt against Parliamentary Democracy although not even a century has elapsed since its universal acceptance and inauguration. There is revolt against it in Italy, In Germany, in Russia, and in Spain, and there are very few countries in which there has not been discontent against Parliamentary Democracy. Why should there be this discontent and dissatisfaction against Parliamentary Democracy? It is a question worth considering. There is no country in which the urgency of considering this question is greater than it is in India. India is negotiating to have Parliamentary Democracy. There is a great need of some one with sufficient courage to tell Indians to beware of Parliamentary Democracy, it is not the best product, as it appeared to be. (p. 101, this voulme)

He found interesting responses to his own interrogations (p. 102, this volume):

The idea became sanctified and was upheld in the name of liberty. Parliamentary Democracy took no notice of economic inequalities and did not care to examine the result of freedom of contract on the parties to the contract, should they happen to be unequal. It did not mind if the freedom of contract gave the strong the opportunity to defraud the weak. The result is that Parliamentary Democracy in standing out as protagonist of Liberty has continuously 'added to the economic wrongs of the poor, the downtrodden and the dis-inherited class. The second wrong ideology which has vitiated Parliamentary Democracy is the failure to realize that political democracy cannot succeed where there is no social and economic democracy. Some may question this proposition. To those who are disposed to question it, I will ask a counter question. Why Parliamentary Democracy collapsed so easily in Italy, Germany and Russia? Why did it not collapse so easily in England and the U. S. A.? To my mind there is only one answer—namely, there was a greater degree of economic and social democracy in the latter countries than it existed in the former. Social and economic democracy are the tissues and the fiber of a Political Democracy. The tougher the tissue and the fiber, the greater the strength of the body. Democracy is another name for equality. Parliamentary Democracy developed a passion for liberty. It never made even a nodding acquaintance with equality. It failed to realize the significance of equality, and did not even endeavour to strike a balance between Liberty and Equality, with the result that liberty swallowed equality and has left a progeny of inequities.

This remarkable paragraph contradicts the previous assumption, formulated in 1919 for the first time, that democracy could transform society. In 1943, he suspected that democracy could only survive if society had been transformed before and was egalitarian enough. Four years later, Ambedkar supported parliamentary democracy again, as Chairman of the Drafting Committee. Presenting the draft of the Constitution to the Assembly on 4 November 1948, he said (pp. 176, 178, this volume):

In the Draft Constitution, there is placed at the head of the Indian Union a functionary who is called the President of the Union. The title of this 'functionary reminds one of the President of the United States. But beyond identity of names there is nothing in common between the forms of government prevalent in America and the form of Government proposed under the Draft Constitution. The American form of Government is called the Presidential system of Government. What the Draft Constitution proposes is the Parliamentary system. The two are fundamentally different. (...) Both systems of Government are of course democratic and the choice between the two is not very easy. A democratic executive must satisfy two conditions—(1) It must be a stable executive and (2) it must be a responsible executive. (...) The Draft Constitution in recommending the Parliamentary system of Executive has preferred more responsibility to more stability.

Here, the word 'stability' is a euphemism for the word 'authority'. A presidential system is potentially more stable because power is concentrated in the hands of one man. And Ambedkar was apprehensive of such a political arrangement given the Indians' tendency to the cult of the personality (p. 196, this volume):

There is nothing wrong in being grateful to great men who have rendered life-long services to the country. But there are limits to gratefulness. As has been well said by the Irish Patriot Daniel O'Connel, 'no man can be grateful at the cost of his honour, no woman can be grateful at the cost of her chastity and no nation can be grateful at the cost of its liberty'. This caution is far more necessary in the case of India than in the case of any other country, for in India, Bhakti or what may be called the path of devotion or hero-worship, plays a part in its politics unequalled in magnitude by the part it plays in the politics of any other country in the world, Bhakti in religion may be a road to the salvation of the soul. But in politics, Bhakti or hero-worship is a sure road to degradation and to eventual dictatorship.

Besides O'Connell, Ambedkar draws his inspiration from John Stuart Mill's recommendation to his fellow countrymen not 'to lay their liberties at the feet of even a great man, or to trust him with powers which enable him to subvert their institutions' (p. 196, this volume). But he's more worried about the capacity of 'great men' to impose their authority over society because of their popularity.[9]

Nevertheless, Ambedkar defends parliamentary democracy and wants to use democracy as a means for promoting national unity and social homogeneity. Independence opened a new chapter and he was prepared to try once again to bridge the gap between caste groups for building a unified political body—and, via this detour, a more egalitarian society. This is the deep meaning of the speech he made in the Constituent Assembly on 9 December 1946 (p. 127, this volume):

I know today we are divided politically, socially and economically. We are a group of warring camps and I may go even to the extent of confessing that I am probably one of the leaders of such a camp. But, Sir, with all this, I am quite convinced that given time and circumstances nothing in the world will prevent this country from becoming one. [Applause] With all our castes and creeds, I have not the slightest hesitation that we shall in some form be a united people [Cheers]. I have no hesitation in saying that notwithstanding the agitation of the Muslim League for the partition of India some day enough light would dawn upon the Muslims themselves and they too will begin to think that a United India is better even for them. [Loud cheers and applauses].

This speech made Ambedkar immediately popular and catapulted him to the Drafting Committee of the Assembly. At that time, he probably believed that a new India was possible and that he could influence the making of the Indian Constitution in such a manner that, in the end, not only politics, but also society would change. All the more so as he tried to give a social dimension to the Constitution of India—what he called 'economic democracy' in his 1 November 1948 speech:

> In my judgment, the directive principles have a great value, for they lay down that our ideal is economic democracy. Because we did not want merely a parliamentary form of Government to be instituted through the various mechanisms provided in the Constitution, without any direction as to what our economic ideal, as to what our social order ought to be, we deliberately included the Directive Principles in our Constitution. (p. 189, this volume)

Economic or Liberal Democracy

There is some tension in Dr Ambedkar's view of democracy between his emphasis on the economic dimension that needs to be added to this political system and his liberal inclination.

Besides his training in social sciences—sociology, political science, and economics—Dr Ambedkar was a lawyer who adhered to the values of political liberalism—as his references to John Stuart Mill (among others) testify.

His interest in the rule of law found expression in a constant promotion of the judiciary from the top to the bottom of the political system. In 1933, when the Village Panchayat Bill was discussed, he arraigned the idea that the five members of these village councils should be endowed with judicial power. He asked whether 'these five gentlemen who will be elected on the basis of adult suffrage will have sufficient judicial training to discharge the duties of judges? Sir, I would like to submit that judicial decisions demand a developed judgment; they demand a vast amount of legal knowledge' (p. 60, this volume). It shows that he looked [at] elected judiciary as not conducive to rule of law and emphasized that he had not found such a system anywhere else in the world.

As Chairman of the Drafting Committee, Dr Ambedkar was to fight in the same manner for the making of a professional, independent judiciary. A clear indication of his attachment to the values of liberal democracy was found then in his proposing an amendment in one plenary session—a rare occurrence because his task consisted especially in defending there the text of the Drafting Committee—in favour of a strict separation of the Executive power and the judiciary. Some representatives opposed it in the name of the authority of the State, by arguing that too strict a legal control would weaken it. Nehru took part in this debate even though his responsibilities as Prime Minister did not let him much time, because he wanted to support Ambedkar's amendment. It was adopted and became Article 50 of the Directive Principles. Ambedkar later defended the setting up of a judicial system of British inspiration. In his view, separation of powers would not, on any account, weaken the State, but rather strengthen democracy.

Besides a strong judiciary—that was to result in the making of the most independent Supreme Court in the world—Dr Ambedkar also wanted to insulate the electoral process from political interferences. Hence his plea for the making of an independent Election Commission which was to give the voting procedure a rare credibility. Though his ideas might indicate a tilt towards liberal democratic institutions but in the given circumstances of newly independent country, probably instituting autonomous institutions was one of the major concerns for making the democracy work.

Defending the values of liberal democracy also meant fighting totalitarianism across the board. The fight of the British against the Nazis was one of the reasons why he supported them during WWII—another reason, of course, was his decision to join the Viceroy's Council as Labour Minister. His assessment of the Nazi threat made his relation with Mahatma Gandhi even more adversial. In July 1942 he declared (p. 92, this volume):

> Except Mr. Gandhi, everyone knows that beyond a certain limit it is worse than useless and even when it succeeds because the British Government, unlike the Nazi Government are not addicted to the use of brute force and do not use unmoral means to suppress a moral cause. Mr. Gandhi will not admit it. That is only because he fortunately has no experience as to how the Nazis will deal with his mass Civil Disobedience. No doubt the Nazis will give Mr. Gandhi a very short shrift and prove that his plan of direct action can be put out of action at the very start.

Dr Ambedkar is a liberal because of his concern for the defense of the individual and his/her rights but he remained equally perturbed by the social inequalities that needed redressal. In May 1956, he pointed out, 'A society to be democratic should open a way to use all the capacities of the individual. Stratification is stunting of the growth of the individual and deliberate stunting is a deliberate denial of democracy' (p. 242, this volume)

In the same vein, Ambedkar opposed the criticisms of the left which wanted to qualify the Indian Republic, from the very first article of the

Constitution, as 'socialist', meaning a particular form of Socialism based on communistic idea as was prevalent in some countries like Union of Soviet Socialist Republic that had seen worst effects on the common masses of dictatorship of Stalin in the name of proletariat. According to him, this form of socialism would have the effect 'simply of destroying democracy', because it was for the government, designated by the people to choose the best form of social organization, as he explained it on 19 November 1948:

> The reason why we have established in this Constitution a political democracy is because we do not install by any means whatsoever a perpetual dictatorship of any particular body of people. While we have established political democracy, it is also the desire that we should lay down as our ideal economic democracy. [...] [Now], there are various ways in which people believe that economic democracy can be brought about; there are those who believe in individualism as the best form of economic democracy; there are those who believe in having a socialistic state as the best form of economic democracy; there are those who believe in the communistic ideas as the most perfect form of economic democracy [.;.].
>
> [In these conditions] we have deliberately introduced in the language that we have used, in the Directive Principles, something which is not fixed or rigid. We have left enough room for people of different ways of thinking, with regard to the reaching of the ideal of economic democracy, to strive in their own way, to persuade the electorate that it is the best way of reaching economic democracy... (pp. 188–9, this volume)

In this context, however, it must be recognized that on some issues Dr Ambedkar had to carry the wishes of the majority (or Congress party which was in majority in Constitution Assembly) in Constitution Assembly, even if the majority view deviated from his own. There were few such occasions and issues including the way he put the Directive Principles on a higher plank for the rulers of the future, where he had made an accommodation, and accepted the position, which deviated, from his own position. For instance in early 1930s, he favoured separate electorate, but had to settle down for reservation of seats in assemblies (under the threat of Gandhi's fast unto death). He favoured reservation in jobs as safeguards against discrimination in both government and private sector, but agreed for reservation of jobs in government sector to begin with. Or converted the Independent Labour party in to the Scheduled Caste Federation in 1942 for some consideration. (That he later corrected by replacing with Republication Party of India).

However, the two most important issues on which he had to make accommodation and carry the wishes of the majority in Constitution Assembly related to Socialism as the best form of economic democracy, and on the issue of right to private property. At first Dr Ambedkar favoured constitutional State Socialism (with Parliamentary Democracy) as the best form of economic democracy, but due to lack of support had to forge this alternative. His strong belief in State Socialism is also reflected when he commented on the aims and objectives of the Constitution while speaking on the Resolution, when he said:

> If this Resolution has a reality behind it and a sincerity, of which I have not the least doubt, coming as it does from the Mover of the Resolution[Nehru, the acclaimed socialist], I should have expected some provision whereby it would have been possible for the State to make economic, social and political justice a reality and I should have from that point of view expected the Resolution to state in most explicit terms that in order that there may be social and economic justice in the country, that there would be nationalisation of industry and nationalisation of land, I do not understand how it could be possible for any future Government which believes in doing justice socially, economically and politically, unless its economy is a socialistic economy. Therefore, personally, although I have no objection to the enunciation of these propositions, the Resolution is, to my mind, somewhat disappointing. I am however prepared to leave this subject where it is with the observations I have made. (pp. 126–7, this volume)

Much against his view, Dr Ambedkar had to carry the view and wishes of majority in the Constituent Assembly in favour of non-inclusion of Socialism. As a way out he brought in the Directive Principles of State Policy to achieve the goal of economic democracy. However, the clearest case of accommodation—carrying the majority view that deviates from his own—relates to the right to private property, Article 31. He disclosed, five years later, in his speech while speaking on the Constitution (Fourth Amendment) Bill 1954 on 19 March 1955 in Rajya Sabha:

> The Article 31 with which we are dealing with, in this amending Bill, is an Article for which the Drafting Committee, and I can take no responsibility whatsoever .We do not take any responsibility for that. That is not our draft. The result was that the Congress Party, at time when Article 31 was framed so divided with in itself that we did not know what to do? What to put and what not to put? There was a section in Congress Party, one section was made by Sardar Vallabhbhai Patel, who stood for full compensation in the

sense, enacted as our land acquisition, namely, market price plus15 percent solarium. That was his point of view, our Prime Minister was against compensation. Our friend, Mr. Pant who had conceived his Zamindari Abolition Bill before the Constitution—wanted a very safe delivery of baby. So he had his own proposition. There was this struggle and left the matter to them to decide in any way they like and nearly embodied what their decision was in Article 31. The Article 31 in my judgement is very ugly thing, something which I do not like to look at. (p. 236, this volume)

We can understand the anguish of Dr Ambedkar, given that fact that he had proposed the nationalization of land in his Memorandum 'State and Minorities' submitted to the Fundamental Rights Committee in 1946. He also advocated the same while speaking on the Objective Resolution in the Constituent Assembly and subsequently included it in the Manifesto of the Republican Party of India conceived by him.

With all these accommodations as Chairman of Drafting Committee, however, Dr Ambedkar believed that only social and economic reforms would take India on the path of a truly democratic trajectory. Hence his famous speech of 1949, after completing his job as Chairman of the Drafting Committee (p. 197, this volume):

On January 26, 1950 [date when the Constitution will be proclaimed], we are going to enter into a life of contradictions. In politics, we will have equality and in the social and economic life, we will have inequality (...). We must remove this contradiction at the earliest possible moment, or else those who suffer from inequality will blow up the structure of political democracy which this assembly has so laboriously built up.

Dr Ambedkar also declared that political democracy would have no meaning if it did not come along with some social democracy. This mark of lucidity demonstrated well that Ambedkar was not gullible of the practical efficiency of the Constitution to which he had devoted so much of his energy, but it does not mean that he doubted the importance of this kind of reform 'from above'. Simply, it was necessary to go farther on this path; that is why he subsequently devoted so much of his energies to the defense of the Hindu Code Bill that could never see the light of the day as he conceived it.

During 1947–50, the tension between the liberal and social dimensions of Dr Ambedkar's democratic ideal could be seen as manageable: in Constitution, both dimensions could be seen as the two faces of the coin, the former epitomized by the Fundamental Rights and the latter by the Directive Principles. This complementarity, however, had to be implemented by the government to become a reality. In this respect, Ambedkar was disappointed. The first shock came from the dilution of the Hindu Code Bill under the aegis of conservative Congressmen, Nehru did not want to oppose frontally. He resigned from Nehru's government in 1951 because of the Prime Minister's dilly-dallying attitude. By then, he was totally disillusioned and did not believe any more that the Indian Constitution was the social charter he had hoped for. In a Lok Sabha debate which took place in 1955, he replied to an MP asking for some clarification (p. 236, this volume):

> My friend says that the last time when I spoke, I said that I wanted to burn the Constitution. Well, in a hurry I did not explain the reason. Now that my friend has given me the opportunity, I think I shall give the reason. The reason is this: We built a temple for a god to come in and reside, but before the god could be installed, if the devil had taken possession of it, what else could we do except destroy the temple? We did not intend that it should be occupied by the Asuras. We intended it to be occupied by the devas. That is the reason why I said I would rather like to burn it.

Dr Ambedkar was naturally frustrated by the fact that the Indian government had not tried to reform society more effectively. And here he seems ready to use mythological terms like Asuras and Devas to make the people understand the issue at hand that he usually did not refer to. What was at stake was the quality of the Indian democracy at large. In May 1956, he made his views explicit on that subject in a statement to the Voice of America (p. 240, this volume).

He looked at democracy as a transformative force, as 'a form and method of government whereby revolutionary changes in the economic and social life of the people are brought about without bloodshed' (BAWS, Vol. 17{III} 2003: 475). Democracy for Ambedkar, thus, was not only confined to State and its apparatus but extended in the societal sphere where the people revere fraternity despite differences. For him, 'Democracy is not merely a form of Government. It is primarily a mode of associated living of conjoint communicated experience. It is essentially an attitude of respect and reverence towards fellowmen' (BAWS, Vol. 1, 1979: 57).

Dr Ambedkar was back to his 1919 assessment: democracy has to live in society for being meaningful and in India the resilience of caste hierarchies made it impossible to prosper. Which meant that his efforts to reform the polity of the country by using constitutional reforms had failed: he had taken the risk to play balls with the political establishment (including the Congress party) but they had not reciprocated as much as he expected. His goals remained the same—democracy—but he had to take a different route for achieving his dream of emancipation.

Since all the political strategies of Ambedkar had limited success by the mid-1950s—from the making of political parties which did not even ensure his election to parliament, to the implementation of the progressive potential of 'his' Constitution—Ambedkar turned to religion and converted to Buddhism. But in this creed, he was still looking at Buddhism as a trans-formative moral and social base for real democracy.

Buddhism as the Crucible of Democracy

At times, it seems that Ambedkar looked at democracy as a western creation that he had learnt from outside and imported. Certainly, he had read most of the European and American political philosophers of democracy and drew most of his inspiration from outside for drafting the Indian Consti-tution. His intellectual affinities with the West developed during his stays in the United States and in England. A good part of his ideas ensued from them. However in the Indian context, he recognized the need of religion of principles that are supportive of equality, freedom, and fraternity. He considered that, 'Religion is absolutely essential for the development of mankind' and diverged from the Marxists' atheism in that respect. But his vision of religion was over-determined by social considerations. He rejected Hinduism because he thought that the caste system was co-substantial to this religion, whereas equality was inherent in Buddhism (BAWS Vol. 17[III], 2003: 540):

> By remaining in the Hindu religion nobody can prosper in any way. Because of the stratification in Hindu religion, it is fact that higher varnas and castes are benefitted, but not the others? The Varna-System of Hindu religion is responsible for such a strange social structure. What improvement can take place from this? Prosperity can be achieved only in the Buddhist religion.
> In the Buddhist religion 75 percent Bhikkhus were Brahmins. 25 percent were the Shudras and others. But the Lord Buddha said, 'O Bhikkhus, you have come from different countries and castes.' Rivers flow separately when

they flow in their provinces, but they lose their identity when they meet the
sea. They become one and the same. The Buddhist Sangh is like an ocean.
In this Sangh all are equal.

Ambedkar's reading of Buddhism does not only have social implications—it
also has political implications. Considering that the 'religion of the Buddha
gives freedom of thought and freedom of self-development to all' (p. 201,
this volume), Ambedkar argues that, 'the rise of Buddhism in India was as
significant as the French Revolution'—a political event in the first place.
Ambedkar saw deep affinities between Buddhism and the French Revolution. In an All-India Radio broadcast speech on 3 October 1954 he declared
(pp. 230–31, this volume):

> Positively, my Social Philosophy, may be said to be enshrined in three
> words: Liberty, Equality and Fraternity. Let no one, however, say that I
> have borrowed my philosophy from the French-Revolution. I have not. My
> philosophy has roots in religion and not in political science. I have derived
> them from the teachings of my Master, the Buddha. In his philosophy, liberty
> and equality had a place. (...) He gave the highest place to fraternity as
> the only real safeguard against the denial of liberty or equality or fraternity
> which was another name for brotherhood or humanity, which was again
> another name for religion.

In that sense, Buddhism is a democratic religion and Ambedkar, eventually
found in this religion the societal values he had tried to promote via political democracy. Between 1919 and 1949–50 he tried to instill in the Indian
society a more fraternal sense of human relations by making assemblies
places of endosmosis, by arguing in favour of a new unity between the
majority and the minorities within the Constituent assembly itself. To no
avail: fraternity never resulted from these political arrangements. Hence
the last resort in conversion to Buddhism, a democratic religion, became
the last resort solution in his eyes by the mid-1950s.

This rediscovery of Buddhism had important implications. If the teachings of the Buddha was democratic, then democracy is not an invention of
the West—as the manner in which Dr Ambedkar drew his inspiration from
so many European and American scholars and leaders suggested—but it's a
product of the Indian history. In his historic speech of 25 November 1949
where Dr Ambedkar presented the final draft of the Indian Constitution
to the Assembly which was to pass it on 26 January 1950, he pointed out
that by becoming a parliamentary democracy 'again', India is back to its
Buddhist roots (p. 195, this volume):

It is not that India did not know Parliaments or Parliamentary Procedure. A study of the Buddhist Bhikshu Sanghas discloses that not only there were Parliaments—for the Sanghas were nothing but Parliaments—but the Sanghas knew and observed all the rules of Parliamentary Procedure known to modern times. They had rules regarding seating arrangements, rules regarding Motions, Resolutions, Quorum, Whip, Counting of Votes, Voting by Ballot, Censure Motion, Regularization, Res Judicata, etc. Although these rules of Parliamentary Procedure were applied by the Buddha to the meetings of the Sanghas, he must have borrowed them from the rules of the Political Assemblies functioning in the country in his time.

Such an 'invention of the tradition' (to use the words of Eric Hobsbawm [1983]) shows that even in his interpretation of the historical impact of Buddhism over India, Dr Ambedkar remains deeply interested in political ideas. This is evident from a tangible fact: on 13 October 1956, the day before he converted to Buddhism, in a grand ceremony in Nagpur, he addressed a press conference in which he announced that he had drafted the constitution of his new party, the Republican Party of India. (He called it the Republican Party of India by reference, at the same time, to Lincoln's American Republican Party and to the Republics of the Buddhist era in India.) In this charter, it was stated that this party would 'stand for the Parliamentary system of Government as the being the best form of Government both in the interest of the public and in the interest of the individual' (BAWS Vol. 17[II], 2003:152). This party would also uphold 'the secular character of the State'. These components of Dr Ambedkar's ideology of Republicanism reflect his liberal values, which are even more obvious in his deep attachment to the rule of law.

***

Democracy is the key to our understanding of Dr Ambedkar and his contribution to India's political history. A multifaceted concept in his view, it is somewhat co-terminus with his trajectory and achievements since it remains associated with his political career in more than one way: as a leader coming from untouchable background Dr Ambedkar tried to use democracy to ensure the representation of his caste fellows in elected assemblies, through positive discrimination and the making of political parties; as a believer in law, he promoted constitutional arrangements; as a progressive statesman, he argued in favour of equality and socialism as pre-conditions, of sustainable democracy. His socialist ideology and resistance to his proposal on constitutional socialism with parliamentary democracy in the Constituent Assembly made him to settle down for alternative solution or the second best solution in liberal mode. On a number of issues like political reservation through reserve seats, in place of separate electorate, reservation in only public sector in place of public and private sector both, Directive Principles of State Policy for social and economic democracy through liberal policies in place of state socialism, are some of the adjustments which Ambedkar had to make but did not dispense with the basic position on these concerns as is revealed in major contributions outside Constituent Assembly viz. in States and Minorities on the eve of end of colonial rule and in the manifesto of Republican Party of India. The influence of the pragmatism of his teacher, John Dewey of Colombia University, clearly reflects in some of these adjustments and accommodations. Nevertheless, his original thinking was rooted in democracy marked by absence of social and economic inequalities but his pragmatism reflects his inclination towards liberal ethos, where individual becomes the focus and it is probably this individual that needed to be freed from the clutches of societal and economic disparities in his model and without addressing the later, the former was not feasible which comes out distinctly. His contribution of *relative majority* to ease the influence of absolute majority in the legislatures and *principle of unanimity* in choice of Cabinet including the Prime minister for addressing the questions of minorities would remain among some of his original contributions in the successful functioning of a democracy. Though he believed in institutionalization for the success of democracy but it was not a one-way traffic, but an arrangement where citizens not only interrelate with others but also allow others to do the same. Thus he did not fix meanings to democracy beyond a certain level but allows the future generations to evolve by defining and redefining their own democracy.

Notes

1. Ambedkar will himself recognize the fact that, because he lived in a cantonment, he 'had a few relations with the outside world' and, consequently, was not at all conscious of his 'untouchability' (quoted in Das 1980 Vol. 4: 65).
2. These recollections of Ambedkar come from a speech given on 17 May 1936 when he spoke about some episodes of his life that shaped his decision to struggle against untouchability (Das 1967, Vol. 2: 67).

3. Probably the reason could be that around this period, i.e., 1928, the right to vote was too limited even for the general electorates due to the conditions of education and property, and that it was further restricted for the depressed classes/untouchables as they lacked these resources more than the general populace and Ambedkar saw a ray of hope in the universal adult franchise that will make all adult members of the Untouchables to vote.

4. The name given to this meeting, 'Conference of the Hindus and untouchable leaders', was paradoxical but revealing: even when Gandhi refused to consider the untouchables as being outside Hinduism, the qualification of 'Hindus' was reserved for the upper caste Congressmen participating in the conference.

5. *Constituent Assembly Debates.* Vol. 5. 1989 (New Delhi : Lok Sabha Secretariat), p. 260.

6. *Constituent Assembly Debates* p. 265.

7. *Constituent Assembly Debates* p. 272.

8. On this notion, see Herrenshmidt (1997: 37).

9. While he thought that parliamentary democracy would make the personalization of power more difficult in India, he was shocked by the way Nehru imposed his views on others. In 1955 he declared in parliament, 'In our country the dogma on which we proceed is that the Prime Minister can do no wrong and that he will do no wrong. Therefore, anything that the Prime Minister proposes to do must be accepted as correct and without question. This devotion in politics to a personality may be excusable in some cases, but it does not seem to me excusable where the fundamental rights are being invaded.'

References

Dr. Babasaheb Ambedkar's Writings and Speeches (BAWS) 1979. Vol. 1. Education Department, Government of Maharashtra, India.

———. 1982. Vol. 2 Education Department, Government of Maharashtra, India.

———. 1991. Vol. 9. Education Department, Government of Maharashtra, India.

———. 1991. Vol. 10. Education Department, Government of Maharashtra, India.

———. 1994. Vol. 13. Education Department, Government of Maharashtra, India.

———. 2003. Vol. 17. Part I, Part II and Part III Education Department, Government of Maharashtra, India.

Das, Bhagwan. 1967 *Thus Spoke Ambedkar.* Vol 2. Bangalore: Ambedkar Sahitya Prakashana.

———. 1980. *Thus Spoke Ambedkar.* Vol 4. Jalandhar: Buddhist Publishing House.

Herrenshmidt, Olivier. 1997. 'L'inégalité graduée ou la pire des inégalités. L'analyse de la société hindoue par Ambedkar', *Archive Européenne de Sociologie,* p. 37.

Hobsbawm, Eric. 1983. 'Introduction: Inventing Traditions', in E. Hobsbawm and T. ranger (eds), *The Invention of Tradition*. Cambridge: Cambridge University Press.

Jaffrelot, C. 2005. *Dr Ambedkar and Untouchability–Analysing and Fighting Caste*. New Delhi: Permanent Black, p. 28.

Keer, Dhanajay. 1954. *Dr Ambedkar: Life and Mission*. Bombay: Popular Prakashan, pp. 298–9.

Pitkin, Hanna F. 1972. *The Concept of Representation*. Los Angeles: University of California Press.

1 Evidence Before the Southborough Committee (27 January 1919)

A BRIEF SKETCH ABOUT THE DOCUMENT

The evidence before the Southborough Committee on 27 January 1919 has been the first major intervention of Ambedkar with regard to the political reforms started by British. It was in the context of British government modifying the Government of India Act after every ten years. It aimed at participation of citizens in the process of government and hence wished for a popular government to provide both the representation of persons and representation of opinions. British regarded India unfit for representative government because of the division of the society on various primordial identities viz. caste, creed, religion, etc. To find a solution to the hurdle of the popular government, Ambedkar put forth his views through a memorandum and with personal appearance before the committee. He brought forth the issues of separate identity, need for separate representation to the depressed classes (untouchables), and making the system of governance more democratic. These initial arguments have been taken from BAWS, Volume I, 1979 (pp. 247–73).

'The most difficult and the most momentous question of Government (is) how to transmit the force of individual opinion and preference into public action. This is the crux of popular institutions'. So says Professor A.B. Hart. But this is only half the definition of popular Government. It is therefore necessary to emphasize the other half which is equal if not more in importance. As the Government is the most important field for the exercise of individual capacities, it is in the interest of the people that no person as such should be denied the opportunity of actively participating in the process of Government. That is to say popular Government is not only Government for the people but by the people. To express the same in a different way, representation of opinions by itself is not sufficient to constitute popular Government. To cover its true meaning it requires personal representation as well. It is because the former is often found without the latter that the Franchise Committee has to see in devising the franchises and constituencies for a popular Government in India, it provides for both, i.e., representation of opinions and representation of persons. Any scheme of franchise and constituency that fails to bring this about fails to create a popular Government.

Success in this task will ultimately depend upon the accuracy of the *de facto* conception of the society which is to be given the popular form of Government. *De facto* India was well portrayed by Lord Dufferin when he described it as a ...

> Population . . . composed of a large number of distinct nationalities, professing various religions, practising diverse rites, speaking different languages, while many of them ... still further separated from one another by discordant prejudices, by conflicting sources of usages, and even antagonistic material interests. But perhaps the most patent characteristic of our Indian cosmos is its division into two mighty political communities as distant from each other as the poles apart—On the one hand the Hindus—with their elaborate caste distinctions—on the other hand, the Mohammedans—with their social equality. To these must be added a host of minor nationalities most of them numbering millions—almost as widely differentiated from one another by ethnological or political distinctions as are the Hindus from the Mohammedans, such as Sikhs, with their warlike habits and traditions and their enthusiastic religious beliefs, the Rohillas, the Pathans, the Assamese, the Baluchis and other wild and martial tribes on our frontiers, the hillmen dwelling in the folds of the Himalayas, our subjects in Burma, Mongol in race and Buddhist in religion, the Gonds, Mhars, Bheels and other non-Aryan people in the centre and south of India, and the enterprising Parsees, with their rapidly developing manufactures and commercial interests. Again, amongst these numerous communities may be found, at one and the same moment, all the various stages of civilization through which mankind has passed from the pre-historic ages to the present days.

Englishmen have all along insisted that India is unfit for representative Government because of the division of her population into castes and creeds. This does not carry conviction with the advanced wing of Indian politicians. When they say that there are also social divisions in Europe as there are in India they are amply supported by facts. The social divisions of India are equaled, if not outdone, in a country like the United States of America. Corresponding to those in the former, we have in the latter men bonded together in a criminal conspiracy and trust or combinations that prey upon the public. Not only are there political sub-divisions but also industrial, scientific, and religious associations, differing in their aims and their attitudes towards each other. Apart from political parties with diverse ends, social sets, cliques and gangs we find in the United States of America more permanent divisions of the population such as the Poles, Dutch, Swedes, Germans, Russians, etc., each with its own language, religious and moral codes and traditions. If social divisions unfit a country for representative Government, it should unfit the United States of America as much as India. But if with all the social divisions, the United States of America is fit for representative Government, why not India? Ask the Indian politicians, so entrenched, it is difficult to dislodge them, and show that the social divisions of India are of a different kind or grant them their contention. Without these two there is no third alternative possible.

In my opinion their contention cannot be granted, for the social divisions of India do matter in politics. How they matter can be best shown by understanding when they do not matter. Men live in a community by virtue of the things they have in common. What they must have in common in order to form a community are aims, beliefs, aspirations, knowledge, a common understanding; or to use the language of the Sociologists, they must be like-minded. But how do they come to have these things in common or how do they become like-minded? Certainly, not by sharing with another as one would do in the case of a piece of cake. To cultivate an attitude similar to others or to be like-minded with others is to be in communication with them or to participate in their activity. Persons do not become like-minded by merely living in physical proximity, any more than they cease to be like-minded by being distant from each other. Participation in a group is the only way of being like-minded with the group. Each group tends to create its own distinctive type of like-mindedness, but where there are more groups than one to be brought into political union, there would be conflict among the differently like-minded. And so long as the groups remain isolated the conflict is bound to continue and prevent the harmony of action. It is the isolation of the groups that is the chief evil. Where the groups allow of endosmosis they cease to be evil. For endosmosis among the groups makes possible a re-socialization of once socialized attitudes. In place of the old, it creates a new like-mindedness, which is representative of the interests, aims, and aspirations of all the various groups concerned. Like-mindedness is essential for a harmonious life, social or political and, as has just been shown, it depends upon the extent of communication, participation or endosmosis. Applying this test to the divisions in India, we must pronounce upon them as constituting an obstacle in the path of realizing a harmonious political life.

The groups or divisions each with its set like-mindedness that are sure to be in conflict may be given as follows:

1. Hindus
2. Mohammedans
3. Christians
4. Parsees
5. Jews, etc.

Except the Hindus the rest of the divisions are marked by such complete freedom of communication from within that we may expect their members to be perfectly like-minded with respect to one another. Regarding the Hindus, however, the analysis must be carried on a little farther. The significant fact about the Hindus is that before they are Hindus they are members of some caste. The castes are so exclusive and isolated that the consciousness of being a Hindu would be the chief guide of a Hindu's activity towards non-Hindu. But as against a Hindu of a different caste his caste-consciousness would be the chief guide of activity. From this, it is plain that as between two Hindus, caste-like-mindedness is more powerful than the like-mindedness due to their both being Hindus. Thus from within the Hindus as from without, there is likely to be a conflict of like-minded persons. There are some who argue that this conflict runs through the whole gamut of the caste system. But this is protesting too much. From the point of view of communication the Hindus, in spite of castes, divide themselves into two significant groups—the touchables and the untouchables. The touchables have enough communication between them to enable us to say that the conflict of like-mindedness so far as they are concerned is not much to be dreaded. But there is a real difference and consequent conflict between the like-mindedness of the touchables and the untouchables. Untouchability is the strongest ban on the endosmosis between them. Their complete isolation accounts for the acuteness of the difference of like-mindedness.

The real social divisions of India then are:

1. Touchable Hindus
2. Untouchable Hindus
3. Mohammedans
4. Christians
5. Parsees
6. Jews

It will not do good to ignore these real divisions in devising a system of policy, if the policy is to take the form of popular Government. But if the success of popular Government depends upon how well the constituencies and franchises transmit the social forces and how well they secure personal representation; we must first study the form, which the conflict between these groups will assume in an election.

In a territorial constituency, which will group together voters belonging to the above groups, a majority of votes will declare a candidate to be a representative for the constituency in question. Now the question arises: is such a candidate, a true representative of the groups, covered by the territorial constituency? Is he a true mirror of the mind of the constituency? Is he a representative of all the interests in the constituency? To be concrete, will a Hindu candidate represent Mohammedan interests? At this stage it must be recalled that the various divisions described above are held together by a community of interests, which are non-secular or purely religious. We cannot say that each division is held together by a community of interests, which are secular or material. If so, then for secular purposes the groups will be broken up. From the point of view of material interests, there are no such people as Mohammedans, Parsees, Hindus, etc. There will be in each of these groups landlords, labourers, capitalists, free traders, protectionists, etc., each of the groups having community of interests which are material will be composed of Hindus, Mohammedans, Parsees, etc. Consequently, a Hindu candidate can very well represent the material interests of the Mohammedans and *vice versa*. There is thus no conflict of material interest in the main among the communities as such. If we suppose that religious interests in future will occupy a subordinate place in the affairs of men, the secular interests of a group can be well represented by a candidate from another group.

From this point of view a territorial constituency will be sufficient for a popular Government. A little more consideration will show that it will be sufficient for only one-half the definition of popular Government. How true it is, will be shown presently. In an electoral fight between the various groups in a territorial constituency the voters will discriminate in favour of a candidate with whom they are in sympathy. But with whom they will be in sympathy is determined for them in advance. Given two candidates belonging to different groups but purporting to represent the same interest, the voters will mark their votes on the person belonging to the same community. Any group yielding a large number of electors will have its own candidate elected. This discrimination on the part of the voters, though it may not leave unrepresented the interests of the members of the minor groups, leaves them without any chance of personal representation.

To those who are busy in devising schemes for the proper and adequate representation of interests and opinions dilating on the importance of personal representation is likely to seem idle. But personal representation is not therefore unimportant. In recent times 'Government for the people' has claimed more attention than 'Government by the people'. In fact there are instances to show that 'Government for the people' can exist in the best sense of the phrase without there being a 'Government by the people'. Yet all political theorists will unanimously condemn such a form of Government. And the why of it is important to know. It will be granted that each kind of association, as it is an educative environment, exercises a formative influence on the active dispositions of its members. Consequently, what one is as a person is what one is as associated with others. A Government for the people, but not by the people, is sure to educate some into masters and others into subjects; because it is by the reflex effects of association that one can feel and measure the growth of personality. The growth of personality is the highest aim of society. Social arrangement must secure free initiative and opportunity to every individual to assume any role he is capable of assuming provided it is socially desirable. A new rule is a renewal and growth of personality. But when an association—and a Government is after all an association—is such that in it every role cannot be assumed by all, it tends to develop the personality of the few at the cost of the many—a result scrupulously to be avoided in the interest of Democracy. To be specific, it is not enough to be electors only. It is necessary to be law-makers; otherwise who can be law-makers will be masters of those who can only be electors.

Territorial constituencies are therefore objected to, and rightly, on the ground that they do nothing to prevent this absurd outcome. They erroneously suppose that electors will vote on the programmes of the candidates without any regard for their persona. As a matter of fact, the electors before they are electors are primarily members of a group. The persona of the candidates does matter with them. Naturally, therefore, as members of a group they prefer the candidate who belongs to their group to another candidate who does not belong to their group though both of them claim to represent the same interest. As a result of this preference the electors of a large group are destined to rise to a higher position of becoming eventual law-makers, while the electors of a smaller group for no fault of theirs are doomed to a lower position of remaining electors. One crux of popular Government is the representation of interests and opinions. The other crux is personal representation. Territorial constituencies fail to create popular Government because they fail to secure personal representation to members of minor groups.

If this is a correct analysis as to how the social divisions operate to the prejudice of the political life of some communities, never was a more improper remedy advocated to meet the situation than proportional representation. Proportional representation is intended to give proportionate representation to views. It presupposes that voters vote for a candidate because of his views and not because of his persona. Proportional representation is ill-suited for the purpose in hand.

We have therefore two possible methods of meeting the situation: either to reserve seats in plural constituencies for those minorities that cannot otherwise secure personal representation or grant communal electorates. Both have their usefulness. So far as the representation of the Mohammedans is concerned, it is highly desirable that they should participate in a general election with seats reserved for them in plural constituencies. The angularity of the division that separates the Hindus and Mohammedans is already sharp and communal representation, it may be urged, sharpens it the more. Communal election, however, seems to be a settled fact, so far as the Mohammedans are concerned and nothing is likely to alter it, even though alteration is likely to be beneficial.

But this argument is mainly intended to concern itself with the representation of the Hindus in general, and of the untouchable Hindus in particular. The discussion of the representation of the Hindus may be best introduced by a quotation, which expresses the newer consciousness that has arisen in the various Hindu groups. It is said:

A community may claim representation only on the ground of separate interests which require protection. In India, such interests are of three kinds only: either they arise out of religious antipathies which are pretty strong in India, or out of the backward state of a community in educational matters, or out of the socio-religious disabilities to which a community may be subject. Confining ourselves to the Hindu communities there are certain communities who, besides being very backward, are suffering under a great social tyranny. The untouchable classes must have their own men in the Council Hall to fight for the redress of their grievances. The non-Brahmins as a class are subjected to the social and intellectual domination of the Brahmin priesthood and may therefore rightly advocate separate representation.

From this it will be seen that the new consciousness among the Hindus while acknowledging the separate interests of the untouchables does not accept the position that the touchable Hindus form a group by themselves. The new consciousness insists on dividing the touchable group into Brahmins and non-Brahmins each with its own separate interests. Separate electorates or reserved seats in mixed electorates are demanded for the three groups in which the Hindus are divided. Before dealing with the problems of the representation of the untouchables something will be said on the question of the Brahmins and non-Brahmins.

That the non-Brahmins are 'backward in educational matters' cannot be said in any way to be their special interest. It is the general interest of all even of those Brahmins who are educationally backward. 'The intellectual and social domination of the Brahmins' is not a matter that affects the non-Brahmins alone. It affects all and it is therefore the interest of all. What remains then as a special interest for the non-Brahmins to require their protection?

The case for separate representation for non-Brahmins fails because they cannot prove to have a common non-Brahmin interest.

But do they fail to secure personal representation? This can be best shown by reference to figures—

Reducing the above figures to the basis of a thousand we have the following interesting result						
	Group I			Group II		
Names of castes	Proportion of population of a caste to every thousand of the population covered	Proportion of voters of a caste to every thousand of the same caste population	Proportion of voters of a caste to every thousand of voters	Proportion of population of a caste to every thousand of the population covered	Proportion of voters of a caste to every thousand of the population of the same caste	Proportion of voters of a caste to every thousand of voters
1	2	3	4	5	6	7
Brahmins	30.2	53.7	197.2	50.8	49.8	367.4
Lingayats	329.4	13.6	545.7			
Marathas	90.2	4.2	46.0	248.8	8.2	300.9
Mahars	69.5	0.1	0.9	74.5	0.2	2.7
Mohammedans	104.4	2.2	28.3	59.2	10.9	95.9
Others	376.2	3.9	181.3	562.2	2.8	232.8

So arranged, the conclusions to be drawn from these figures are highly important.

The Brahmins, given a uniform franchise for all, though a small minority so far as numbers are concerned becomes a majority so far as the total of voters is concerned as is the case in Group II.

Though with a uniform franchise the non-Brahmin communities like the Lingayats and Marathas do not fail to figure on the voters' list, the proportion of their voters to their population is insignificant as compared with the proportion which the Brahmin voters bear to the Brahmin population.

The proportion of the Brahmins to their voters is really extravagant. It is justified neither by faith in them nor by their own numbers. The Lingayats though they can legitimately complain that the proportion of their voters is small will succeed in securing personal representation. The Marathas though larger in numbers than the Brahmins, besides the very small proportion of their voters suffer on the voters' list and very likely will fail to secure personal representation for themselves.

So argued, the case for special provision of the Marathas can be sustained and should be admitted.

The question is in what form the provision should take. In my opinion such provision instead of taking the form of separate electorates of reserved seats should take the form of a low pitched franchise. The franchise for the non-Brahmin should be lower than that for the Brahmin. By this arrangement the Marathas would improve their position on the voters' list and the altogether favoured position of the Brahmin would be equalized. It is in the interest of all that the Brahmin should not play such a preponderant part in politics as he has been doing hitherto. He has exerted a pernicious influence on the social life of the country and it is in the interest of all that his pernicious influence should be kept at a minimum in politics. As he is the most exclusive he is most anti-social.

Even the authors of the report on constitutional reforms are not in favour of a limited or uniform franchise. They say, 'We consider that the limitations of the franchise, which it is obviously desirable to make as broad as possible, should be determined rather with reference to practical difficulties than to any prior considerations as to the degree of education or amount of income which may be held to constitute a qualification. It is possible that owing to unequal distribution of population and wealth it may be necessary to differentiate the qualifications for a vote not merely between provinces, but between different parts of the same province' (p. 147). To this

I should like to add that we should differentiate the qualifications for a vote not merely between provinces or parts thereof but between communities of the same province. Without this differentiation some communities with a small but wealthy or educated population will secure more votes than a large community consisting of poor and uneducated members. Uniformity in franchise should be dispensed with. An important result will be that communal representation or reservation of seats for some non-Brahmin communities who are now clamouring for it would be avoided.

The untouchables are usually regarded as objects of pity but they are ignored in any political scheme on the score that they have no interests to protect. And yet their interests are the greatest. Not that they have large property to protect from confiscation. But they have their very *persona* confiscated. The socioreligious disabilities have dehumanized the untouchables and their interests at stake are therefore the interests of humanity. The interests of property are nothing before such primary interests.

If one agrees with the definition of slave as given by Plato, who defines him as one who accepts from another the purposes which control his conduct, the untouchables are really slaves. The untouchables are so socialized as never to complain of their low estate. Still less do they ever dream of trying to improve their lot, by forcing the other classes to treat them with that common respect which one man owes to another. The idea that they have been born to their lot is so ingrained in their mind that it never occurs to them to think that their fate is anything but irrevocable. Nothing will ever persuade them that men are all made of the same clay, or that they have the right to insist on better treatment than that meted out to them.

The exact description of the treatment cannot be attempted. The word untouchable is an epitome of their ills and sufferings. Not only has untouchability arrested the growth of their personality but also it comes in the way of their material well-being. It has also deprived them of certain civil rights. For instance, in Konkan the untouchables are prohibited from using the public road. If some high caste man happens to cross him, he has to be out of the way and stand at such a distance that his shadow will not fall on the high caste man. The untouchable is not even a citizen. Citizenship is a bundle of rights such as (1) personal liberty, (2) personal security, (3) rights to hold private property, (4) equality before law, (5) liberty of conscience, (6) freedom of opinion and speech, (7) right of assembly, (8) right of representation in a country's Government and (9) right to hold office under the State. The British Government by gradual growth may be said to have conceded these rights at least in theory to its Indian subjects. The right of representation and the right to hold office under the State are the two most important rights that make up citizenship. But the untouchability of the untouchables puts these rights far beyond their reach. In a few places they do not even possess such insignificant rights as personal liberty and personal security, and equality before law is not always assured to them. These are the interests of the untouchables. And as can be easily seen they can be represented by the untouchables alone. They are distinctively their own interests and none else can truly voice them. A free trade interest can be voiced by a Brahmin, a Mohammedan, or a Maratha equally well. But none of these can speak for the interests of the untouchables because they are not untouchables. Untouchability constitutes a definite set of interests which the untouchables alone can speak for.

Hence it is evident that we must find the untouchables to represent their grievances which are their interests and, secondly, we must find them in such numbers as will constitute a force sufficient to claim redress.

Now, will a general territorial electorate provided for the adequate return of the untouchables to the law-making body? Referring back to the figures we find that the untouchables (represented in the table by the Mahars), though they formed 69.4 in every thousand of the population, did not claim even a voter from their class. Under such circumstances it is impossible for them to elect their own man in a general electorate. On the other hand they must despair of any votes being cast by the touchable Hindus for an untouchable candidate. The gradation of castes produces a certain theological basis which cuts the untouchables both ways: in the minds of the lower orders it creates a preference for the higher orders while it creates a contempt for the lower orders in the minds of the higher orders. Thus the ascending scale of preference and the descending scale of hatred and contempt beggars the untouchables both ways. Without giving a single vote to the untouchables the touchables are sure to make a large draft on the already meagre voting strength of the untouchables... ... ...

What the franchise should be is a very important question. There is a line of argument which urges that franchise should be given to those only who can be expected to make an intelligent use of it. As against this view it can be said in the words of Prof. L.T. Hobhouse that it is true that 'the success of democracy depends on the response of voters to the opportunities given them. But conversely the opportunities must be given in order to call forth the response. The exercise of popular Government is itself all education . . . enfranchisement itself may precisely be the stimulus needed to awaken interest. The ballot alone effectively liberates the quiet citizen from the tyranny of the shouter and the wire-puller. An impression of existing inertness alone is not a sufficient reason for withholding responsible Government or restricting the area of suffrage.' Taking into consideration that suffrage is an education and that there are groups with unequal distribution of wealth and education among them and that these groups are not sympathetically like-minded, the authors of the reports rightly argue that the case for uniformity of franchise cannot be sustained.

But in the case of the untouchables there are as few reasons for curtailing the number of their representatives as the reasons for widening their electorate are many. If under a given franchise the untouchables do not muster strong as electors, it is not their fault. The very untouchability attached to their person is a bar to their moral and material progress. The principal modes of acquiring wealth are trade, industry, or service. The untouchables can engage in none of these because of their untouchability. From an untouchable trader no Hindu will buy. An untouchable cannot be engaged in lucrative service. Military service had been the monopoly of the untouchables since the days of the East India Company. They had joined the Army in such large numbers that the Marquis Tweedledale in his note which he submitted to the Indian Army Commission of 1859 wrote, 'It should never be forgotten that India was conquered with the help of the low-caste men.' But after the mutiny when the British were able to secure soldiers from the ranks of the Marathas, the position of the low-caste men who had been the prop of the Bombay Army became precarious, not because the Marathas were better soldiers but because their theological bias prevented them from serving under low-caste officers. The prejudice was so strong that even the non-caste British had to stop recruitment from the untouchable classes. In like manner, the untouchables are refused service in the Police Force. In a great many of the Government offices it is impossible for an untouchable to get a place. Even in the mills a distinction is observed. The untouchables are not admitted in Weaving Departments of the Cotton Mills though many of them are professional weavers. An instance at hand may be cited from the school system of the Bombay Municipality. This most cosmopolitan city ruled by a Corporation with a greater freedom than any other Corporation in India has two different sets of schools . . . one for the children of touchables and the other for those of the untouchables. This in itself is a point worthy of note.

But there is something yet more noteworthy. Following the division of schools it has divided its teaching staff into untouchables and touchables. As the untouchable teachers are short of the demand, some of the untouchable schools are manned by teachers from the touchable class. The heart-killing fun of it is that if there is a higher grade open in untouchable school service, as there is bound to be because of a few untouchable trained teachers, a touchable teacher can be thrust into the grade. But if a higher grade is open in the touchable school service, no untouchable teacher can be thrust into that grade. He must wait till a vacancy occurs in the untouchable service ! ! ! Such is the ethics of the Hindu social life. Under it if the untouchables are poor, the committee, it may be hoped, will not deny them representation because of their small electoral roll but will see its way to grant them adequate representation to enable the untouchables to remove the evil conditions that bring about their poverty. At present when all the avenues of acquiring wealth are closed, it is unwise to require from the untouchables a high property qualification. To deny them the opportunities of acquiring wealth and then to ask from them a property qualification is to add insult to injury. Just what sort of franchise and just what pitch are required to produce sufficient voting strength from the untouchables? In absence of data, I leave it to the Committee to decide. It would be better to pitch the franchise so low as to educate into political life as many untouchables as possible. They are too degraded to be conscious of themselves. I only wish to emphasize that in deciding upon the representation of the untouchables the Committee looking to their interests at stake will not let the extent of the electorate govern the number of representatives, but will rather let the number of representatives govern the extension of the electorate.

In this connection it would not be improper to remind the Committee of Lord Morley who is reported to have said that 'the object of Government was that the Legislative Councils should represent truly and effectively with reasonable approach to the balance of real social forces, the wishes and needs of the communities concerned. This could not be done by Algebra, Arithmetic, Geometry or Logic, but by a wide outlook. He saw no harm as to a compromise that while numbers should be the main factor in determining the extent of representation modifying causes might influence the number of representatives.' It is therefore proposed that the untouchables of the Bombay Presidency should be allowed to elect 9 members through the constituencies made up as above. These 9 members will further form a constituency to elect one member from among themselves to represent the untouchables in the Imperial Legislative Council leaving 8 members to represent the untouchables in the Bombay Legislative Council.

Besides communal electorates there are other schemes in the field for the representation of the untouchables. It would not be proper to close this statement without a word of comment on those Schemes.

The Congress has denied communal representation except in the case of Mohammedans and it also denies the extensive use of nomination; the only way then left, open to the untouchables is to fight in a general electorate. Now this is as it should be if all were equally free to fight. To educate the untouchables by Shastras into pro-touchables and the touchables into anti-untouchables and then to propose that the two should fight out at an open poll is to betray signs of mental aberration or a mentality fed on cunning. But it must never be forgotten that the Congress is largely composed of men who are by design political Radicals and social Tories. Their chant is that the social and the political are two distinct things having no bearing on each other. To them the social and the political are two suits and can be worn one at a time as the season demands. Such a psychology has to be laughed at because it is too interested to be seriously taken into consideration either for acceptance or for rejection. As it pays to believe in it, it will die a hard death. Starting from this unnatural premise the Congress activities have been quite natural. Those who attend the Congress do not care to attend the National Social Conference held in the same pandal. In fact those who attend the Congress had once started a campaign to refuse the use of the pandal to the Conference which was once refused the pandal in the city of Poona, the roosting place of the intelligentsia of our Presidency, as the Congress is a non-national or anti-national body, its views on communal electorates are worthy of no serious consideration.

The moderates in their separate meeting have been more kindly than just. They proposed the reservation of seats for backward communities in plural constituencies. They have not specified the number of seats for the untouchables. But the general sense of many enlightened moderates and others kindly inclined is that one or two representatives of the untouchables in the Legislative Council would suffice. It is impossible to agree with these gentlemen though they are entitled to gratitude for this much sympathy. One or two representatives of the untouchables are as good as having none.

A Legislative Council is not an old curiosity shop. It will be a Council with powers to make or mar the fortunes of society. How can one or two untouchables carry a legislative measure to improve their condition or prevent a legislative measure worsening their state? To be frank, the untouchables cannot expect much good from the political power to be given over to the high caste Hindus. Though the power may not be used against the untouchables and one cannot be altogether sure of this, it may not be used for their betterment. A Legislative Council may be sovereign to do anything it likes, but what it will like to do depends upon its own character. The English Parliament, we may be certain, though it is sovereign to do anything, will not make the preservation of blue-eyed babies illegal. The Sultan will not, though he can, change the religion of Mohammed just as the Pope will not, though he can, overthrow the religion of Christ. In the same way legislature, mainly composed of high caste men, will not pass a law removing untouchability, sanctioning inter-marriages, removing the ban on the use of public streets, public temples, public schools; in short, cleansing the person of the untouchables. This is not because they cannot, but chiefly because they will not. A legislature is the product of a certain social condition and its power is determined by whatever determines society. This is too obvious to be denied. What may happen in future can be guessed from what has happened in the past. The high caste men in the Council do not like any social question being brought before the legislature, as may be seen from the fact of the Resolution introduced by the Honourable Mr Dadabhoy in 1916 in the Imperial Legislative Council. That it was adversely criticized by many who claimed to evince some interest in the untouchables is too well known to need repetition. But what is not well known is that though the resolution was lost the mover was not pardoned; for the very moving of such a nasty resolution was regarded as a sin. At a subsequent election the mover had to make room for the Honourable Mr Khaparde, who once wrote in an article: 'Those who work for the elevation of the untouchables are themselves degraded.'

Isn't this sympathy of the higher castes for the untouchables, sympathy with a vengeance?

Those who tell that one or two members would suffice for the untouchables fail to grasp the true import of political right. The chief import of a political right though technically summed up in the power to vote does lie either in voting upon for laws or for those who make laws; neither does it consist in the right to speak for or against a certain measure nor in being able to say 'yea or nay' upon roll-call; to be able to put into a ballot-box a piece of paper with a number of names written thereon is an act which, like those mentioned above, of itself possesses no value which stamps it as inherently superior to many of the most ordinary transactions of daily life. They are educative but as much as any transaction is. The chief significance of suffrage or a political right consists in a chance for active and direct participation in the regulation of the terms upon which associated life shall be sustained. Now the terms upon which the associated life between the touchables and untouchables is carried on today are the most ignominious to the former and highly detrimental to the latter. To make effective the capacities of a people there must be the power to fix the social conditions of their exercise. If the conditions are too obdurate, it is in the interest of the untouchables as well as of the touchables that the conditions should be revised. The untouchables must be in a position to influence the revision. Looking to the gravity of their interests, they should get their representation as proposed in proportion to their population. One or two is only kind but neither just nor sufficient. As Lord Morley says in an earlier quotation, 'needs not numbers should govern the extent of representations'.

Recently there is brought into the forefront a rival scheme for the representation of the untouchables by the Depressed Class Mission. The scheme is known as co-option. The scheme proposes that the representatives of the untouchables should be nominated by the co-option of the elected members of the Council. Whether one should laugh or cry at the solicitude of the Mission for the untouchables it is rather difficult to decide. To cry is to believe that such a silly scheme would ever be adopted. The best way is to laugh it out. From the scheme can be easily seen that what is some times called benevolent interest in others may be an unwilling mask for an attempt to dictate to them what their good shall be, instead of an endeavour to agree with them so that they may seek and find the good of their own choice. The Mission, it must be said, was started with the intention of improving the condition of the Depressed Classes by emancipating them from the social tyranny of their high caste masters. But the Mission has fallen on such bad times that it is forced to advocate a scheme by which its wards or their representatives will be bounden slaves of their past masters. The masters and the mission have thus met and evolved a scheme which will keep the Depressed classes eternally depressed without any hope of deliverance. Such tactics do not deceive the untouchables ignorant as they are; much less will they deceive the Franchise Committee. From another point of view the scheme of the Mission is unacceptable. It is aggravating to see the Mission proposing a scheme for the representation of the untouchables while persistently refusing to admit an untouchable in its governing council. Interested and officious as it is, its scheme must be rejected.

Nomination even though by Government in itself to be preferred to the former kind of nomination, is to be objected to from the standpoint of the untouchables. Apart from restricting the freedom of the representatives it fails to give political education which is the urgent need of all communities, much more of the untouchables.

At this stage we must consider the argument against communal representation. The first argument raised by the authors of the report is to the effect 'that the history of self-government among the nations who have developed it is decisively against' communal representation. But on an earlier page the authors say that the difference of caste and creeds must be taken 'into account as presenting a feature of Indian Society which is out of harmony with the ideas on which elsewhere in the world representative institutions rest' (p. 97). In writing the former the later analysis of the situation must have vanished from their minds, else we must say that the authors could hold two opposing views at the same time. Presented in juxtaposition, the authors must be expected to agree to communal representation on the score of an exceptional remedy required to meet an exceptional situation.

Another and chief argument against communal representation is that it will perpetuate social divisions. The fun of it is that those who uphold the social divisions are the loudest in their expression of this adverse argument. The committee will please note that those who are the opponents of communal representation on this score are also the staunchest opponents of Mr Patel's Inter-Caste Marriage Bill as a caste-breaking bill. The sincerity of those who bring forward this argument is seriously to be doubted. But as even the authors of the report have put it as a second count against communal representation, this particular argument must be met if possible.

Does communal representation perpetuate social divisions? If you look upon communal representation as making electoral Colleges of social divisions, the criticism may be said to be valid. This is true only if it is presupposed that the divisions are no real divisions and that they don't matter. This is as false a pre-supposition as that of inviting India which is made when it is said that Englishmen are unsocial. Communal Representation is a device to ward off the evil effects of the divisions. To those who, while agreeing to this particular benefit of communal representation, object to it on the score that it perpetuates the divisions it can be shown that there is another perspective from which it can be said that communal representation instead of perpetuating the social divisions is one of the ways of dissolving them.

While communal electorates will be co-terminous with social divisions their chief effect will be to bring together men from diverse castes who would not otherwise mix together into the Legislative Council. The Legislative Council will thus become a new cycle of participation in which the representatives of various castes who were erstwhile isolated and therefore anti-social will be thrown into an associated life. An active participation in an associated life, in its turn, will not leave unaffected the dispositions and attitudes of those who participate. A caste or a religious group to-day is a certain attitude. So long as each caste or a group remains isolated its attitude remains fossilized. But the moment the several castes and groups begin to have contact and co-operation with one another the resocialization of the fossilized attitude is bound to be the result. If the Hindus become resocialized with regard to their attitude towards Mohammedans, Christians, etc., and the Mohammedans, Christians, etc., become resocialized with regard to their attitudes towards the Hindus, or the touchable Hindus with regard to the untouchables, caste and divisions will vanish. If caste is an attitude and it is nothing else, it must be said to be dissolved when that particular attitude symbolizing the caste is dissolved. But the existing set attitude representing the diverse castes and groups will be dissolved only if the diverse groups meet together and take part in a common activity. Such changes of disposition and attitudes will not be ephemeral but will, in their turn influence associated life outside the Council Hall. The more opportunities are created for such conjoint activities the better. The resocialization will then be on a larger scale and bring about a speedier end of caste and groups. Thus those who condemn communal representation on the score of perpetuating the existing divisions will welcome it, on reflection, as a potent solvent for dissolving them.

The importance and necessity of communal and adequate representation of untouchables is beyond question. The depth of emotion with which the untouchables speak on this topic must have been easily gauged when the untouchables of the Madras Presidency told Mr Montagu that there would be bloodshed if Home Rule for India was not accompanied by communal representation to the untouchables. The authors of the Report however are actuated by a faith in the intelligentsia to effect all reforms fox the elevation of the untouchables from permanent degradation and ostracism. They say 'they find the educated Indian organizing effort not for political ends alone but for various forms of public and social service'. As the authors have connived at the demands of the untouchables on this score it is but proper to investigate whether their faith is well grounded. On education and its social value the words of Joseph Addison are not too stale to be recalled. He said, 'There can be no greater injury to human society than that good Talents among men should be held Honourable to those who are endowed with them without any regard how they are applied. The Gifts of Nature and the Accomplishments of Art are valuable but as they are exerted in the interest of virtue or governed by the Rules of Honour, we ought to abstract our minds from the observation of an excellence in those we converse with, till we have taken some notice or received some good information of the Disposition of their Minds, otherwise they make us fond of those whom our reason and judgment will tell us we ought to abhor.'

Statistics will show that the intelligentsia and the Brahmin caste are exchangeable terms. The disposition of the intelligentsia is a Brahmin disposition. Its outlook is a Brahmin outlook. Though he has learned to speak in the name of all, the Brahmin leader is in no sense a leader of the people. He is a leader of his caste at best, for he feels them as he does for no other people. It is not intended to say that there are no Brahmins who feel for the untouchables. To be just, there are a few more moderate and rational Brahmins who admit the frightful nature of the institution of untouchability in the abstract and perceive the dangers to society with which it is fraught. But the great majority of the Brahmins are those who doggedly deny the horrors of the system in the teeth of such a mass of evidence as never was brought to bear on any other subject and to which the experience of every day contributes its immense amount; who, when they speak of freedom, mean the freedom to oppress their kind and to be savage, merciless and cruel, and whose inalienable rights can only have their growth in the wrongs of the untouchables. Their delicate gentility will neither bear the Englishmen as superior nor will it brook the untouchables as equal. 'I will not tolerate a man above me, and of those below none must approach too near' sums up the true spirit of their social as well as political creed. Those who speak against the anti-social spirit of the Brahmin leaders are often cautioned that in their denunciation they do not pay sufficient regard to the existence of the first class of Brahmin leaders. This is no doubt the case. Noble but very rare instances of personal and pecuniary sacrifice may be found among them just as may be found to be tender in the exercise of their unnatural power. Still it is to be feared that this injustice is inseparable from the state of things with which humanity and truth are invoked to deal. The miserable state of the untouchables is not a bit more tolerable because some tender hearts are bound to show sympathy, nor can the indignant tide of honest wrath stand still because in its course it overwhelms a few who are comparatively innocent among a host of guilty.

The trend of nationalism in India does not warrant us to believe that the few who are sympathetic will grow in volume. On the other hand it is the host of guilty that time is sure to multiply. With the growth of political agitation, the agitation for social reform has subsided and has even vanished The Prarthana Samaj, the Brahmo Samaj with their elevating influence have become things of the past. The future has few things like these in store. The growth of education if it is confined to one class, will not necessarily lead to liberalism. It may lead to the justification and conservation of class interest; and instead of creating the liberators of the downtrodden, it may create champions of the past and the supporters of the *status quo*. Isn't this the effect of education so far? That it will take a new course in future *ceteris paribus*, there is no ground to believe. Therefore, instead of leaving the untouchables to the mercy of the higher castes, the wiser policy would be to give power to the untouchables themselves who are anxious, not like others, to usurp power but only to assert their natural place in society.

This gigantic world war, however motivated, has yielded what is known as the principle of self-determination which is to govern international relations of the future. It is happy to note that the pronouncement of the 20th August 1917 declared the application of the principle to India—a principle which enunciates the rule that every people must be free to determine the conditions under which it is to live. It would be a sign of imperfect realization of the significance of this principle if its application were restricted to international relations, because discord does not exist between nations alone, but there is also discord between classes from within a nation. Wittingly our Indian politicians in their political speeches and harangues hold to the *de jure* conception of the Indian people. By the *de jure* conception they conceive of the Indian people as by nature one and emphasize the qualities such as praiseworthy community of purpose and welfare, loyalty to public ends and mutuality of sympathy which accompany this unity. How the *de jure* and *de facto* conceptions conflict, it is hoped, the committee will not fail to realize. As an instance the following may be noted. The moral evil to the Indian people of their conquest and subjugation by the British is a theme which is very attractive to the Brahmin politicians, who never fail to make capital out of it. The moral evils were once portrayed by John Shore in his 'Notes on Indian Affairs' written in 1832. The late Honourable Mr Gokhale once voiced the same feeling when speaking about the 'excessive costliness of the foreign agency'. He said:

> There is a moral evil which, if anything, is even greater. A kind of dwarfing or stunting of the Indian race is going on under the present system. We must live all the days of our life in an atmosphere of inferiority and the tallest of us must bend, in order that the exigencies of the existing system may be satisfied. The upward impulse, if I may use such an expression, which every schoolboy at Eton and Harrow may feel, that he may one day be a Gladstone or Napoleon or a Wellington, and which may draw forth the best efforts of which he is capable, is denied to us. The full height to which our manhood is capable of rising can never be reached by us under the present system. The moral elevation which every self-governing people feel cannot be felt by us. Our administrative and military talents must gradually disappear, owing to sheer disuse till at last our lot as hewers of wood and drawers of water in our own country, is stereotyped.

I beg to invite the attention of the Committee whether these sentiments which have been voiced by a Brahmin (a noble Brahmin to be sure) to the disgrace of the British bureaucracy cannot be more fittingly voiced by the untouchables to the disgrace of the Brahmin oligarchy? May it be said to the credit of the bureaucracy, that it has disproved the charge of being wooden and shown itself susceptible to feeling by proposing changes in the system of the Government which has dwarfed the personality of those for whom it was devised. But can the oligarchy claim anything half as noble? Their belief is that the Hindu social system has been perfected for all time by their ancestors who had the superhuman vision of all eternity and supernatural power for making infinite provision for future ages. This deep ingrained ethnocentrism has prevented a reconstruction of Hindu Society and stood in the way of a revision of vested rights for the common good. A farce of a conference for the removal of untouchability was enacted in March 1918 in Bombay. Doctor Kurtakoti, the Shankaracharya of Karvir fame, though promised to attend, left for Northern India just a day or two before the conference met, on some urgent business. Mr Tilak is credited with a short speech at the conference which has for the good luck of Mr Tilak remained unreported. But this was only lip sympathy shown to hoodwink the untouchables for when the draft of the proclamation removing untouchability was presented to Mr Tilak, it is known on creditable evidence that he refused to honour it with his signature.

Here is disclosed a patent disharmony within a nation and therefore a proper field for the application of the principle of self-determination. If the advanced classes are clamouring for its application to India and if the powers that be have sanctioned it, however partially, to ward off the future stunting and dwarfing of the Indian people, may not the untouchables with justice claim its benefit in their own interest? Admitting the necessity of self-determination for the untouchables communal representation cannot be withheld from them, for communal representation and self-determination are but two different phrases which express the same notion.

Supplementary Written Statement of Mr Bhimrao R. Ambedkar

The object of this supplement is primarily, to show how the scheme of representation which I have recommended for the untouchables of the Bombay Presidency in my previous statement can be fitted into the scheme of representation proposed by the Government of Bombay for the composition of the Legislative Council.

First I wish to propose certain changes in number of seats assigned by the Government to the various main constituencies. ...

As regards the method of election proposed for I, II, III, IV, & V of the above constituencies, I agree with the Government.

The Government has reserved 3 seats for the Sindh Hindus. I have proposed 4 of them, one of which should be earmarked for the untouchables of Sind to be filled by a communal electorate.

For the 6 cities I have reserved 17 seats. Of this I propose that Bombay should be given 10. Of the 10 seats the untouchables of the city should be given 1 seat, also to be filled by a communal electorate.

So far it is shown how the Sind untouchables and their fellows in Bombay can be provided for. In addition to these two seats the untouchables of the Presidency proper, excluding the city of Bombay, should be given 7 seats. The constituencies among which these 7 seats are to be distributed, I have indicated on page 7 of my previous statement. It is in this fashion that the 9 seats for the untouchables of the Presidency should be carved out. The Government of Bombay finds difficulty in defining the Depressed Classes.

The difficulty is not a real difficulty, for, for all practical purposes the untouchables and the Depressed classes are the same. Knowing full well the degradation of the untouchables, the callousness of the Bombay Government is appalling. By refusing to make provision for the representation of the Depressed classes the Government have deliberately thrown the gravest of interests into the greatest of perils—a calamity which I am sure the Committee will avert... ....

I have differed from the Government of Bombay on the number of representatives to be given to the Mohamedans. Of the two bases, population and the Congress Scheme, the Government of Bombay have preferred the latter without even making a show of reasoning. In doing so they have contravened the most considered opinion of the authors of the Reforms Scheme who say that there is no basis other than that of negotiation for the proportion of Mohammedan representation fixed in the Congress League Scheme. It must be urged that looking to its composition the Congress is a body whose vicarious promises can never be binding on the vast population who have played no part in its deliberations.

The Mohammedans of this presidency form 20 per cent of the total population. On the basis of population therefore, they are entitled only to 20 seats out of the 100 elective seats. But tempering population by need I think 24 seats ought to satisfy them. Any excess over this cannot be tolerated as it will be at the cost of the other communities. Of these 24, the 7 districts of Sind on the basis of 2 per district will return 14 Mohammedans. The other 10 seats may be distributed as follows:

		Population	No. of Respondents
(1)	Bombay City ...	179,246	2
(2)	Northern Division ...	342,96	2
(3)	Central Division ...	367,509	3
(4)	Southern Division ...	457,997	3
			Total 10

I should prefer linguistic grouping to divisional grouping even in the case of the Mohammedans. I fail to see how a Mohammedan from Thana can have any affiliation with a Mohammedan of Surat though both the districts come under the same division. To group together for political purposes people who are ethnically different is absurd Mr Bhimrao R. Ambedkar called and examined Sir Frank Sly: He was a professor in the Sydenham College of

Commerce. He graduated from the Elphinstone College, Bombay, and was an M.A. of the Columbia University, New York. He was a Mahar by caste and his statement dealt largely with the depressed classes.

So far as the Hindu community was concerned, he divided them into two classes, touchables and untouchables; a distinction which was unmistakable in practice and more convenient than a division by castes. He recognized also a distinction between Brahmins and non-Brahmins, but this was of less importance. The distinction between Brahmin and non-Brahmin would not make much difference as regards the attitude of voter to a candidate, but the distinction between touchable and untouchable would make a very great difference.

He did not think there was any necessity for communal electorates for non-Brahmins as, if three-member constituencies were granted according to his supplementary statement, non-Brahmins would get some seats. From the figures in para 16 of his written statement he intended to show that on a uniform property qualification, a community which might be in a minority with regard to population might be in a majority in respect of voting strength; some of the communities that he had mentioned might be minorities in the whole province, but majorities in particular districts. They should try to reduce the fever for communal representation as much as possible, and he therefore recommended three-member constituencies.

He wanted a variation of the franchise for the untouchables; but, if constituencies with more than two members were adopted, the lowering of the franchise became a matter of less importance. In the case of a small constituency, for instance, the Marathas, it might be desirable to group them.

If a particular community had a majority of votes in a constituency, there was no need for that community to have separate communal representation. If the untouchables had a majority of votes in a particular constituency, he would not ask for communal representation. It was because they were in a minority and would always remain so on a uniform franchise that he asked for separate representation. His justification for asking for a low franchise was that as a result of being untouchable, the untouchables had no property; they could not trade because they could not find customers. He remembered a case in which a Mahar woman was taken to the police court for selling water-melons. He was not aware of the conditions outside the Bombay Presidency. In the mills in the Bombay Presidency the untouchables were not yet allowed to work in the weaving department; in one case an untouchable did work in the weaving department of a mill saying that he was a Mohammedan, and when found out, he was severely beaten.

The definition of an 'untouchable' as a person who would cause pollution by his touch, was a satisfactory one for electoral purposes. It was not the case that some castes were considered to be untouchable in some districts and touchable in others.

According to his classification the untouchables amounted to about 8 per cent of the population, but he had proposed 9 seats which would make about 9 per cent. These seats should be filled by separate communal election.

He was aware that the untouchable in his present state of development was in no way qualified to give a responsible vote. In the whole Bombay Presidency there were one B.A. and 6 or 7 matriculates among the depressed classes. The proportion of those who were literate in English was very small, but not much smaller than in the case of the backward classes. The depressed classes, especially the Mahars and the Chamars, were fit to exercise the vote. He would also give them the votes by way of education. He could find at least 25 or more men amongst them who had passed the 6th or the 7th Standards of a High School, and, although the number was not large, the 9 seats which he suggested for the depressed classes could be filled from amongst them. Such a candidate in practical matters would be as good as a graduate although, the latter might be able to express himself better.

He was opposed to any system under which the representatives of the depressed classes were drawn from other classes. Representation by missionaries, for instance, would not be representation in any real sense of the word.

He suggested large constituencies for the depressed classes; if such large constituencies had been accepted for the Mohammedans he did not see why they were not practicable in the case of the depressed classes.

In order to obtain the required number of seats for the depressed classes he would reduce the number of seats suggested by Government for the Mohammedans, from 18 to 10. This reduction was justifiable, as on the population basis the Mohammedans were only entitled to 20 per cent of the seats. He did not consider the Congress League Pact as binding on all.

Mr Hailey: Untouchables were persons to whom certain rights of citizenship had been denied. For instance, it was the right of every citizen to walk down the street, and if a man were prevented from doing so, even temporarily, it was an infringement of his right. Whether a man was prevented from exercising his rights by law or social custom, made very little difference to him. Government had recognized custom and persons belonging to the untouchable classes were not employed in Government service.

He suggested the lowering of the franchise qualification in the case of the depressed classes, as it should be the object of the Government to improve the lot of the community.

From an examination of the Census Report he would say that the problem of touchable and non-touchable existed in Sind, as although the greater proportion of the population there were Mohammedans, there were also Hindus. If special provision was going to be made for the Hindus in Sind, he did not see why special provision should not be made for the depressed classes also.

Mr Banerjee: The depressed classes would be able to find 9 men who were able to speak English and who could represent their cause in the Council. The 6th standard was the class below the matriculation, and a man who had passed the 6th standard would be able to follow the debates in the Council. They had about 25 persons who had passed that standard.

For political purposes there would be no difficulty in defining the depressed classes, who were the same as the untouchables. No one who was not a member of a depressed class would think of trying to make himself out to be such, though such a thing might occur in the case of the backward classes.

He would accept 8 representatives as the minimum for the depressed classes, and they should be elected. Nominated representative would not be in a position adequately to represent their interests.

Mr Crump: He had no experience of the problem and conditions of the untouchable classes in Sind, and could not say anything with regard to the statement that there was only one such class, viz., the Bhangis, there—His information was that the total Hindu population in Sind was 837,426 and the total of the untouchable classes was 135,224.

Mr Natarajan: His view was that British rule in India was meant to provide equal opportunities for all, and that in transferring a large share of the power to popular assemblies, arrangements should be made whereby the hardships and disabilities entailed by the social system should not be reproduced and perpetuated in political institutions. As regards the exact position at present, he admitted that, for instance, at the Parel school which was meant for the depressed classes, there were many higher-caste pupils, who came there because it was a good school. Similarly as a professor he, being a member of a depressed class, had pupils of all classes and found no difficulty in dealing with his higher caste pupils. If the untouchable classes were recognized by Government by the grant of seats, their status would be raised and their powers would be stimulated. He was not very particular about the number of their seats; all he wanted was something adequate.

2 Dr Ambedkar with the Simon Commission (17 May 1929)

A BRIEF SKETCH ABOUT THE DOCUMENT

Dr Ambedkar became a member of the Bombay Legislative Council in 1927. He was re-nominated in 1932. In 1937, he returned to the Bombay Legislative Assembly in the General Elections. In 1928–9 he was elected a member of the committee to associate with the Simon Commission. He prepared a comprehensive report for the changes in the Constitution of the Bombay Presidency, expressing his views on composition and powers of the Provincial Executive, Provincial Legislature, Provincial Autonomy, and Public Service. In this section, we have focused on his ideas on Franchise, Electorates and Distribution of Seats, which are crucial for the purpose of democracy. The excerpts in this chapter have been taken from BAWS, Volume 2, 1982 (pp. 315-69).

..... My colleagues have recommended that the franchise in urban areas should remain as it is and that in rural areas the land revenue assessment should be halved. I am unable to agree to this. My colleagues have treated the question of franchise as though it was a question of favour rather than of right. I think that such a view is too dangerous to be accepted as the basis of political society in any country. For if the conception of a right to representation is to be dismissed as irrelevant; if a moral claim to representation is to be deemed as nothing but a metaphysical or sentimental obstruction; if franchise is considered a privilege to be given or withheld by those in political power according to their own estimate of the use likely to be made of it, then it is manifest that the political emancipation of the unfranchised will be entirely at the mercy of those that are enfranchised. To accept such a conclusion is to accept that slavery is no wrong. For slavery, too, involves the hypothesis that men have no right but what those in power choose to give them. A theory which leads to such a conclusion must be deemed to be fatal to any form of popular Government, and as such I reject it in toto.

My colleagues look upon the question of franchise as though it was nothing but a question of competency to put into a ballot box a piece of paper with a number of names written thereon. Otherwise they would not have insisted upon literacy as a criterion for the extension of the franchise. Such a view of the franchise is undoubtedly superficial and involves a total misunderstanding of what it stands for. If the majority had before its mind the true conception of what franchise means they would have realized that franchise, far from being a transaction concerned with the marking of the ballot paper, 'stands for direct and active participation in the regulation of the terms upon which associated life shall be sustained and the permit of good carried on.' Once this conception of franchise is admitted, it would follow that franchise is due to every adult who is not a lunatic. For, associated life is shared by every individual and as every individual is affected by its consequences, every individual must have the right to settle its terms. From the same premises it would further follow that the poorer the individual the greater the necessity of enfranchising him. Form in every society based on private property the terms of associated life as between owners and workers are from the start set against the workers. If the welfare of the worker is to be guaranteed from being menaced by the owners, the terms of their associated life must be constantly resettled. But this can hardly be done unless the franchise is dissociated from property and extended to all property-less adults. It is therefore clear that judged from either point of view the conclusion in favour of adult suffrage is irresistible. I accept that conclusion and recommend that the franchise should be extended to all adults, male and female, above the age of 21.

Political justice is not the only ground for the introduction of adult suffrage. Even political expediency favours its introduction. One of the reasons why minorities like the Mohamedan insist upon communal electorates is the fear that in a system of joint electorates the voters of the majority community would so largely influence the election that seats would go to men who were undesirable from the standpoint of the minority. I have pointed out in a subsequent part of the report that such a contention could be effectively disposed of by the introduction of adult suffrage. The majority has given no thought to the importance of adult suffrage as an alternative to communal electorates. The majority has proceeded as though communal electorates were a good to be preserved and have treated adult suffrage as though it was an evil to be kept within bonds. My view of them is just the reverse. I hold communal electorates to be an evil and adult suffrage to be a good. Those who agree with me will admit that adult suffrage should be introduced not only because of its inherent good but also because it can enable us to get rid of the evil of communal electorates. But even those whose political faith does not include a belief in adult suffrage, will, I am sure, find no difficulty in accepting this view. For it is only commonsense to say that a lesser evil is to be preferred to a greater evil and there is no doubt that adult suffrage, if it is at all an evil, is a lesser evil than communal electorates. Adult suffrage, which is supported by political justice and favoured by political expediency, is also, I find, demanded by a substantial body of public opinion. The Nehru Committee's report, which embodies the views of all the political parties in India except the Non-Brahmins and the Depressed Classes, favours the introduction of adult suffrage. The Depressed Classes have also insisted upon it. The Sindh Mohamedan Association, one Mohamedan member and one Non-Brahmin member of the Government of Bombay, have expressed themselves in favour of it. There is thus a considerable volume of public opinion in support of adult franchise. My colleagues give no reason why they have ignored this volume of public opinion.

Two things appear to have weighed considerably with my colleagues in their decision against the introduction of adult suffrage. One is the extent of illiteracy prevalent in the country. No one can deny the existence of illiteracy among the masses of the country. But that this factor should have any bearing on the question of franchise is a view the correctness of which I am not prepared to admit. First of all, illiteracy of the illiterate is no fault of theirs. The Government of Bombay for a long time refused to take upon itself the most important function of educating the people, and, when it did, it deliberately confined the benefit of education to the classes and refused to extend it to the masses.

It was not until 1854, that Government declared itself in favour of mass education as against class education. But the anxiety of Government for the spread of education among the masses has gone very little beyond the passing of a few resolutions. In the matter of financial support Government always treated education with a most niggardly provision. It is notorious, how Government, which is always in favour of taxation refused to consent to the proposal of the Honourable Mr Gokhale for compulsory primary education, although it was accompanied by a measure of taxation. The introduction of the Reform has hardly improved matters. Beyond the passing of a Compulsory Primary Education Act in the Presidency there has not been any appreciable advance in the direction of mass education. On the contrary there has been a certain amount of deterioration owing to the transfer of education to local authorities which are manned, comparatively speaking, by people who being either indifferent or ignorant, are seldom keen for the advancement of education.

In the case of the Depressed Classes the opportunity for acquiring literacy has in fact been denied to them. Untouchability has been an insuperable bar in their way to education. Even Government has bowed before it and has sacrificed the rights of the Depressed Classes to admission in public schools to the exigencies of the social system in India. In a resolution of the year 1856 the Government of Bombay in rejecting the petition of a Mahar boy to a school in Dharwar observed:

The question discussed in the correspondence is one of very great practical difficulty

1. There can be no doubt that the Mahar petitioner has abstract justice in his side; and Government trust that the prejudices which at present prevent him from availing himself of existing means of education in Dharwar may be are long removed.

2. But Government are obliged to keep in mind that to interfere with the prejudices of ages in a summary manner, for the sake of one or few individuals, would probably do a great damage to the cause of education. The disadvantage under which the petitioner labours is not one which has originated with this Government, and it is one which Government cannot summarily remove by interfering in his favour, as he begs them to do.

The Hunter Commission which followed after the lapse of 26 years did say that Government should accept the principle that nobody be refused admission to a Government College or School merely on the ground of caste. But it also felt it necessary to say that the principle should 'be applied with due caution' and the result of such caution was that the principle was never enforced. A bold attempt was, no doubt, made in 1921 by Dr Paranjpye, when he was the Minister of Education. But as his action was without any sanction behind it, his circular regarding admission of the Depressed Classes to Schools is being evaded, with the result that illiteracy still continues to be a deplorable feature of the life of the Depressed Classes.

To the question that is often asked how can such illiterate people be given the franchise, my reply therefore is, who is responsible for their illiteracy? If the responsibility for illiteracy falls upon the Government, then to make literacy a condition precedent to franchise is to rule out the large majority of the people who, through no fault of their own, have never had an opportunity of acquiring literacy provided to them. Granting that the extension of franchise must follow the removal of illiteracy what guarantee is there that efforts will be made to remove illiteracy as early as possible? The question of education like other nation-building questions is ultimately a question of money. So long as money is not forthcoming in sufficient amount, there can be no advance in education. How to find this money is therefore the one question that has to be solved. That a Council elected on the present franchise will never be in a position to solve the problem is beyond dispute. For the simple reason that money for education can only be provided by taxing the rich and the rich are the people who control the present Council. Surely the rich will not consent to tax themselves for the benefit of the poor unless they are compelled to do so. Such a compulsion can only come by a radical change in the composition of the Council which will give the poor and illiterate adequate voice therein. Unless this happens the question of illiteracy will never be solved. To deny them that right is to create a situation full of injustice. To keep people illiterate and then to make their illiteracy the ground for their non-enfranchisement is to add insult to injury. But the situation indeed involves more than this. It involves an aggravation of the injury. For to keep people illiterate and then to deny them franchise which is the only means whereby they could effectively provide for the removal of their illiteracy is to perpetuate their illiteracy and postpone indefinitely the day of their enfranchisement.

It might be said that the question is not who is responsible for illiteracy; the question is whether illiterate persons should be given the right to vote. My answer is that the question cannot be one of literacy or illiteracy: the question can be of intelligence alone. Those who insist on literacy as a test and insist upon making it a condition precedent to enfranchisement in my opinion, commit two mistakes. Their first mistake consists in their belief that an illiterate person is necessarily an unintelligent person. But everyone knows that, to maintain that an illiterate person can be a very intelligent person, is not to utter a paradox. Indeed an appeal to experience would fortify the conclusion that illiterate people all over the world including India have intelligence enough to understand and manage their own affairs. At any rate the law presumes that above a certain age every one has intelligence enough to be entrusted with the responsibility of managing his own affairs. The illiterate might easily commit mistakes in the exercise of the franchise. But then the Development Department of Bombay has fallen into mistakes of judgment equally great which though they are condemned, are all the same tolerated. And even if they fall into greater errors it may still be well that they should have franchise. For all belief in free and popular Government rests ultimately on the conviction that a people gains more by experience than it loses by the errors of liberty and it is difficult to perceive why a truth that holds good of individuals in non-political field should not hold good in the political field. Their second mistake lies in supposing that literacy necessarily imports a higher level of intelligence or knowledge than what the illiterate possesses. On this point the words of Bryce might be quoted. In his survey of 'Modern Democracies' he raises the question how far ability to read and write goes towards civic competence and answers thus:

> Because it is the only test practically available, we assume it to be an adequate test. Is it really so? Some of us remember, among the English rustics of sixty years ago shrewd men, unable to read but with plenty of mother wit, and by their strong sense and solid judgment quite as well qualified to vote as are their grand-children today who read a newspaper and revel in the cinema.
>
> The Athenian voters were better fitted for civic franchise than most of the voters in modern democracies. These Greek voters learnt politics not from the printed and, few even from any written page, but by listening to accomplished orators and by talking to one another. Talking has this advantage over reading, that in it mind is less passive. It is thinking that matters, not reading, and by thinking, I mean the power of getting at facts,

and arguing consecutively from them. In conversation there is a clash of wits, and to that some mental exertion must go. But in these days of ours reading has become substitute for thinking. The man who reads only the newspaper of his own party, and reads its political intelligence in a medley of other stuff, narratives of crimes and descriptions of football matches, need not know that there is more than one side to a question and seldom asks if there is one, nor what is the evidence for what the paper tells him. The printed page, because it seems to represent some unknown power, is believed more readily than what he hears in talk. He takes from it statements, perhaps groundless, perhaps invented, which he would not take from one of his follows in the workshop or the counting house. Moreover, the Tree of Knowledge is the Tree of the Knowledge of Evil as well as of Good. On the Printed Page Truth has no better chance than Falsehood, except with those who read widely and have the capacity of discernment. A party organ, suppressing some facts, misrepresenting some others, is the worst of all guides, because it can by incessantly reiterating untruth produce a greater impression than any man or body of men, save only ecclesiastics clothed with a spiritual authority, could produce before printing was invented. A modern voter so guided by his party newspapers is no better off than his grandfather who eighty years ago voted at the bidding of his landlord or his employer or (in Ireland) of his Priest. The grandfather at least knew whom he was following, while the grandson, who only reads what is printed on one side of a controversy may be the victim of selfish interests who own the organs which his simplicity assumes to express public opinion or to have the public good at heart. So a democracy that has been taught only to read and not also to reflect and judge, will not be better for the ability to read.

It seems to me that too much is being made out of the illiteracy of the masses in India. Take the English voter and inquire into his conduct as a voter and what do we find? This is what the *Times Literary Supplement* of August 21, 1924, says about him:

The mass of the people have no serious interest. Their votes decide all political issues, but they know nothing of politics. It is a disquieting, but too well-founded reflection that the decision about tariff reform or taxation or foreign policy is now said by men and women who have never read a dozen columns of serious politics in their lives. Of the old narrow electorate of eight years ago probably at least two-thirds eagerly studied political speeches on the question of the day. Today not five per cent, of the voters read either debates or leading articles. The remnant, however remarkable, is small. Democracy as a whole is as content with gross amusement as Bottles was with vulgar ones, and like him it leases his mind to its newspaper which makes his Sundays much more degrading than those which he spent under his Baptist Minister. This is the atmosphere against whose poisonous gases the schools provide in vain the helmet of their culture.

Surely if British Democracy—say the British Empire is content to be ruled by voters such as above, it is arguable that Indians who are opposed to adult suffrage are not only unjust and visionaries but are protesting too much and are laying themselves open to the charge that they are making illiteracy of the masses an excuse to pocket their political power. For, to insist that a thorough appreciation of the niceties of political creeds and the ability to distinguish between them are necessary tests of political intelligence is, to say the least, hypercritical. On small political questions no voter, no matter in what country he is, will ever be accurately informed. Nor is such minute knowledge necessary. The most that can be expected from the elector is the power of understanding broad issues and of choosing the candidate who in his opinion will serve him best. This, I make bold to say, is not beyond the capacity of an average Indian.

The other thing which apparently weighed with my colleagues in refusing to accept adult suffrage is the analogy of the countries like England. It is argued that the extension of the franchise from forty shilling freehold in 1429 to adult suffrage in 1832 there were less than 500,000 persons who had the right to vote in the election of members of Parliament; that it was not until the Reform Act of that year that the number of voters was increased to nearly 1,000,000; that no further step was taken to lower the franchise till the passing of the Act of 1867 which increased it to 2,500,000; that the next step was taken 17 years after when the Act of 1884 increased it again to 5,500,000; and that adult suffrage did not come till after a lapse of 34 years when People's Representation Act of 1918 was passed. This fact has been used for very different purposes by different set of peoples. A set of politicians who are social tories and political radicals use this in support of their plea that the legislature can be given full powers although it may not be fully representative and in reply to this argument of their opponents that the transference of power to a legislature so little representative will be to transfer it to an oligarchy. By others in support of their plea that in the matter of franchise we must proceed slowly and go step by step as other nations have done. To the second group of critics my reply is that there is no reason why we should follow in the footsteps of the English nation in this particular matter. Surely the English people had not devised any philosophy of action in the matter of franchise. On the other hand, if the extension was marked by such long intervals it was because of the self-seeking character of the English ruling classes. Besides, these is no reason why every nation should go through the same stages and enact the same scenes as other nations have done. To do so is to refuse to reap the advantage which is always open to those who are born later. To the other section of critics my reply is that their contention as a fact is true, that Parliament did exercise full powers of a sovereign state even when it represented only a small percentage of the population. But the question is with what results to the nation? Anyone who is familiar with the history of social legislation by the unreformed Parliament as told by Lord Shaftesbury certainly will not wish the experiment to be repeated in this country. This result was the inevitable result of the restricted franchise which obtained in England. The facts relied upon by these critics in my opinion do not go to support a government based upon a restricted franchise is a worse form of government in that it gives rise to the rule of oligarchy. Such a result was never contemplated by the authors of the Joint Report. Indeed they were so conscious of the evil that in paragraph 262 of their Report they were particular enough to say that among the matters for consideration the Statutory Commission should consider the working of the franchise and the constitution of electorates, including the important matter of the retention of communal representation. 'Indeed we regard the development of a broad franchise as the arch on which the edifice of self-government must be raised: for we have no intention that our reforms should result merely in the transfer of powers from a bureaucracy to an oligarchy.'

What is however the remedy for preventing oligarchy? The only remedy that I can think of is the grant of adult suffrage. It is pertinent to remark that the members of the Ceylon Commission of 1928 who like the authors of the Joint Report were conscious that 'the grant of a responsible government to an electorate of these small dimensions would be tantamount to placing an oligarchy in power without any guarantee that the interests of the remainder of the people would be consulted by those in authority' and who felt it 'necessary to observe that His Majesty's Government is the trustee not merely of the wealthier and more highly educated elements in Ceylon but quite as much of the peasant and the coolie, and of all those poorer classes which form the bulk of the population' and who held that 'to hand over the interests of the latter to the unfettered control of the former would be a betrayal of its trust,' came 'to the conclusion that literacy should not remain as one of the qualifications for voters at election of State Council.' They said 'the development of responsible government requires, in our opinion, an increasing opportunity to the rank and file of the people to influence the Government and the franchise cannot be fairly or wisely confined to the educated classes.' If adult franchise can be prescribed for Ceylon the question that naturally arises is why should it not be prescribed for India? Similarity in the political, social, economic, and educational conditions of the two countries is so striking that to treat them differently in the matter of franchise is to create a distinction when there is no real difference to justify the same. Analogy apart and considering the case purely on merits it is beyond doubt that of the two if any one of them is more fitted to be trusted with the exercise of adult it is the people of India and more so the people of the Bombay Presidency wherein the system of adult suffrage is already in vogue in the village panchayats.

Electorates

The existing Legislative Council is composed of 114 members, of whom 26 are nominated and 86 are elected. The nominated members fall into two groups (a) officials to represent the reserved half of the Government and (b) the non-officials to represent (1) the Depressed Classes, (2) Labouring Classes, (3) Anglo-Indians, (4) Indian Christians and (5) the Cotton Trade. Of the elected members (1) some are elected by class-electorates created to represent the interests of the landholders, commerce and industry, some by reserved electorates for Maratha and allied castes and the rest, by communal electorates which are instituted for the Muhammadans and the Europeans. The question is whether this electoral structure should be preserved without alteration. Before any conclusion can be arrived at, it is necessary to evaluate it, in the light of considerations both theoretical as well as practical.

Nominated Members

Against the nominated members it is urged that their presence in the Council detracts a great deal from its representative character. Just as the essence of responsible self-government is the responsibility of the Executive to the Legislature, so the essence of representative government lies in the responsibility of the legislature to the people. Such a responsibility can be secured only when the legislature is elected by the people. Not only does the system of nominated member make the house unrepresentative, it also tends to make the Executive irresponsible. For by virtue of the power of nominations, the Executive on whose advice that power is exercised, appoints nearly 25 per cent, of the legislature with the result that such a large part of the house is in the position of the servants of the Executive rather than its critics. That the nominated non-officials are not the servants of the Government cannot go to subtract anything from this view. For the nominated non-official can always be bought and the Executive has various ways open to it for influencing an elected member with a view to buy up his independence. A direct conferment of titles and honours upon a member, or bestowal of patronage on his friends and relatives, are a few of such methods. But the nominated non-official members are already in such an abject state of dependence that the Executive has not to buy their independence. They never have any independence to sell. They are the creatures of the Executive and they are given seats on the understanding, if not on the condition, that they shall behave as friends of the Executive. Nor is the Executive helpless against a nominated member who has the audacity to break the understanding. For, by the power of renomination which the Executive possesses, it can inflict the severest penalty by refusing to renominate him and there are instances where it has inflicted that punishment. Like the King's veto, the knowledge that this power to renominate exists, keeps every nominated member at the beck and call of the Executive.

Another evil arising from the system of nomination must also be pointed out. The nominated non-official members were to represent the interests of certain communities for whose representation the electoral system as devised, was deemed to be inadequate just as the nominated official members were appointed to support the interests of government. The regrettable thing is that while the nominated officials served the interests of government, the nominated non-officials failed to serve the interests of their constituents altogether. Indeed a nominated non-official cannot serve his community. For more often that not the interests of the communities can only be served by influencing governmental action, and this is only possible when the Executive is kept under fire and is made to realize the effects of an adverse vote. But this means is denied to a nominated member by the very nature of his being, with the result that the Executive, being assured of his support, is indifferent to his cause and the nominated member, being denied his independence, is helpless to effect any change in the situation of those whom he is nominated to represent. Representation by nomination is thus no representation. It is only mockery.

Another serious handicap of the system of nomination is that the nominated non-officials are declared to be ineligible for ministership. In theory there ought not to be limitations against the right of a member of the legislature to be chosen as a minister of an administration. Even assuming that such a right is to be limited, the purpose of such limitation must be the interests of good and efficient administration. Not only that is not the purpose of this limitation but that the limitation presses unequally upon different communities owing to the difference in the manner of their representation and affects certain communities which ought to be free from its handicap. Few communities are so greatly in need of direct governmental action as the Depressed Classes for effecting their betterment. It is true that no degree of governmental action can alter the face of the situation completely or quickly. But making all allowance for this, no one can deny the great benefits that wise legislation can spread among the people. All these classes do in fact begin and often complete their lives under a weight of inherited vices and social difficulties, for the existence of which society is responsible, and of the mitigation of which much can be done by legislation. The effect of legislation to alter the conditions under which the lives of individuals are spent has been recognized everywhere in the world. But this duty to social progress will not be recognized unless those like the Depressed Classes find a place in the Cabinet of the country. The system of nomination must therefore be condemned. Its only effect has been to produce a set of eventually subordinate the care of the constituents to the desire for place.

Elected Members

Class Electorates

These class electorates a heritage of the Morley-Minto Reforms. The Morley-Minto Scheme was an attempt at make-believe. For under it the bureaucracy without giving up its idea to rule was contriving to create legislatures, by arranging the franchise and the electorates in such a manner as to give the scheme the appearance of popular rule without the reality of it. To such a scheme of things, these class electorates were eminently suited. But the Montagu Chelmsford Scheme was not a make-believe. It contemplated the rule of the people. Consequently it was expected to suggest the abolition of such class electorates. Owing, however, to the powerful influence, which these classes always exercised, the authors of the Report were persuaded to recommend their continuance, which recommendation was given effect to by the Southborough Committee. Whatever the reason that led to the retention of these class electorates, there is no doubt that their existence cannot be reconciled with the underlying spirit of popular government. Their class character is a sufficient ground for their condemnation. In a deliberative assembly like the legislature, where questions of public interest are decided in accordance with public opinion, it is essential that members of the Council who take part in the decision should each represent that opinion. Indeed no other person can be deemed to be qualified to give a decisive vote on the issues debated on the floor of the house. But the representatives of class interests merely reflect the opinions one might say, the prejudices of their class, and should certainly be deemed to be disqualified from taking part in the decision of issues which lie beyond the ambit of the interests of their class. Notwithstanding their class character as members of legislature they acquire the competence to vote upon all the issues whether they concern their own class or extend beyond. This, in my opinion, is quite subversive of the principle of popular government. It might be argued that representatives of such class interests are necessary to give expert advice on those sectional issues with which the unsectional house is not familiar. As against this, it is necessary to remember that in a democracy, the ultimate principle is after all self-government and that means that final decision on all matters must be made by popularly elected persons and not by experts. It is moreover not worthy that the advice of such people is not always serviceable to the house. For, their advice invariably tends to become eloquent expositions of class ideology rather than careful exposition of the formulae in dispute.

Assuming, however, that it is necessary either to safeguard the interests of these classes or to tender advice to the house on their behalf, it is yet to be proved that these interests will not secure sufficient representation through general electorates. Facts, such as we have, show that they can. Taking the case of the Inamdars, though they have been given three seats through special electorates of their own, they have been able to secure 12 seats through the general electorates. Indeed by virtue of the solidarity which they have with other landholding members of the Council, they felt themselves so strong in numbers that only a few months back they demanded a ministerial post for the leader of their class. Besides, it is not true that without class-electorates there will be no representation of the interests of these classes in the Council. Such interests will be amply safeguarded by a member belonging to that class, even if he is elected by a general constituency. This will be clear if we bear in mind that a member taking his seat in the legislature, although he represents directly his constituency, yet indirectly he does represent himself and to that extent also his class. Indeed, from the very nature of things this tendency on the part of a member, indirectly to represent himself, although it might be checked, controlled and over-ruled, so surely manifests itself that it throws, and must necessarily throw, direct representation into the background. No one for instance can believe that a European gentleman representing a Chamber of Commerce will only represent the interests of commerce and will not represent the interests of the European community because he is elected by a Chamber of Commerce and not by the general European community. It is in the nature of things that a man's self should be nearer to him than his constituency. There is a homely saying that a man's skin sits closer to him than his shirt and without any imputation on their good faith so it is with the members of the legislature. It is the realization of this fact which has led the English people who at one time wished that the shipping trade, the woollen trade and the linen trade should each have its spokesman in the House of Commons, to abandon the idea of such class-electorates. It is difficult to understand why a system abandoned elsewhere should be continued in India. It is not necessary in the interests of these classes and it is harmful to the body politic. The only question is whether or not persons belonging to the commercial and individual classes can secure election through the general constituencies. I know of nothing that can be said to handicap these classes in the race of election. That there is no handicap against them is proved by the success of Sardars and Inamdars in general election. Where Inamdars and Sardars have succeeded there is no reason why representatives of commerce and industry should not.

Reserved Electorates

Three objections can be raised against the system of reserved electorates. One is that it seeks to guarantee an electoral advantage to a majority. It is true that the Marathas and the allied castes form a majority in the Marathi speaking part of the Presidency both in population as well as in voting strength and as such deserve no political protection. But it must be realized that there is all the difference in the world between a power informed and conscious of its strength and power so latent and suppressed that its holders are hardly aware of that they may exercise it. That the Marathas and the allied castes are not conscious of their power, is sufficiently evident if we compare the voting strength of the Marathas and the allied castes in those constituencies wherein, seats are reserved for them, with the rank of their representatives among the different candidates contesting the elections. In every one of such constituencies the Maratha voters, it must be remembered, have a preponderance over the voters of other communities. Yet in the elections of 1923 and 1926, out of the seven seats allotted to them, they could not have been returned in three had it not been for the fact that the seats were reserved for them. It is indeed strange that the candidates of a community which is at the top in the electoral roll, should find themselves at the bottom, almost in a sinking position. This strange fact is only an indication that this large community is quite unconscious of the power it possesses, and is subject to some influence acting upon it from without.

The second ground of objection, urged by the members of the higher classes who are particularly affected by the system of reserved seats, is that it does an injustice to them in that it does not permit them the benefit of a victory in a straight electoral fight. It is true that the system places a restriction upon the right of the higher classes to represent the lower classes. But is there any reason why 'the right to represent', as distinguished from 'a right to representation', should be an unrestricted right? Modern politicians have spent all their ingenuity in trying to find out the reason for restricting the right to vote. In my opinion there is a greater necessity why we should strive to restrict the right of a candidate to represent others. Indeed, there is no reason why the implications of the representative function should not define the condition of assuming it. It would be no invasion of the right to be elected to the Legislature to make it depend, for example, upon a number of years' service on a local authority and to rule out all those who do not fulfil that condition. It would be perfectly legitimate to hold that that service in a legislative assembly is so important in its results, that proof of aptitude and experience must be offered before the claim to represent can be admitted. The argument for restricting the rights, of the higher classes to represent the lower classes follows the same line. Only it makes a certain social attitude as a condition precedent to the recognition of the right to represent. Nor can it be said that such a requirement is unnecessary. For aptitude and experience are not more important than the social attitude of a candidate towards the mass of men whom he wishes to represent. Indeed, mere aptitude and experience will be the cause of ruination if they are not accompanied and regulated by the right sort of social attitude. There is no doubt that the social attitude of the higher classes towards the lower classes is not of the right sort. It is no doubt always said to the credit of these communities that they are intellectually the most powerful communities in India. But it can with equal truth be said that they have never utilized their intellectual powers to the services of the lower classes. On the other hand, they have always despised, disregarded and disowned the masses in belonging to a different strata, if not to a different race than themselves. No class has a right to rule another class, much less a class like the higher classes in India. By their code of conduct, they have behaved as the most exclusive class steeped in its own prejudices and never sharing the aspirations of the masses, with whom they have nothing to do and whose interests are opposed to theirs. It is not, therefore, unjust to demand that a candidate who is standing to represent others shall be such as shares the aims, purposes and motives of those whom he desires to represent

The third objection to the system of reserved electorates is that it leads to inefficiency inasmuch as a candidate below the line gets the seat in supersession of a candidate above the line. This criticism is also true. But here, again, there are other considerations which must be taken into account. First of all, as Professor Dicey rightly argues, 'it has never been a primary object of constitutional arrangement to get together the best possible Parliament in intellectual capacity. Indeed, it would be inconsistent with the idea of representative government to attempt to form a Parliament far superior in intelligence to the mass of the nation.' Assuming, however, that the displacement of the intellectual classes by the candidates belonging to the non-intellectual classes is a loss, that loss will be more than amply recompensed by the natural idealism of the backward communities. There is no doubt that the representatives of the higher orders are occupied with the pettiest cares and are more frequently concerned with the affairs of their own class than with the affairs of the nation. Their life is too busy or too prosperous and the individual too much self-contained and self-satisfied for the conception of the social progress to be more than a passing thought of a rare moment. But the lower orders are constantly reminded of their adversity, which can be got over only by a social change. The consciousness of mutual dependence resulting from the necessities of a combined action makes for generosity, while the sense of untrained powers and of undeveloped faculties gives them aspirations. It is to the lower classes that we must look for the motive power for progress. The reservation of seats to the backward Hindu communities makes available for the national service such powerful social forces, in the absence of which any Parliamentary government may be deemed to be poorer.

Communal Electorates

That some assured representation is necessary and inevitable to the communities in whose interests communal electorates have been instituted must be beyond dispute. At any rate, for some time to come the only point that can be open to question is, must such communal representation be through communal electorates? Communal electorates have been held by their opponents to be responsible for the communal disturbances that have of late taken place in the different parts of the country. One cannot readily see what direct connection there can be between communal electorates and communal disturbances. On the contrary it has been argued that by satisfying the demand of the Mohamedans, communal electorates have removed one cause of discontent and ill-feeling. But it is equally true that communal electorates do not help to mitigate communal disturbances and may in fact help to aggravate them. For communal electorates do tend to the intensification of communal feeling and that they do make the leaders of the two communities feel no responsibility towards each other, with the result that instead of leading their people to peace, they are obliged to follow the momentary passions of the crowd.

The Mohamedans who have been insisting upon the retention of the communal electorates take their stand on three grounds.

In the first place they say that the interests of the Mohamedan community are separate from those of the other communities, and that to protect these interests they must have separate electorates. Apart from the question whether separate electorates are necessary to protect separate interests, it is necessary to be certain that there are any interests which can be said to be separate in the sense that they are not the interests of any other community. In the secular, as distinguished from the religious field, every matter is a matter of general concern to all. Whether taxes should be paid or not, if so, what and at what rate; whether national expenditure should be directed in any particular channel more than any other; whether education should be free and compulsory; whether Government lands should be disposed of on restricted tenure or occupancy tenure; whether State aid should be granted to industries; whether there should be more police in any particular area; whether the State should provide against poverty of the working classes by a scheme of social insurance against sickness, unemployment or death; whether the administration of justice is best served by the employment of honorary magistrates, and whether the code of medical ethics or legal ethics should be altered so as to produce better results, are some of the questions that usually come before the Council. Of this list of questions, is there any which can be pointed out as being the concern of the Mohamedan community only? It is true that the Mohamedan community is particularly interested in the question of education and public service. But there again it must be pointed out that the Mohamedan community is not the only community which attaches particular importance to these questions. That the non-Brahmin and the depressed classes are equally deeply interested in this question becomes evident from the united effort that was put forth by all three in connection with the University Reform Bill in the Bombay Legislative Council. The existence of separate interests of the Mohamedan community is therefore a myth. What exists is not separate interests but special concern in certain matters.

Assuming, however, that separate interests do exist, the question is, are they better promoted by separate electorates than by general electorates and reserved seats? My emphatic answer is that the separate or special interests of any minority are better promoted by the system of general electorates and reserved seats than by separate electorates. It will be granted that injury to any interest is, in the main, caused by the existence of irresponsible extremists. The aim should therefore be to rule out such persons from the councils of the country. If irresponsible persons from both the communities are to be ruled out from the councils of the country, the best system is the one under which the Mohamedan candidates could be elected by the suffrage of the Hindus and the Hindu candidates elected by the suffrage of the Mohamedans. The system of joint electorates is to be preferred to that of communal electorates, because it is better calculated to bring about that result than is the system of separate electorates. At any rate, this must be said with certainty that a minority gets a larger advantage under joint electorates than it does under a system of separate electorates. With separate electorates the minority gets its own quota of representation and no more. The rest of the house owes no allegiance to it and is therefore not influenced by the desire to meet the wishes of the minority. The minority is thus thrown on its own resources and as no system of representation can convert a minority into a majority, it is bound to be overwhelmed. On the other hand, under a system of joint electorates and reserved seats the minority not only gets its quota of representation but something more. For, every member of the majority who has partly succeeded on the strength of the votes of the minority if not a member of the minority, will certainly be a member for the minority. This, in my opinion, is a very great advantage which makes the system of mixed electorates superior to that of the separate electorates as a means of protection to the minority. The Mohamedan minority seems to think that the Council is, like the Cardinals' conclave, convened for the election of the Pope, an ecclesiastical body called for the determination of religious issues. If that was true then their insistence on having few men but strong men would have been a wise course of conduct. But it is time the community realized that Council far from being a religious conclave is a secular organization intended for the determination of secular issues. In such determination of the issues, the finding is always in favour of the many. If this is so, does not the interest of the minority itself justify a system which compels others besides its own members to support its cause?

The second ground on which the claim to separate electorates is made to rest is that the Mohamedans are a community by themselves; that they are different from other communities not merely in religion but that their history, their traditions, their culture, their personal laws, their social customs and usages have given them such a widely different outlook on life quite uninfluenced by any common social ties, sympathies or amenities; that they are in fact a distinct people and that they do so regard themselves even though they have lived in this country for centuries. On this assumption it is argued that if they are compelled to share a common electorate with other communities, the political blending consequent upon it will impair the individuality of their community. How far this assumption presents a true picture, I do not step to consider. Suffice it to say, that in my opinion it is not one which can be said to be true to life. But conceding that it is true and conceding further that the preservation of the individuality of the Mohamedan community is an ideal which is acceptable to that community one does not quite see why communal electorates should be deemed to be necessary for the purpose. India is not the only country in which diverse races are sought to be brought under a common Government. Canada and South Africa are two countries within the British Empire where two diverse races are working out a common system of government. Like the Hindus and the Mohamedans in India, the British and the Dutch in South Africa and the British and the French in Canada are two distinct communities with their own distinctive cultures. But none has ever been known to object to common electorates on the ground that such a common cycle of participation for the two communities for electoral purposes is injurious to the preservation of their individualities. Examples of diverse communities sharing common electorates outside the Empire are by no means few. In Poland there are Poles, Ruthenians, Jews, White Russians, Germans, and Lithuanians. In Latvia, there are Latvians, Russians, Jews, Germans, Poles, Lithuanians, and Esthonians. In Esthonia, there are Germans, Jews, Swedes, Russians, Latvians, and Tartars. In Czechoslovakia, there are Czechs, Slovaks, Germans, Magyars, Ruthenians, Jews, and Poles. In Austria, there are Germans, Czechs, and Slovenes; while in Hungary there are Hungarians. Germans, Slovaks, Roumanians, Ruthenians. Croatians, and Serbians. All these groups are not mere communities. They are nationalities each with a live and surging individuality of their own, living in proximity of each other and under a common Government. Yet none of them have objected to common electorates on the ground that a participation in them would destroy their individuality.

But it is not necessary to cite cases of non-Muslim communities to show the futility of the argument. Cases abound in which Mohamedan minorities in other parts of the world have never felt the necessity of communal electorates for the preservation of their individuality against what might be termed the infectious contagion of political contact with other communities. It does not seem to be sufficiently known that India is not the only country where Mohamedans are in a minority. There are other countries, in which they occupy the same position. In Albania, the Mohamedans form a very large community. In Bulgaria, Greece and Roumania they form a minority and in Yugoslavia and Russia they form a very large minority. Have the Mohamedan communities there insisted upon the necessity of separate communal electorates? As all students of political history are aware the Mohamedans in these countries have managed without the benefit of separate electorates; nay, they have managed without any definite ratio of representation assured to them. In India, at any rate, there is a consensus of opinion, that as India has not reached a stage of complete secularization of politics, adequate representation should be guaranteed to the Mohamedan community, lest it should suffer from being completely eclipsed from the political field by the religious antipathy of the majority. The Mohamedan minorities, in other parts of the world are managing their affairs even without the benefit of this assured quota. The Mohamedan case in India, therefore, overshoots the mark and in my opinion, fails to carry conviction.

The third ground on which it is sought to justify the retention of separate communal electorates of the Mohamedans, is that the voting strength of the Mohamedans in a mixed electorate may be diluted by the non-Mohamedan vote to such an extent that the Mohamedan returned by such a mixed electorate, it is alleged, will be a weak and instead of being a true representative of the Mohamedans will be a puppet in the hands of the non-Mohamedan communities. This fear has no doubt the look of being genuine, but a little reasoning will show that it is groundless. If the mass of the non-Muslim voters were engaged in electing a Mohamedan candidate, the result anticipated by the Mohamedans may perhaps come true if the non-Muslims are bent on mischief. But the fact is that at the time of general election there will be many non-Mohamedan candidates standing for election. That being the case, the full force of all the non-Muslim voters will not be directed on the Mohamedan candidates. Nor will the non-Mohamedan candidates allow the non-Mohamedan voters to waste their votes by concentrating themselves on the Mohamedan candidates. On the contrary, they will engage many voters, if not all, for themselves. If this analysis is true, then it follows that very few non-Mohamedan voters will be left to participate in the election of the Mohamedan candidates, and that the fear of the Mohamedans of any mass action against Muslim candidates by non-Muslim voters is nothing but a hallucination. That the Mohamedans themselves do not believe in it is evident from what are known as the 'Delhi' proposals. According to these proposals, which have been referred to in an earlier part of this report, the Mohamedans have shown their willingness to give up communal electorates, in favour of joint electorates, provided the demand for communal Provinces and certain other concessions regarding the representation of the Muslims in the Punjab and Bengal are given to them. Now, assuming that these communal Provinces have no purpose outside their own, and it is an assumption which we must make, it is obvious that the Mohamedan minority in any province must be content with such protection as it can derive from joint electorates. It is therefore a question as to why joint electorates should not suffice without the addition of communal Provinces when they are said, to suffice with the addition of communal Provinces. But this consideration apart, if there is any substance in the Muslim view that the watering of votes is an evil which attaches itself to the system of joint electorates, then the remedy in my opinion does not lie in the retention of communal electorates. The remedy lies in augmenting the numbers of the Mohamedan electors to the fullest capacity possible by the introduction of adult suffrage, so that the Mohamedan community may get sufficiently large voting strength to neutralize the effects of a possible dilution by an admixture of the non-Muslim votes.

All this goes to show that the case for communal electorates cannot be sustained on any ground which can be said to be reasonable. What is in its favour is feeling and sentiment only. I do not say that feeling and sentiment have no place in the solution of political problems. I realize fully that loyalty to Government is a matter of faith and faith is a matter of sentiment. This faith should be secured if it can be done without detriment to the body politic. But communal representation is so fundamentally wrong that to give in to sentiment in its case would be to perpetuate an evil. The fundamental wrong of the system, has been missed even by its opponents. But its existence will become apparent to any one who will look to its operation. It is clear that the representatives of the Muslims give law to the non-Muslims. They dispose of revenue collected from the non-Muslims. They determine the education of the non-Muslims, they determine what taxes and how much the non-Muslims shall pay. These are some of the most vital things which Muslims as legislators do, whereby affect the welfare of the non-Muslims. A question may be asked by what right can they do this? The answer, be it noted, is not by right of being elected as representatives of the non-Muslims. The answer is by a right of being elected as the representatives of the Muslims! Now, it is a universally recognized canon of political life that the Government must be by the consent of the governed. From what I have said above communal electorates are a violation of that canon. For, it is government without consent. It is contrary to all sense of political justice to approve of a system which permits the members of one community to rule other communities without their having submitted themselves to the suffrage of those communities. And if as the Mohamedans allege that they are a distinct community with an outlook on life widely different from that of the other communities, the danger inherent in the system becomes too terrible to be passed over with indifference.

Such are the defects in the existing structure of the Council. It was framed by the Southborough Committee in 1919. The nature of the framework prepared by that Committee was clearly brought forth by the Government of India in their Despatch No. 4 of 1919 dated 23rd April, 1919, addressed to the Secretary of State in which they observed:

> Before we deal in detail with the report (of the Southborough Committee) one preliminary question of some importance suggests itself. As you will see, the work of the Committee has not to any great extent been directed towards the establishment of principles. In dealing with the various problems that came before them they have usually sought to arrive at agreement rather than to base their solution upon general reasonings.

My colleagues have not cared to consider the intrinsic value of the framework as it now stands. They have no doubt recommended that the system of nominations should be done away with and in that I agree with them. But excepting that they have kept the whole of the electoral structure intact, as though it was free from any objection. In this connection I differ from them. As I have pointed out, the whole structure is faulty and must be overhauled. I desire to point out that the object of the Reforms are embodied in the pronouncement of August, 1917, declares the goal to be the establishment of self-governing institutions. The electoral structure then brought into being was only a half-way house towards it and was justified only because it was agreed that a period of transition from the rule of the bureaucracy to the rule of the people, was a necessity. This existing electoral structure can be continued only on the supposition that the present system of divided government is to go on. The existing system of representation would be quite incompatible with a full Government and must therefore be over-ruled.

There is also another reason why the present system of representation should be overhauled. Representative government is everywhere a party government. Indeed a party government is such a universal adjunct of representative government that it might well be said that representative government cannot function except through a party government. The best form of party government is that which obtains under a two-party-system both of ensuring stable as well as responsible government. An executive may be made as responsible as it can be made by law to the legislature. But the responsibility will only be nominal if the legislature is so constituted that it could not effectively impose its

Will on the executive. A stable government requires absence of uncertainty. An executive must be able to plan its way continuously to an ordered scheme of policy. But that invokes an unwavering support of a majority. This can be obtained only out of a two-party-system. It can never be obtained out of a group system. Under the group system the executive will represent not a general body of opinion, but a patch-work of doctrines held by the leaders of different groups who have agreed to compromise their integrity for the sake of power. Such a system can never assure the continuous support necessary for a stable government since the temptation to reshuffling the groups for private advantage is ever present. The existing Council by reason of the system of representation is, to use the language of Burke, 'a piece of joinery so crossly indented and whimsically dovetailed, a piece of diversified mosaic, a tessellated pavement without cement, patriots and courtiers, friends of government and open enemies. This curious show of a Legislature utterly unsafe to touch and unsure to stand on' can hardly yield to a two-party-system of government, and without a party system there will neither be stable government nor responsible government. The origin of the group system must be sought in the formation of the electorates. For, after all, the electorates are the moulds in which the Council is cast. If the Council is to be remodelled so that it may act with efficiency, then it is obvious that the mould must be recast.

In making my suggestions for the recasting of the electoral system I have allowed myself to be guided by three considerations: (1) Not to be led away by the fatal simplicity of many a politician in India that the electoral system should be purely territorial and should have no relation with the social conditions of the country, (2) Not to recognize any interest, social or economic, for special representation which is able to secure representation through territorial electorates, (3) When any interest is recognized as deserving of special representation, its manner of representation shall be such as will not permit the representatives of such interest the freedom to form a separate group.

Of these three considerations the second obviously depends upon the pitch of the franchise. In another part of this Report I have recommended the introduction of adult suffrage. I am confident that it will be accepted. I make my recommendations therefore on that basis. But in case it is not, and if the restricted franchise continues, it will call for different recommendations, which I also proposed to make. For the reasons given above and following the last mentioned consideration I suggest that—

  I. If adult suffrage is granted there shall be territorial representation except in the case of the Mohamedans, the Depressed Classes, and the Anglo-Indians.

  II. If the franchise continues to be restricted, all representation shall be territorial except in the case of the Mohamedans, the Depressed Classes, Anglo-Indians, the Marathas and the allied castes and labour.

  III. That such special representation shall be by general electorates and reserved seats and of labour by electorate made up of registered trade unions.

From these suggestions it will be seen that I am for the abolition of all class electorates, such as those for (1) Inamdars and Sardars, (2) Trade and Commerce, whether Indian or European, (3) Indian Christians, and (4) Industry; and merge them in the general electorates. There is nothing to prevent them from having their voice heard in the Councils by the ordinary channel. Secondly, although I am for securing the special representation of certain classes, I am against their representation through separate electorates. Territorial electorates and separate electorates are the two extremes which must be avoided in any scheme of representation that may be devised for the introduction of a democratic form of government in this most undemocratic country. The golden mean is the system of joint electorates with reserved seats. Less than that would be insufficient, more than that would defeat the ends of good government. For obvious reasons I make an exception in the case of the European community. They may be allowed to have their special electorates. But they shall be general electorates and not class electorates.

3 On Village Panchayats Bill (October 1931– March 1933)

A BRIEF SKETCH ABOUT THE DOCUMENT

Decentralization of powers is an important component of democratic functioning. During 1932–33, the village panchayats in India was discussed four times in the Bombay Legislative Council. Ambedkar expressed himself on the issue that is part of BAWS, volume II, 1982 (pp. 104–22). Raising various concerns against the making of village panchayats, he did find that the existing panchayats were against the idea of democracy itself.

Dr. B. R. Ambedkar: Mr. President, I have listened with very great interest to the speech delivered by the Honourable Minister in charge of this Bill. Sir, I must also say that I have listened to it with very grave concern. I am sure there can be no two opinions on the fact that this Bill deals with some very vital issues. It not only deals with the question of self-government in so far as it affects the civic amenities of the rural population of this Presidency, but it also affects the question of the life, liberty, and property of the rural population. Having regard to these vital issues involved in this Bill, I am bound to say that the Honourable Minister, in justice to all the interests concerned, ought to have given a longer period for the consideration of the implications involved in this Bill. Sir, he has chosen to satisfy his conscience by barely complying with the requirements of the law by allowing seven days to pass before the Bill was brought for consideration. May I say that in my opinion not only seven days but seven months are necessary for the consideration of this Bill? And I suggest that there would be nothing wrong even now in the Honourable Minister sending this Bill for circulation in order to elicit the opinion of the general public on the issues involved in this Bill. That course I would request him with all due respect to adopt, but if he does not, I would like to address to him two other considerations which, in my opinion, are very important considerations. Sir, I would like to say that, in my opinion, the present Government is not competent to undertake this piece of legislation. The Government is aware that the present system of administration is a discredited system. I am not using that in any carping sense. I am only trying to depict the facts as we all know them. Sir, no section of the population of this country is satisfied with the administration and the working of this Government. Indeed, if one wants to state facts as they are, there is a powerful section in this country which is not prepared to admit and to acknowledge the moral authority of this Government to rule. Sir, we also know that we are on the threshold of a new constitution. We know that the constitution of India for a government of the people, by the people and for the people is on the anvil. We all know and I think we are justified in hoping that this new constitution will be forged within the short period of a year or two, and that a new government, supported fully by all sections of the community, will be installed. Sir, having regard to that consideration, I would like to point out to the Honourable Minister and to those honourable members who are occupying the Treasury Bench that they in their present position are no better than caretakers. Sir, by common consent a caretaker cannot undertake substantial alterations in the premises he is appointed to look after. At the most, during the interval before the real occupant comes to occupy his abode, he may undertake repairs in order to keep the building in working order.

I would also like to point out to the Honourable Minister the analogy of parliamentary life. In England where parliamentary system has been in operation for centuries now, when a Ministry is defeated and when the defeated Ministry does not resign outright and allow the reins to pass into the hands of the opposition but chooses to make its appeal to the electorate, it is an accepted convention of the constitution that the Ministry so situated must not undertake any legislation of any consequential importance. All that they can do is to look after the administration pending the decision of the electorate so that the new Government may not be embarrassed by anything that may be undertaken by such a Government. I ask the Honourable Minister whether he does not wish to abide by the conventions of the parliamentary constitution. I leave it to him to decide.

Sir, I do not find any reason why the Honourable Minister should rush with this measure with such terrific speed, if I may say so, with only seven days' notice. I do not find that there is any very great urge, that there is any very great necessity and urgent call upon him by the people of this Presidency to introduce this measure. So far as I am aware, no political party in this country has made this measure a party cry. I do not know that the Liberals, the Responsivists or the Non-Brahmins or the Congress members who were in this House during the last Legislative Council had ever insisted that they looked upon the introduction of the village panchayats as a fundamental part of their programme. I know of no such thing. Not only that, but I do not find that the masses themselves are clamouring for this measure. If you read the report of the Committee made in 1925 on this question appointed to report upon the working of the Village Panchayat Act of 1920, what do you find? You find this. There are in this Presidency as many as 30,000 villages, on a rough calculation. The Act was passed in 1920 permitting the people to apply for the application of that Act voluntarily. What is the result? The result is that the Sind people set their face against the introduction of village panchayats, so that we do not find a single village panchayat instituted in the province of Sind. In the presidency proper, there is a paltry figure of 323 or something like that. I submit that it is a sad commentary on the civic spirit of the people. Apart from that, it is a proof positive that the people are not anxious for the introduction of village panchayats. I do not wish to go into the reasons of that at this stage, but I am certain that my honourable friend the Minister for Local Self-Government will accept that that is a correct analysis of the situation. Not only that, but I would like to suggest that the reason why he has super-added the judicial functions to the village panchayats is to sweeten the pill so that it may be swallowed more readily. In view of these considerations, I think it would be advisable for the Honourable Minister to postpone the Bill *sine die* so that it may be considered in all its implications on its merits by a new Government which will be fully representative of the people of this Presidency.

Coming to the merits of the Bill itself, Sir, I find that the Bill has two parts. The first part deals with the functions of the panchayat as a body for local self-government. I should like to say at once that I have no objection in principle to the policy of devolution; if it is found that the local boards of this Presidency are overburdened by the functions which are placed upon them by the Local Board Act and if by reason of that they are unable to discharge their functions efficiently, then I say 'by all means institute village panchayats so as to disburden the local boards.' Sir, if the desire is to constitute panchayats for their own sake, then to my mind it is a reversion to a very dangerous system. Many have eulogised the ancient system of village panchayats. Some have called them 'rural republics'. Whatever be the merits of these rural republics, I have not the slightest hesitation in saying that they have been the bane of public life of India.

Mr. Pestanshah N. Vakil: Question.

Dr. B. R. Ambedkar: If India has not succeeded in producing nationalism, if India has not succeeded in building up a national spirit, the chief reason for that in my opinion is the existence of the village system. It made all people saturated with local particularism, with local patriotism. It left no room for larger civic spirit. None whatever. Under the ancient village panchayats, India, instead of being a country of a united people, became a loose conglomeration of village communities with no common tie except common allegiance to a common King. I am glad to say, Sir, that this is not my opinion alone. A member of the committee which was appointed in 1925 expressed himself in that same strain. I refer to the minute of my friend Mr R.G. Pradhan. This is what he stated in that minute:

The excessive village patriotism and village spirit which these communities fostered proved very fatal to the growth of a strong Indian nationality based on the realisation of the territorial unity of India as a whole or of the racial unity of each of our natural territorial divisions.

Mr. Pestanshah N. Vakil: Is Mr R.G. Pradhan a historian?

Dr. B. R. Ambedkar: I do not think that we need bring historians here; we ought to be beware of historians. In these days when you are striving for bringing about a national spirit, in these days when you are striving for bringing about a common nationality and a common sense of Indian citizenship, in my opinion we ought to do nothing which will nullify and which will dilute that sense. I would like to leave this aspect of the matter at that so far as I am concerned.

My next objection is to the constitution of the panchayats themselves. The Bill, as the honourable member has pointed out, provides that the village panchayats shall be elected on the basis of adult suffrage both for males and females. I may at once state that, so far as I am concerned, I say 'so far so good', but I should like to make it clear to the Honourable Minister that, speaking for the depressed classes, I have not the slightest hesitation in saying that adult suffrage is not sufficient for us. The Honourable Minister has forgotten that the depressed classes are in a minority in every village, a miserable minority, and assuming that he adopts adult suffrage, he will readily admit I am sure that adult suffrage cannot convert a minority into a majority. Consequentially I am bound to insist that if these village panchayats come, there shall be special representation for the minorities. At any rate, there shall be special representation for the depressed classes, and others of course will speak for themselves.

I know, Sir, that there is a section in this House who will at once jump and say that this is communalism. Now I agree that this is communalism. But I am also convinced that communalism must be my policy. I am not ashamed of it.

Mr. J. B. Petit: Is that compatible with nationalism? *Dr. B. R. Ambedkar:* Oh, yes. Why not? *Mr. J. B. Petit:* I am glad to hear that.

Dr. B. R. Ambedkar: I will say that India cannot proceed, in my opinion at any rate, on the path of political progress without communalism. Without communalism there can be no self-government for India. That is the proposition that I would assert without fear of challenge.

Speaking for the depressed classes, therefore, I can never accept the principle of self-government for India unless I am satisfied that every self-governing institution has provisions in it which give the depressed classes special representation in order to protect their rights, and until that is done, I am afraid it will not be possible for me to assent to the first part of the Bill.

Sir, in respect of this, I am glad to find that two members of the committee which was set up in 1925 to discuss this question supported the plea of the depressed classes for special representation. I refer to the minute of Mr R.G. Pradhan. This is what he said:

> I am of opinion that provision should be made for the representation of the depressed classes on the village panchayats by nomination. The nomination should be made either by the Collector or the President of the district local board, preferably the latter. It is eminently desirable in the interests of the proper representation of the depressed classes and much more with a view

to raising their general status and making the other classes realise their communal identity with them that there should be at least one member of the depressed classes in every village panchayat. In cases, therefore, where no member of these classes has been able to get in by election, recourse should be had to nomination.

Sir, I should also like to refer to the minute of my honourable friend Mr P.R. Chikodi. He also wrote a separate minute and this is what he said:

I think it is necessary that some arrangements ought to be made to secure on panchayats the representation of the depressed classes by means of nomination or by the system of reserved seats in villages where there are at least 50 adult persons belonging to these classes. It is not likely at present that any representative of these stands a chance of being elected at an open election, the failure of such an attempt having come to my notice very lately.

In this connection, I would also like to draw the attention of the Hindu members of this honourable House to the recent events that have happened. I refer to the Poona Pact between the Caste Hindus and the Depressed Classes that was signed on the 24th of last month. Many members, I am sure, must have read the terms of that Pact, but I should like to draw particular attention to one section of it. In that section it has been agreed that the right of the depressed classes to representation in all local bodies shall be accepted and an endeavour shall be made in order to give effect to that part of the agreement. Sir, I would like to draw the attention of the Hindu members to that part of the Pact and I am sure whatever may have been the opinions before 24th of last month, they will now loyally abide by the terms of that Pact.

Now, Sir, I come to what I call the second part of this Bill. I ought to have stated at the very start that when I read this Bill, I was inclined to say that this Bill was, like the curate's egg, bad in parts only. But after having read the whole Bill and gone through all the provisions of the Bill. I am obliged to revise my opinion. I now think that it is worse than the curate's egg. It is not only bad in some parts but it is rotten in others. I refer, Sir, to the judicial provisions of the Village Panchayats Bill. Sir, I do not know what is the view of the Honourable Minister for Local Self-Government as to the requisites of a proper judiciary which could be trusted to deal with civil and criminal justice. I was expecting to hear from him on that point in the course of the opening remarks which he addressed to this House, but he was silent on that point. I think it will be agreed that a judiciary before it could be entrusted with the duties of discharging civil and criminal justice, must have three requisites. It must be trained in law, it must be impartial in its outlook, and I submit, it must be independent in position. Let us apply these three requisites to the provisions of this Bill. What does the Honourable Minister provide in this Bill? He says, 'We shall elect a panchayat based on adult suffrage, consisting of five or seven members; those gentlemen will hold office for three years. During the course of these three years they shall not only discharge the functions of a local self-governing body, but in addition to that they will also discharge the functions of trying certain criminal and civil cases.' That is, in substance, the provision of this Bill.

Now, the first question that I would like to ask the Honourable Minister is this: Does he expect that these five gentlemen who will be elected on the basis of adult suffrage will have sufficient judicial training to discharge the duties of judges? Sir, I would like to submit that judicial decisions demand a developed judgment; they demand a vast amount of legal knowledge. (Laughter.) Let there be no laughter, because it is a serious matter. Just take this into consideration. We are all agog when members of the I.C.S. want to have certain places reserved for them in the High Court or in the judiciary. What is the reason for our objection? If I have understood the objection correctly, it is this, that these gentlemen who have passed the I.C.S. examination have no judicial training, and not having judicial training, we cannot entrust them with judicial powers. That is the gravamen of the objection. They not only want justice, but they want judges who are competent to discharge their duties. Now, I ask the Honourable Minister whether he thinks that a population which is illiterate, which is steeped in ignorance, which is swallowed up in superstition, can produce five good men who can be entrusted to discharge the duties of judges.

Mr. M. M. Karbhari: Are we so bad as that?

Dr. B. R. Ambedkar: I do not know we may have a difference of opinion on that. But that is my contention. And, supposing it may not be held necessary for these gentlemen to have the necessary legal training. I think we ought at least to expect this much, that they should have proper notions of right, of duty, of equity and good conscience. A population which is hidebound by caste, a population which is infected by ancient prejudices, a population which flouts equality of status and is dominated by notions of gradations in life, a population which thinks that some are high, that some are low—can it be expected to have the right notions even to discharge bare justice? Sir, I deny that proposition, and I submit that it is not proper to expect us to submit our life and our liberty and our property to the hands of these panchas.

The next proposition that I would like to place before this House is this: Is it possible to expect this panchayat to be an impartial body of judges? Let us consider the facts as they are. No honourable member of this House, I am sure, will deny that there are very few villages which are not rent by faction feuds. There are quarrels between the Brahmins and non-Brahmins

Dewan Bahadur D. R. Patil: They will remain for ever.

Dr. B. R. Ambedkar: So much the worse for you if they do. There are, I submit, Sir, factions between Brahmins and non-Brahmins, and I think I may as well cite a case, in view of the fact that the honourable member Rao Bahadur Kale is laughing at the suggestion, from what I know of his own district, namely, Satara. I remember at one time the feud between the Brahmins and non-Brahmins had gone to such an extent in a certain village in Satara District that a complete boycott of the Brahmins was proclaimed by the non-Brahmins. They could not get a barber to shave them; they could not get the village Baniya to sell them provisions; they could not get people to do any service for them. The Brahmin had either to grow a beard or walk seven miles to Satara to have a shave. So, there are quarrels between the depressed classes and the non-Brahmins.

An Honourable Member: They are over.

Dr. B. R. Ambedkar: Unfortunately, far from being over, they have become the order of the day. Not only are there quarrels amongst the Hindus themselves, but there are quarrels between the Hindus and the Mahomedans, and these quarrels are of no ordinary importance, they are serious. I would like the Honourable Minister and the House to consider whether a panchayat elected in an atmosphere of this sort would be impartial enough to distribute justice between men of different castes and men of different creeds. That is a proposition, I submit, which the House and the Honourable Minister should consider seriously.

The next question I would like to ask is, does the Honourable Minister expect that the judiciary he is bringing into being will be an independent judiciary? Sir, what is his proposition? His proposition is that the judiciary shall be elected, because that is what the provisions for a panchayat means. The panchayat which will administer justice will be a panchayat elected by the adult population of the village. I would like to ask him whether he expects that a judge who has to submit himself to the suffrage of the masses will not think twice before doing justice, whether, while giving justice he is offending the sensibility of the voter. Suppose there was a Hindu-Mahomedan riot; suppose a Mahomedan was brought up before a panchayat for an offence which is triable by the panchayat; suppose one Hindu member of the panchayat thought that there was justice on the side of the Mahomedan. Does the Honourable Minister and does the House think that this gentleman, who may have to submit himself to an election within the course of a few months or a year, will think that he ought to do justice to the Mahomedan rather than keep his seat? What will he do?

Dewan Bahadur D. R. Patil: A riot case is not triable by a panchayat.

Dr. B. R. Ambedkar: I am giving it as an example; it may be for some other offence.

Sir, I have never seen anywhere a judiciary that is elected. The only country where we know that the judiciary is elected is America, and you know that it has brought judges into disrepute in all the American Commonwealth and has small justice a by-word for corruption. I am sure my honourable friend does not want us to have that experiment tried on us. In view of this, I must say at once, as I do not wish to trespass too much upon the time of the House, that I cannot accept the principle embodied in the second part of the Bill, that judicial powers, both civil and criminal, should be handed over to a panchayat, which, in substance, is an elective judiciary. Sir, I am bound to say, watching as I have been the affairs that are going on in this presidency and especially what is happening to the depressed classes, that so far as we are concerned we can never consent to judicial affairs being administered by a panchayat. Ours is a very peculiar and, if I may say so, a very pitiable position. We are a small body of people, occupying a corner of a village. We are never looked upon as part and parcel of the village community. Although living in the village, we are all the same an alien body, whose progress is looked upon with great jealousy by the rest of the community. My honourable friend Mr Kamat shakes his head, and therefore I think I must read to him from the report of the State Committee, which I did not want to do. In paragraph 102 of that Committee's report, the condition of the depressed classes in the village is described at great length. This is what the Committee say:

> Although we have recommended various remedies to secure to the Depressed Classes their rights to all public utilities, we fear that there will be difficulties in the way of their exercising them for a long time to come. The first difficulty is the fear of open violence against them by the orthodox

classes. It must be noted that the Depressed Classes form a small minority in every village, opposed to which is a great majority of the orthodox who are bent on protecting their interests and dignity from any supposed invasion by the Depressed Classes at any cost. The danger of prosecution by the Police has put a limitation upon the use of violence by the orthodox classes and consequently such cases are rare.

The second difficulty arises from the economic position in which the Depressed Classes are found today. The Depressed Classes have no economic independence in most parts of the Presidency. Some cultivate the lands of the orthodox classes as their tenants at will. Others live on their earnings as farm labourers employed by the orthodox classes and the rest subsist on the food or grain given to them by the orthodox classes in lieu of service rendered to them as village servants. We have heard of numerous instances where the orthodox classes have used their economic power as a weapon against those Depressed Classes in their villages, when the latter have dared to exercise their rights, and have evicted them from their land, and stopped their employment and discontinued their remuneration as village servants. This boycott is often planned on such an extensive scale as to include the prevention of the Depressed Classes from using the commonly used paths and the stoppage of sale of the necessaries of life by the village Bania. According to the evidence sometimes small causes suffice for the proclamation of a social boycott against the Depressed Classes. Frequently it follows on the exercise by the Depressed Classes of their right to the use of the common well, but cases have been by no means rare where a stringent boycott has been proclaimed simply because a Depressed Class man has put on the sacred thread, has bought a piece of land, has put on good clothes or ornaments, or has carried a marriage procession with a bridegroom on the horse through the public street.

That Sir, is our position. We are a besieged people, so to say, and I cannot allow, and I cannot consent to so much judicial power, both civil and criminal to be handed over to a people who are perpetually in an organized conspiracy to defect our aims and objects.

An Honourable Member: No, no.

Dr. B. R. Ambedkar: I perfectly sympathize with the Honourable Minister's underlying purpose. If I have understood him correctly, all that he wants is that the villagers should get justice cheaply, and it should be more easily accessible to them. I believe that is the underlying motive he has for the judicial provisions he has made in his Bill. If that is so, then I think that there is a better method of doing that. It is not necessary to give the judicial powers to the village panchayats. We have already in existence what are called honorary bench magistrates in towns. It should be perfectly possible to extend that system whereby we can divide each district into judicial circles extending over an area of two or three miles suited to convenience, and for Government to nominate—I emphasize the word 'nominate'—three or more persons to discharge the judicial functions in that circle. These three gentlemen would on one day sit as magistrates to deal with criminal cases and on another day they will sit as civil judges to try civil cases. By this method, you will secure cheap justice, easy justice, at the same time you will secure a judiciary that will be independent of local influence, a judiciary that will be free from the disadvantages of an elective system. I think, Sir, this ought to satisfy the requirements of the case. At any rate, I have to make it plain that, if the Honourable Minister insists that the Bill be put through as it is with all the provisions in it, especially those provisions which he regards as matters of principles, I must say that I shall oppose this Bill. (Applause.)

4 Democracy Must Give Respectful Hearing to All Who are Worth Listening to (4 January 1938)

A BRIEF SKETCH ABOUT THE DOCUMENT

This is an address delivered by Ambedkar at Sholapur during the Matang Conference on 4 January 1938. It was reported by the 'Times of India'. It was the first focused speech by Ambedkar, expressing his views on the working of parliamentary democracy. He was critical of the way parliamentary democracy got confined to a particular political party, in this case the Congress party in India, terming it the greatest malaise, a disease and sickness for the people at large. It is in BAWS, Volume 17 Part III, 2003 (pp. 168–9).

..... In the political situation that has grown up in this country, there has grown the habit among the people of paying homage to only one political party, the Congress.

'I am no believer,' continued he, 'in Democracy as an ideal to be pursued in all circumstances and in all claims; and having regard to the present-day conditions in India, Democracy is a most unsuitable system of Government. At any rate, for some time India needs the strong hand of an enlightened autocrat.'

'In this country we have,' observed he, 'Democracy, but it is a Democracy which has ceased to exercise its intelligence. It has bound itself hand and foot to one organization and only one. It is not prepared to sit in judgment over the doings or thinking of this organization. I consider it the greatest malaise, a disease and a sickness. It has affected all our people. They are intoxicated.' 'Unfortunately,' he added, 'the Indian people are by tradition men who have more faith and less wit. Anyone who does anything out of the ordinary, does something so eccentric as to be called in other countries an insane person, acquires in this country the status of a Mahatma or Yogi. And people follow him as the sheep follow the shepherd'.

I am sure that if this continues we could reap no benefit from the political advancement which this country has secured under the act. Dr Ambedkar emphatically stated that, 'democracy must learn that its safety lies in having more than one opinion regarding the solution of any particular problem, and in order that people may be ready to advice with their opinions, democracy must learn to give a respectful hearing to all who are worth listening.'

'I am glad,' he concluded, 'that the Sholapur Municipality has set an example in voting an address to me who do not belong to an organization which claims to be the only organization in the country and which all people are in a mood to uphold at present.'

5 If Democracy Dies It Will Be Our Doom (18–20 July 1942)

A BRIEF SKETCH ABOUT THE DOCUMENT

Three conferences were held in Nagpur from 18 to 20 July 1942, namely 1) The All-India Depressed Classes Conference; 2) The Depressed Classes Women's Conference; and 3) The Samata Sainik Dal Conference. During these conferences Ambedkar addressed the issues separately. He termed the Nazi emergence as a war between democracy and dictatorship and stressed upon the need for Indians to stand for democracy. These are the excerpts from BAWS, Volume 17 part III., 2003 (pp. 248–83).

All-India Depressed Classes Conference

.....Dr B.R. Ambedkar was given prolonged ovation as he rose to speak.

Address by Dr Ambedkar

Mr. President, Ladies, and Gentlemen,

In this Conference, the first and initial difficulty with which one is faced is the question of language. In this vast gathering vast number of people are from the Marathi speaking area to whom one must speak in the

Marathi language if they are to understand the proceedings of this Conference. Besides the vast Marathi-speaking audience we have also present in this Conference representatives of the Scheduled Castes from other than Marathi-speaking Provinces.

We have in our midst representatives of the Scheduled Castes from other Provinces as well. I see some from Bengal, from Bihar, from Madras, from Andhra, from Punjab and from various other places. It is quite obvious that if they are to follow our proceedings it is necessary to speak in English. To avoid this difficulty I have decided to speak twice—once in English and again in Marathi, so that both sections may know what I have to say. Today I propose to speak in English. Tomorrow I will address you in Marathi.

I might as well tell you how the idea of the holding of this Conference originated. As you will recall, I was called in April last to be present in Delhi to meet Sir Strafford Cripps, who had come to India as an agent of His Majesty's Government with proposals for constitutional changes and who was charged with the duty of negotiating with the different political parties in India for the acceptance of those proposals. Before I went to Delhi, I had invited representatives of the Scheduled Castes in different provinces in India to meet me in Delhi for consultation. When I communicated to them the results of my talks with Sir Strafford Cripps we all felt that the proposals Sir Strafford Cripps had brought with him were a death-blow to the interests of the Scheduled Castes. I expressed my views on the Cripps proposals in a statement to the press which I hope you have all read. But it was felt that common and united action on the part of the Scheduled Castes from all over India was a great necessity—and that it was only common action that could save us from the impending political doom. This Conference has been the result of the wish expressed by the Scheduled Castes all over India through their representatives who met at Delhi and has therefore the backing of the Untouchable India as a whole. That is why we have here present among us representatives of the Scheduled Castes all over India. There was a great rivalry among the different Provinces as to where it should be held. Bengal, Punjab, U.P., C.P. and Bombay each wanted to have the credit of hold the Conference. Ultimately all agreed to allow the Central Provinces to have the credit to hold the Conference. There was however one condition on which they had insisted, namely that I should preside over the Conference no matter where it was held. In deference to the wishes of all I had agreed to preside. The Conference is taking place according to that plan. I am sure we never had a conference so vast and so successful, and I am sure we are all grateful to our C.P. friends. It is their enthusiasm, it is their efforts which had made the Conference the success which it is. The only deviation which has taken place from the original plan is the change in the Presidentship. In my place we have our friend Rao Bahadur N. Shivraj presiding over this Conference. At the time when I agreed to preside I was a free man with the freedom of a politician, and could have presided over the Conference and said what I thought I should say. The limitations of office were then non-existent. But before the Conference could take place, there came the announcement that I was appointed a Member of the Viceroy's Executive Council. This brought in the limitations of office and I thought it would be better to have another person who could speak for the Scheduled Castes with freedom and authority. Rao Bahadur N. Shivraj can speak with freedom, and I have no doubt that he can also speak with authority. He has long laboured in the cause of our people. He represents our people in the Central Legislature. By his education there are very few who are as well qualified as he is. He is B.A., B.L. of the Madras University. He has been a practicing lawyer and he has been a professor of Law in Madras for over ten years. Indeed, a better person than him could not have been found to preside over this Conference, and I am indeed very happy that he has been chosen to take my place.

While I am a Member of Government of India, you will have the responsibility of keeping up our movement and making it effective so that it may lead to the result we all hope to achieve. I shall help you, I shall advise you. But I shall not be able to participate in it. That is a fact you must all bear in mind. It is, therefore, all the more necessary that before I transfer the responsibility to others, I must render account of my stewardship of this movement of the Untouchables which has been associated with me and has been carried on under my guidance if not under my aegis during the last 20 years. It is necessary for me to do so in order that those on whom this responsibility will fall should know where the Scheduled Castes stand *vis-a-vis* other communities in this country, what has been done and what remains to be done for their emancipation.

It is a matter of immense satisfaction that the Untouchables have made great strides along all sides. I will particularize only three. They have acquired a degree of political consciousness which few communities in India have acquired. Secondly they have made considerable progress in education. Thirdly, they are securing a foothold in the institutions and in the public service of the country.

The modern generation of Untouchables are not in a position to realize the immensity of the progress made by the Untouchables. For the simple reason that they do not know how things stood when the movement began 20 years ago. I well remember the first meeting addressed in Bombay after I returned from England as a Barrister-at-Law. Except the organizers of the meeting, there was not a single member in the audience—some persons were sitting on the doorsteps of houses smoking pipes and others were chatting in corners by themselves. No one thought of attending the meeting. See the difference. You have here an audience of 75000 people. Education has made a good progress as compared to that 20 years ago. In Poona alone there are 50 boys studying in colleges. There are altogether about 500 Untouchables who have graduated from the various universities. Some are doctors. Some have become barristers. Many of our brethren are members of Municipalities, District and Local Boards. Years ago our children were denied education. Years ago Untouchables were not permitted to be Members of Local Boards and Municipalities for fear of causing pollution. All this has now changed. Our progress in public service has not been as rapid as we wish. In some respects the Untouchables have an entry. I must mention the Police and the Army. The Police Department was closed to the Untouchables and not even a constable's place was open to the Untouchables. This has changed in some Provinces at least. Our people are now recruited in the Police Service. I must also mention the Army. Up to 1892, Mahars were everywhere in the Army and there were Armies of Mahars. After 1892 the entry of the Mahars in the Army was stopped. During the Great War of 1914, recruitment of the Mahars in the Army was restarted and one battalion of the Mahars was formed. After the last War that battalion was again disbanded. Now, however, our regiments are again being formed. Commissions are being granted to our young men and 5 or 6 of our young men have received King's Commission and are holding posts of responsibility and honour in the Army. The greatest progress that we have made is to be found among our women folk. Here you see in this Conference these 20000 to 25000 women present. See their dress, observe their manners, mark their speech. Can any one say that they are Untouchable women. The progress made by our women is the most astonishing and encouraging feature of our movement and it is of course the most gratifying feature.

This is a record of progress of which we may all be legitimately proud. It is a progress for which we have not to thank anybody. It is not the result of Hindu charity. It is an achievement which is entirely the result of our own labour. The question is how can we maintain this progress. That is a question we must never forget to ask ourselves. Progress in the competition of communities is the result of power. This power may be economic, it may be social or it may be political. Have we power to sustain our progress? Have we economic power? I am sure we have none. We are a class of serfs. Have we social power? I am sure we have none. We are a degraded portion of humanity. The only thing, therefore, we can depend upon for our continued progress is the capture of political power. I have no doubt that is our only salvation, and that without it we will perish. It is on this question that we must concentrate all our attention. It is a question of life and death for us. What are our prospects in the matter of capturing political power? It is better if I sum up the forces which are helping us and the forces which are working against us. With the knowledge of such forces, you will be better able to frame your policy and forge your sanctions.

Let me begin by telling you what has been the keynote of my politics. You may be familiar with it but it is well to re-state it. My basis of my politics lies in the proposition that the Untouchables are not a sub-head or a sub-section of the Hindus, and that they are a separate and a distinct element in the national life of India, as separate and distinct as the Muslims and like the Muslims of India the Untouchables are entitled to separate political rights as against the Hindus of India. This is the keynote of my politics. No one will misunderstand me or my politics if he bears that in mind. Having stated the fundamental basis of my politics I will proceed to sum up the forces working for and against our claim for separate political rights. To begin with the Round Table Conference, the Round Table Conference was a very vast affair, and I do not wish to trouble you with all the details of what took place there. I will confine myself to what happened to the Untouchables. There was a contest between me and Mr Gandhi. Mr Gandhi contested that the Untouchables were a sub-section of the Hindus and consequently if any political power was to devolve from the hands of the British it should pass undivided into the hands of the Hindus who could be trusted to look after the interests of the Untouchables. The position taken up by me was totally different; I contended that the Untouchables formed separate and distinct element in the life of the country. The Hindus who are their hereditary enemies could not be trusted and far from using the political power for raising the Untouchables the fear was that they would use it for perpetuating their subjection, and it was, therefore, absolutely necessary that there should be political partition between the Untouchables and the Hindus so that the Untouchables may get political power in their own hands to use it to promote their welfare or to use it to save themselves against the tyranny and oppression of the Hindus. I do not want to dilate upon what the Mahatma or other Hindus did by way of manoeuvring to defeat the claim. It is sufficient to say that at the Round Table Conference the Untouchables won and the Mahatma lost. The Communal Award was the result of this contest. Its great virtue lies in the fact that the Untouchables were recognized in the national life of India and entitled to claim separate political rights. That is the importance of the Communal Award.

Mr Gandhi, at first, did not accept the Communal Award. He started a fast unto death to compel the British Government to unsettle a settled fact. He failed in the fast as he failed at the Round Table Conference in defeating the claim of the Untouchables to be treated as a distinct element separate from the Hindus and, entitled to separate political recognition. In the Poona Pact which was the result of his fast, he had to admit the main contention I had put forth at the Round Table Conference.

In the first round, the victory had gone to the Untouchables. Our position remained intact even after the war had commenced and the Congress had come to occupy a doposition in Indian politics. Indeed, our claim was reassured and sustained by the declaration of the Viceroy made on the 8th August 1940 in which it was made clear that the Muslims and the Untouchables were distinct and separate elements in the National life of India and that the British. Government will not enforce a constitution which has not the support of the Muslims and the Depressed Classes.

I have spoken so far of the strength of our position. I must now speak to you of the forces that tend to weaken our position. One major factor which has been working to weaken our position is Gandhi and Gandhism. By signing the Poona Pact, I helped to save the life of Mr Gandhi. But Mr Gandhi accepted the Poona Pact not as a gentleman signing an agreement with the intention to honour his word but as a crafty person seeking to find a way out of a difficulty. For, I want you to remember that Mr Gandhi, notwithstanding the Poona Pact which saved him from death, never gave his true and honest consent to the principle underlying the Poona Pact. He remained a determined opponent of the claim of the Untouchables for a separate political recognition and has ever since done everything possible to oppose our claim and to undermine our position. I want you to bear in mind that Mr Gandhi is our greatest opponent. I do not like to use the word enemy, though there is enough justification for it. There are some among us who were deluded by the artificiality of his phraseology. But, I must warn you that you would be making the greatest mistake if you forget to take note of the fact that among the adverse forces which are weakening your side and against which you have to concentrate your forces in winning your battle for political freedom, the most formidable force is Mr Gandhi.

The second factor which has weakened our position must be ascribed to thee change in the attitude of His Majesty's Government, Up to the declaration of 8th August 1940, the Government's view was that the Untouchables were distinct and a separate element and they constituted so important an element that their consent was necessary for any constitutional changes that may be desired. But in the proposals of His Majesty's Government which were sent down with Strafford Cripps, His Majesty's Government took a, complete *volte-face*. For, Sir Strafford Cripps proclaimed without blush or without remorse that only the consent of the Hindus and the Muslims was enough for giving effect to the constitutional changes involved in the Cripps proposals; that the consent of the Untouchables was not necessary. In plain terms the Untouchables had ceased to be regarded as an important element in the national life of India. It passes one's comprehension how 60 to 70 millions of Untouchables have ceased to be an important element within a few months. It is a complete somersault on the part of His Majesty's Government. It is a great betrayal of the Untouchables. Whatever the reasons for this betrayal and however strong may be your feelings at so unjust and indecent an act on the part of His Majesty's Government, the fact must be recognized that this has been the greatest breach in our war. There is a third circumstance of an adverse character to which I think I must not fail to draw your attention. There was a time when there was a solidarity of feeling based on community of interest among the different minority communities in India, among whom the Muslim Community was a premier community. That solidarity is now gone. This is principally due to the change in the vision of the Muslim community brought about by the Muslim League. The Muslim League when it was resuscitated by Mr Jinnah after the 1937 election began with the ideology that the Musalmans were a minority, and as a minority they needed the strength of other minorities to support and sustain them. So firm was the faith of the Muslim League in the scheme of mutual strength that the Muslim League had taken up the cause of other minorities and passed resolutions pledging its support to their claims and had stood out not merely as an advocate of the Muslim cause but as a champion of all the other minorities in India. This attitude of the League has undoubtedly been of great help to the Untouchables as the attitude of the Untouchables had always been to the Muslims of India. But the League's attitude has undergone a complete change. The Muslim League ever since the Resolution on Pakistan was passed has ceased to regard the Muslims as a community. It holds that the Muslims are a nation. That is not all. The Muslim League further believes that it has nothing to do with the other communities, that it has nothing to do with the Hindu community but it has also nothing to do with other minority communities. The Muslim League alignment is simple. It is an alignment of Muslim as against all other Non-Muslim without distinction or discrimination. This change in the attitude of the League cannot but have serious consequences for the Untouchables. It means that the Untouchables have lost an ally. But it may mean more than the loss of an ally The Muslim League has not only come to set up a new and a different alignment of Muslims *versus* Non-Muslims, it has set up a new equation of values. That equation is a simple equation. It says that the Muslims, whatever their numbers, are just equal to the Non-Muslims and therefore, in any political arrangement the Muslims must get fifty per cent. To this equation no one can consent. Not only it is against arithmetic; it is also against the interests of all non-Muslim including the Untouchables. Having regard to these changes in the political standpoint of the Muslim League the Untouchables may be said not only to have lost an ally but also to have lost a friend. For, if the League insists on fifty per cent representation in everything, there can be no doubt that the Muslims and the Untouchables will come in conflict.

I have, so far, given you an idea as to what was our position in Indian politics and what forces have been working to undermine that position. Let me now give you an idea of what I think should be your political demands. It is very necessary that you should formulate them in clear terms. It will clarify the position. Our people will know what we stand for. Our opponents will have notice of our demands.

In the first place, you must insist upon being recognized as an independent and separate element in the national life of India. The theory that they are only a sub-section of the Hindus must be fought tooth and nail. Failure to get the Untouchables recognized as a distinct element, separate from the Hindus, will keep them submerged and lead to their suppression and degradation. Next, you must ask for provision being made in the constitution for a sum of money to be set apart annually in the budget of every Province for the education of the Untouchables. You must demand such a sum not only for primary education but also for higher education: Higher education is more important to us at this stage than primary education. From the standpoint of leadership, from the standpoint of filling in high administrative posts, higher education is to the Untouchables a great necessity. Thirdly, you should demand that a number of posts in the public services shall be reserved for the Untouchables subject, of course, to the rule of minimum qualification. This is very essential. We suffer from bad administration and not from bad laws. The administration is bad because it is in the hands of the Caste Hindus, who carry their social prejudices into administration and persistently deny to the Untouchables for one reason or another the principle of equal benefit to which they are entitled. Good laws can do you no good unless you have good administration and you can have good administration when you have persons belonging to the Untouchables holding high administrative posts from which they could watch how other Hindu Civil Servants are behaving towards the Untouchables and to check them, control them and prevent them from doing mischief. It is, however, not enough to ask for mere reservation. It is necessary to insist that such reservation shall be given effect to within a stated period. This is far more essential than mere reservation. For, unless you fix a period, the reservation will not come. It will be evaded on one ground or another and of course on the usual but unfathomable ground that no suitable candidate was available. We all know that to a Hindu, if he is the appointing authority, no candidate from the Untouchables would be a suitable candidate. Fourthly, you must insist upon securing representation for the Untouchables in the Central and Provincial Executives. These are key positions. It is those who occupy these positions who have the power to give direction to the course of events. They alone can control any mischief that they may be threatened of and they alone can force new and salutary changes in social, political, and economic affairs. The Untouchables must insist that their representatives are placed in these key positions. This time it must not be left to understanding or convention. The Hindus cannot be trusted to abide by their plighted word. You must see that a provision in this behalf is made part of the constitution.

Then, there is the last demand which the Untouchables must insist upon. It is the last, but it is by no means the least in importance. Indeed, I am convinced that it is the most vital demand which to my mind must override every other demand. I refer to the project of having new settlements of the Untouchables, separate and independent, of the Hindu villages. Why have the Untouchables been the slaves and serfs of the Hindus for so many thousand years? To my mind the answer lies in the peculiar organization of Hindu villages. You are spread out all over India some 7,00,000 Hindu villages, good to every Hindu village there exists a small settlement of Untouchables. This settlement of Untouchables is usually numerically very small as compared with the Hindu village to which it is attached. Secondly, this settlement of Untouchables is economically without any resource and without any opportunity for improvement. It is invariably a settlement of landless population. Being Untouchable it could not sell anything, for nobody would buy from an Untouchable. It is wholly a population, destitute, and dependent for its livelihood upon the Hindu village. It lives by begging food or by offering its labour for a paltry wage. In this setting you can well understand why the Untouchable has remained in a degraded condition for so many centuries. As against the Hindu village, the Untouchables simply cannot offer any resistance. They are numerically small and they are economically poor. While this village system continues to exist in its present form, the Untouchables will never achieve their independence, whether social, or economic, and will never get over the inferiority complex which they have developed as a result of their state of social and economic dependence. The village system must, therefore, be broken. It is the only way that is open for the Untouchables if they really wish to emancipate themselves from the stranglehold which the Hindus have acquired over them through the village system. My suggestion is that you should insist upon a provision being made in the Constitution for the formation of new and independent villages exclusively of Untouchables at the public cost to be undertaken by the Central Government. There is a good deal of cultivable land which belongs to Government and which is unoccupied. This could be reserved for the purpose of giving effect to this scheme of new villages of Untouchables. Government could buy from private individuals outlying vacant land and use it for the same purpose. It would not be difficult to induce the Untouchables to shift from their present habitats to these new villages and settle there as independent farmers. The process may take time. But, that does not matter. It is so vital that we must insist upon the scheme being made by the constitution itself a matter of obligation upon the Central Government.

There is one other point about which I must speak to you a few words. That is about the necessity of forming one central all-India political organization to act as the mouth-piece of the Untouchables of India. We have been carrying on our political activities through our provincial organizations. I find that even in provinces there is a multiplicity of political organizations. Any ambitious person who wants to parade himself as a President or a Secretary founds an association with himself as President or the Secretary. He needs do nothing more than get a printed letter paper having the name of the association and his name as President or Secretary. This is a state of anarchy which you must put a stop to at once. There is only one way by which this can be done. And that is by establishing an all-India organization with provincial branches and to abolish all existing organizations. This will give you the strength you need and enable you to work in a manner that will help you to build a united front. I hope you will take up this matter in right earnest.

I have told you what I have thought and felt regarding the problem of the Untouchables and I hope you will give it your best consideration.

Perhaps, in closing I may refer to our attitude to the war. From the beginning we have supported the war efforts. I am sure we shall continue to lend it our support. We have our political demands which, we insist, shall be satisfied. But we have given our support to the war efforts without making the satisfaction of our demands being a condition precedent. It is not that we value the satisfaction of our demands as of lesser importance, than the successful conclusion of the war. We do not lay down any conditions for our support to the war because we feel that the successful issue of the war will help us better in the realization of our political demands than the loss of the war. This is a war between democracy and dictatorship—not an enlightened dictatorship but a dictatorship of the most barbarous character based not on any moral ideal but on racial arrogance. If any dictatorship needs to be destroyed, it is this vile Nazi Dictatorship. Amidst all the political dissensions that one witnesses in this country, amidst all uncertainties of the future which some feel, we are trying to forget what a menace to our future this Nazism, if it wins, is going to be. What is more important is that its racial basis is a positive danger to Indians. If this is a correct view of the situation, it seems to me that there lies on us a very heavy duty to see that democracy does not vanish from the earth as a governing principle of human relationship. If we believe in it, then, we must both be true and loyal to it. We must not only be staunch in our faith in democracy but we must resolve to see that in whatever we do, we do not help the enemies of democracy to uproot the principles of liberty, equality and fraternity.

On that point I hope we are all agreed and if you agree with me, then if follows that we must strive along with other democratic countries to maintain the basis of democratic civilization. If democracy lives, we are sure to reap the fruits of it. If democracy dies, it will be our doom. On that there can be no doubt.

There is nothing more that I have to say to you on this occasion. I am happy to be in the midst of you. I shall be happy to serve you in future as I have done in the past. If we all work together and strive together, we will not fail, for our cause is the cause of justice, and the cause of humanity.

....Friends, during the last ten years the political movement has taken great strides. Still I am sure the resolutions which you have passed today mark the beginning of a new era so far as the Untouchables are concerned. As you know, I am taking up from tomorrow the duties of my new office. I, therefore, consider it to be my duty to render to you an account of my stewardship during the past twenty years (Dr Ambedkar here repeated in Marathi the account of the political, economic and social progress made by the Depressed Classes during the past twenty years.).

I must tell you that between the condition of the Muslims and the Untouchables there is a substantial difference, although both are known as minority communities. The Muslim Community is very rich as compared to our Community. They were rulers in this Country till the British came. They have; thus, superior status behind them and their progress is decidedly far in advance of us. We had been oppressed for centuries. Our economic condition is one of extreme poverty. We cannot simply compare ourselves with the Muslims on the ground of population alone. We have to work up ourselves from the beginning relying entirely on our own efforts. We have to raise our Community. Due to my new appointment the responsibility for shouldering the task now rests upon others. I have no love for office. I am quite alright as I was. I do not consider that there is any difference between 'the hon'ble Dr. Ambedkar' and the simple 'Dr. Ambedkar'. What I consider most important with regard to my appointment is that a convention is now established that them should be a seat for the representative of the Depressed Classes on the Executive Council of the Governor General. This is death-blow to Brahminism. Therein lies the importance of my appointment. It was not in the interest of Brahminism to have such a convention at all. I consider this a great victory for the Untouchables.

There are many people who are not well disposed towards me. I am by nature given to live alone and spend my time in reading. Many people consider this nature of mine as an indication that I do not treat the people properly and avoid them. I assure you that I do not mean any insult to anyone. My time is limited. I have to do many things and I have no assistance.

Many Hindus look upon me as their enemy. They complain that I speak hard to injure their feelings. I know I have kind heart and I have many friends even among Brahmins. But even a kind hearted man has to speak the truth. When he sees his kith and kin being treated worst than dogs and their future progress blocked by all means, how can they expect me to treat them kindly as though they have done nothing. I try to suppress my feelings and treat my opponents with honour but guilty conscience feels the pinch, although my treatment to my opponents is never unkind.

I am definitely of opinion that in this Country political rights must be shared between the Hindus, the Musalmans and the Depressed Classes. The Depressed Classes must by law have a proper share in the Government of the Country along with the Hindus and the Musalmans. The future constitution can only work if it rests on these three pillars. To achieve this, you must all come together under one flag and have only organization. If we have not so far achieved the position in the Constitution which is due to us, it is because we have not been united. If you all unite and work under one organization, I have no doubt that you will reach the position you are entitled to.

Congress is a big organization and its influence is spread far and wide. Some naturally ask why this is so, and why our organization is not so spread. There are two things at the command of the Congress. The Congress have the whole Press of India behind it. It gets full publicity. We can get no publicity from the nationalist Hindu Press. Secondly, the Congress has money at its command. You will remember that the Congress collected a fund of one crore of rupees. This large fund forms the secret of its success. But for the work of our Community I have never asked for funds. What progress and organization we have achieved we have done so without the help of any funds at all. I must, however, tell you that it is very necessary to collect funds to build up our organization and without funds our community will not be able to march forward and to keep pace with the other already well-organized communities.

In public life mistakes do occur, but these should not discourage us. Through errors only we can find out our weakness and put them right.

I am very happy to note your decision today to have one organization for the whole of India. You must now in each Province establish its branches and you must see that all the existing organizations are merged in this one All-India Federation.

It is my great desire that there should be buildings of our organizations not only in each Province but in each town to serve as a centre of office and activity. Last night, I was talking to Mr Dashrath Patil of Bela (Nagpur). I told him to purchase a piece of land and erect a building in Nagpur for our organization: You call do that with a sum of rupees twenty to twenty-five thousand. If you will do this and invite me to lay the foundation stone of such a building at Nagpur, it shall give me the greatest pleasure to accept your invitation. (At this stage Mr Sitaram Hadke presented a purse of rupees two hundred and fifty on behalf of Bhanklxda Basti, Nagpur.) Mr Ambedkar accepted the purse and made it over to Mr Dashrath Patil to apply it for the building fund....

The All-India Depressed Classes Women's Conference

Address by Dr Ambedkar

I am very happy to have this occasion of addressing you. There cannot be an occasion of greater happiness to anyone interested in the advancement of the Depressed Classes than to witness this gathering of women. That you would assemble in such vast number—almost 20,000 to 25,000 strong—would have been unthinkable 10 years ago. I am a great believer in Women's organization. I know what they can do to improve the condition of society if they are convinced. In the eradication of social evils they have rendered great services. I will testify to that from my own experience. Ever since I began to work among the Depressed Classes, I made it a point to carry women along with men. That is why you will see that our Conferences are always mixed Conferences. I measure the progress of a community by the degree of progress which women have achieved, and when I see this assembly, I feel both convinced and happy that we have progressed. I shall tell you a few things which I think you should bear in mind.

Learn to be clean; keep free from all vices. Give education to your children. Instill ambition in them. Inculcate on their minds that they are destined to be great. Remove from them all inferiority complex. Don't be in a hurry to marry: marriage is a liability. You should not impose it upon your children unless financially they are able to meet the liabilities arising from marriage. Those who marry will bear in mind that to have too many children is a crime. That Parental duty lies in giving each child a better start than its parents had. Above all, let each girl who marries stand up to her husband, claim to be her husband's friend and equal, and refuse to be his slave. I am sure if you follow this advice you will bring honour and glory to yourself and to the Depressed Classes.

6   Objections to Cripps' Proposals (20 July 1942)

A BRIEF SKETCH ABOUT THE DOCUMENT

During the Second World War the British wanted to get the support of the Indians against the Nazis. In this light, Sir Stafford Cripps formulated some proposals for the benefit of Indians. These included the constitution of Constituent Assembly. This is a statement by B. R. Ambedkar showing how the Cripps' Proposals would affect the Untouchables adversely by subjugating and undermining their concerns. This statement was given on 20 July 1942 and is now part of BAWS, Volume 9, 1991 (pp. 336–43).

The War Cabinet proposals show a sudden *Volte Face* on the part of His Majesty's Government. The putting forth of these proposals, which were denounced by them as an invasion of minority rights, is an indication of their complete surrender of right to win might. This is Munich mentality, the essence of which is to save oneself by sacrificing others, and it is this mentality which is writ large on these proposals. It is reported that the American and English people are annoyed at Indians not welcoming the proposals of His Majesty's Government relating to the constitutional advancement of India and thereby allowing the mission of Sir Stafford Cripps to fail. One can forgive the Americans for their attitude, but surely the English people and Sir Stafford Cripps ought to know better. It does not seem to have been sufficiently realized that the proposals of His Majesty's

Government now put forth as the best are the very proposals which have been rejected and condemned by His Majesty's Government as the worst, only a few months previously. Those who realize this cannot but help saying that this is the ugliest part of the whole business of constitutional advance, which His Majesty's Government is now suddenly and contrary to its previous declarations, rushing to undertake. The proposals fall into three parts: (1) There is to be a constituent assembly with a right to frame the Constitution for India. This Assembly is to have the fullest power to frame such constitution as the majority in the Assembly may choose to decide. (2) The new Constitution is not to include all of the present Provinces of India but only such Provinces as may be willing to be bound by it. For this the Provinces have been given a right to decide whether they shall join the new Constitution or stay out of it. This is left to be done by a plebiscite in which a bare majority is declared enough to decide the issue. (3) The Constituent Assembly shall be required to enter into a treaty with the British Government. The treaty is to contain provisions for the safety and security of racial and religious minorities. After such a treaty is signed, the British Government is to withdraw its sovereignty and the Constitution framed by the Constituent Assembly is to come into operation.

Such, in brief outline, is the scheme of His Majesty's Government.

The proposal regarding Constituent Assembly is not a new proposal. It was put forth by the Congress when the war broke out and what is important is that this proposal of the Congress was rejected by His Majesty's Government. This is what Mr Amery said in the House of Commons on August 14, 1940, regarding Constituent Assembly:

> Congress leaders ... have built up a remarkable organization, the most efficient political machine in India.... If only they had succeeded, if the Congress could, in fact speak, as it professes to speak, for all the main elements in India's national life, then however advanced their demands, our problem would have been in many respects far easier than it is today. It is true that they are numerically the largest single party in British India, but their claim in virtue of that fact to speak for India is utterly denied by very important elements in India's complex national life. These others assert their right to be regarded not as mere numerical minorities but as separate constituent factors in any future Indian policy. The foremost among these elements stands the great Muslim community. They will have nothing to do with a Constitution framed by a Constituent Assembly elected by a majority vote in geographical constituencies. They claim the right in any constitutional

discussions to be regarded as an entity and are determined only to accept a Constitution whose actual structure will secure their position as an entity against the operations of a mere numerical majority. The same applies to the great body of what are known as the *Scheduled Castes* who feel, in spite of Mr. Gandhi's earnest endeavours on their behalf, that, as a community, they stand outside the main body of the Hindu Community which is represented by the Congress.

This statement was made by Mr Amery when he was elucidating the announcement made by the Viceroy on 8 August 1941 in which he had given the following pledge to the minorities on behalf of His Majesty's Government:

> There are two main points which have emerged. On these two points. His Majesty's Government now desire me to make their position clear. The first is as to the position of the minorities in relation to any future constitutional scheme. ... It goes without saying that they (H. M. Government) could not contemplate the transfer of their present responsibilities for the peace and welfare of India to any system of government whose authority is directly denied by large and powerful elements in India's national life. Nor could they be parties to the coercion of such elements into submission to such a government.

Again on the 23 April 1941, Mr Amery referred to the demand of the Constituent Assembly and expressed himself in the following terms:

> India's future Constitution should be devised by Indians for themselves and not by the British Government. India's future Constitution should be essentially an Indian Constitution, framed in accordance with the Indian conception of Indian conditions and Indian needs. The only essential condition is that the Constitution itself and the body which is to frame it, must be the outcome of agreement between principal elements in India's national life.

Such were the views and pledges given by His Majesty's Government regarding Constituent Assembly, which is now conceded. Regarding the demand for Pakistan, it was a demand put forward by the Muslim League. This demand was also rejected by His Majesty's Government. This is what Mr Amery said in regard to it in the House of Commons on 1 August 1940:

> This reaction against the dangers of what is called the Congress Raj or Hindu Raj has gone so far as to lead to a growing demand from Muslim quarters for a complete breaking up of India into separate Hindu and Muslim

dominions. I need say nothing to-day of the manifold and to my mind, insuperable objections to such a scheme, at any rate in its extreme form. I would only note that it merely shifts the problem of permanent minorities to somewhat smaller areas, without solving it.

Again on 23 April 1941, he referred to it in his speech in the House of Common and spoke about it in the following terms:

> I am not concerned here to discuss the immense practical difficulties in the way of this so-called Pakistan project nor need I go back to the dismal record of India's history in the 18th century or to the disastrous experience of the Balkan countries before our eyes, to-day, in order to point out the terrible dangers inherent in any break up of the essential unity of India, at any rate in its relation to the outside world. After all, there is no British achievement in India of which we have reason to be proud than the unity ... we have given her.

Such were the views of His Majesty's Government only a year ago regarding Constituent Assembly and Pakistan.

It is quite obvious that the proposal for a Constituent Assembly is intended to win over the Congress, while the proposal for Pakistan is designed to win over the Muslim League. How do the proposals deal with the Depressed Classes? To put it shortly, they are bound hand and foot and handed over to the caste Hindus. They offer them nothing; stone instead of bread. For the Constituent Assembly is nothing short of a betrayal of the Depressed Classes. There can be no doubt as to what the position of the Depressed Classes will be in the Constituent Assembly; nor can there be any doubt regarding the political programme of the Constituent Assembly. In the Constituent Assembly, there may be no representatives of the Depressed Classes at all because no communal quotas are fixed by these proposals. If they are there, they cannot have a free, independent and decisive vote. In the first place, the representatives of the Depressed Classes will be in a hopeless minority. In the second place, all decisions of the Constituent Assembly are not required to be by a unanimous vote. A majority vote is enough to decide any question no matter what its constitutional importance is. It is clear that under this system the voice of the Depressed Classes in the Constituent Assembly cannot count. In the third place, the present system of proportional representation by which the members to the Constituent Assembly are to be elected under the terms contained in His Majesty's proposals cannot but result in the caste Hindus having virtually the right to nominate the representatives of the Depressed Classes to the Constituent Assembly. Such representatives of the Depressed Classes will be the tools of the caste Hindu. In the fourth place, the Constituent Assembly will be filled with the Congressites who will form the dominant majority party able to carry out its own programme. There is no doubt that Mr Gandhi, whatever may be said about his endeavours in the matter of the social uplift of the Depressed Classes, is totally opposed to giving political recognition to the Depressed Classes in the Constitution as a separate and distinct element in the national life of India. That being the case, the programme of the majority party in the Constituent Assembly will be to wipe out the political safeguards already granted to the Depressed Classes in the present Constitution. Any one, who realizes what is implied in the Constituent Assembly, will admit that His Majesty's Government by their proposals have literally thrown the Depressed Classes to the wolves. It may be said that while there is the Constituent Assembly which may deny constitutional safeguards to the Depressed Classes, His Majesty's Government have been careful to include in their proposals the provisions for a treaty with the Constituent Assembly the object of which is to secure the interests of the Depressed Classes. This proposal of a treaty is evidently borrowed from the plan adopted by His Majesty's Government for the settlement of the Irish dispute. The proposal regarding the treaty does not say what are the safeguards His Majesty's Government will decide to include in the treaty. This is an important point because there may be a difference of opinion between His Majesty's Government and the Depressed Classes on the nature, number and method of the political safeguards that may be necessary to protect the interests of the Depressed Classes under the new Constitution. The second and equally important question about the treaty is what is going to be the sanction behind the treaty. Will the treaty be a part of the Constitution framed by the Constituent Assembly, so that any provision in the Constitution which is repugnant with the treaty will be null and void? Or, will the treaty be just a treaty between the two governments; the Indian National Government and His Majesty's Government, as any trade treaty? If the treaty is to be of the former kind, it will be the law of the land and will have legal sanction of the Indian Government behind it. If, on the other hand, the treaty is to be of the latter kind, it is obvious it will not be the law of the land and will have no legal sanction behind it. Its sanction will be political sanction. Now a treaty cannot override the Constitution framed by the National Government for the obvious reason that such a thing, as was found in the case of Irish Free State, is incompatible with Dominion Status. The only sanction behind such a treaty will be political sanction. It is obvious that the use of such sanction must depend upon the colour of the Government and the state of public opinion. Given this fact, the questions that arise are two: (1) What are the means which His Majesty's Government will have at its disposal to enforce the treaty obligations? (2) Secondly, will His Majesty's Government be prepared to use these means to coerce the Indian National Government to abide by the terms of the treaty? With regard to the first question, it is obvious that the means for enforcing the treaty are twofold—use of force and trade war. As to the military force, the Indian army will not be available. It will be entirely transferred to the control of the new Indian National Government. His Majesty's Government will have therefore lost this means of enforcing the treaty. It is impossible to believe that His Majesty's Government will send its own army to compel the National Government to obey the treaty. A trade war is not possible. It is a suicidal policy and the experience of the Irish war with the Irish Free State for the recovery of land annuities shows that a nation of shopkeepers will not sanction it even though it may be for their interest and honour. The treaty therefore is going to be an empty formula, if not a cruel joke, upon the Depressed Classes. His Majesty's Government has sent out these proposals to be welcomed by Indians. But neither His Majesty's Government nor Sir Stafford Cripps have offered any explanation as to why they are offering to Indians the very proposals which His Majesty's Government had been condemning in scathing terms only a few months ago. A year ago, His Majesty's Government said that they would not grant Constituent Assembly because that would be a coercion of the minorities. His Majesty's Government is now prepared to grant Constituent Assembly and to coerce the minorities. A year ago, His Majesty's Government said that they will not allow Pakistan because that is Balkanization of India. To-day, they are prepared to allow the partition of India. How can the Government of a Great Empire lose all sense of principle? The only explanation is that His Majesty's Government has, as a result of the course of the war, become panic-stricken. The proposals are the result of loss of nerve. How great is the panic that has overtaken His Majesty's Government can be easily seen if one compared the demands made by the Congress and the Muslim League and the concessions made to them by these proposals. The Congress demanded that the Constitution should be framed by a Constituent Assembly by a mere majority vote. On the other hand, when the Viceroy announced that the British Government will not be a party to the coercion of the minorities involved in the demand by the Congress, the Working Committee of the Congress at its meeting at Wardha held on 22 August 1940, passed the following resolution:

The Committee regrets that although the Congress has never thought in terms of coercing any minority, much less of asking the British Government to do so, the demand for a settlement of a Constitution though through a Constituent Assembly of duly elected representatives has been misrepresented as coercion and the issue of minorities has been made into an insuperable barrier to Indians progress.

The Working Committee added:

The Congress had proposed that minority rights should be amply protected by agreement with the elected representatives of the minorities concerned.

This shows that even the Congress did not demand that the decision of minority rights should be included in the purview of the Constituent Assembly. His Majesty's Government has, however, given them the additional right to decide this minority rights issue by a bare majority vote. With regard to the question of Pakistan, the same attitude is noticeable. The Muslim League did not demand that Pakistan must be conceded immediately. All that the Muslim League had asked for was that at the next revision of the Constitution, the Mussalmans should not be prevented from raising the question of Pakistan. The present proposals have gone a step beyond and distinctly give to the Muslim League the right to create Pakistan. These are constitutional proposals. They are intended to lead India to wage a total war in which Hindus, Mussalmans, Depressed Classes and Sikhs are called upon wholeheartedly to participate. Yet Sir Stafford Cripps, either with the consent or without the consent of His Majesty's Government, has been making discrimination between major parties and minor parties. The major parties are those whose consent is necessary. Minor parties are those with whom consultation is believed to be enough. This is new distinction. Certainly it was never made in the prior pronouncements either of His Majesty's Government or of the Viceroy. The pronouncement spoke of the 'consent of the principal elements in the national life of India.'

So far as the Depressed Classes are concerned, I am not aware of any pronouncement in which the Depressed Classes were placed on a lower plane than the one given to the Mussalmans. I quote the following from the speech of the Viceroy made in Bombay on January 10, 1941, from which it will be seen that the Depressed Classes were bracketed with the Mussalmans:

> There are insistent claims of the minorities. I need refer only to two of them; the great Muslim minority and the Scheduled Classes—there are the guarantees that have been given to the minorities in the past, the fact that their position must be safeguarded and that those guarantees must be honoured.

This invidious distinction now sought to be made is a breach of faith with those minorities whose position has been lowered by this discrimination. From a constitutional point of view of total war, it is bound to cause more disaffection and disloyalty in the country. It is for the British to consider whether in this attempt to win the friendship of those who have probably already decided to choose other friends, they should lose those who are their real friends. The proposals show a sudden *volte face* on the part of His Majesty's Government. The putting forth of those proposals which were denounced by them as an invasion of minorities' rights is an indication of their complete surrender of right to win might. This is Munich Mentality the essence of which is to save oneself by sacrificing others and it is this mentality which is writ large on those proposals. My advice to the British Government is that they should withdraw these proposals. If they cannot fight for right and justice and their plighted word they should better make peace. They can thereby at least save their honour....

7 Indians' Destiny Is Bound Up with the Victory of Democracy (28 July 1942)

A BRIEF SKETCH ABOUT THE DOCUMENT

Continuing his crusade for the victory of democracy against the dictatorship of the Nazis during the Second World War, Ambedkar argued that Indians need to realize two things: one that their destiny is bound up with the victory of democracy against Nazism and two, once democracy wins no power can stop India to achieve its independence (provided Indians care to unite themselves). Here his visionary zeal is reflected wherein not only the world will be benefiting due to the defeat of dictatorship but the Indians will also realize long awaited freedom. 'The Times of India' reported his ideas on 28 July 1942, which are part of the BAWS, Volume 17, part II, 2003 (pp. 328–32).

'No one can expect consistency from Mr. Gandhi. But everybody did and had a right to expect a sense of responsibility from him. There can be no doubt that, Mr. Gandhi's present move to launch a mass movement is both irresponsible and insane,' observed the Hon. Dr. B. R. Ambedkar, Labour Member, Government of India, to a representative of The Times of India, prior to his departure to Delhi on Monday evening.

'Why does Mr. Gandhi not try the other method, namely, bringing about unity among all parties? Why does he not call a conference of leaders of all the different parties to find out their demands and settle if there is any dispute?'

These questions were asked by Dr Ambedkar. He added: 'Duty requires that those who do not believe in Mr. Gandhi's movement must take steps to prevent his threatened action from taking shape.'

'It is difficult to understand why Mr. Gandhi should think it necessary to enter upon so hazardous a plan of action at so perilous a time in the history of India' Dr. Ambedkar said:

'To me some points are quite clear. As to India's reaching its political goal, no one can deny that the transfer of power from the British to the hands of Indians has been continuous and of late rapid—except those who affect a certain degree of passion for independence. Barring such passionate patriots, it can be said without exaggeration that the British *vis-a-vis* Indians are in the last ditch. That the British do not wish to entrench themselves in the last ditch and prevent the political advancement of India to its final goal is equally clear. If any proof was necessary, the Cripps Proposals are there. They conceded Independence and Constituent Assembly both of which have been the demands which the Congress has been making.

After the Cripps Proposals it is hard to believe Mr Gandhi when he says that the British do not intend to transfer power to the hands of Indians. It is a positive and deliberate untruth.

'That the Cripps Proposal have fallen through does not, to my mind, affect the fact that the British Government are committed to independence if Indians prefer it to Dominion Status.

Short-Sighted View

One does not know what led the Congress to reject the Cripps Proposals even when they conceded Independence and Constituent Assembly. If the failure to transfer defence be the reason for starting a mass movement, I am sure very few will accept the soundness of so short-sighted view. In the first place the Congress claimed from the British only a declaration of their war aims and did not claim their implementation during the war. Secondly, there is no Indian politician so far as I know, competent to run the technical and military side of the Defence department. Indians have neglected to study this subject. In these circumstances, it is foolish to ask for Indian control of defence; for, such control when in the hands of an ignorant person can only be nominal. Thirdly, when all departments were transferred, as was contemplated by the Cripps Proposals, it was childish to quarrel over the non-transfer of the Defence Department. Any man with commonsense would know that the reserved department could not have held out on matters insisted upon by the transferred departments if they are necessary and reasonable. This is what had happened to the special powers of the Governors when the Congress took office in 1937. It is surprising that the Congress should have forgotten its own experience in this matter.

'I am clearly of the opinion that the Congress deserves on sympathy in this move for causing disorder. It has rejected the best opportunity it was given to serve the country. Looking at it from this point of view, I cannot see how this move, proposed to be taken by Mr. Gandhi, can be held to be in the interests of the country.

'It seems to me that Mr. Gandhi is merely trying to retrieve the prestige which he and the Congress have lost since the war started.

'The Congress can live with prestige in either of two ways. It can live by the glamour of direct action or it can live by the patronage which office gives. Mr. Gandhi compelled the Congress to give up office and he refused to be a party to direct action. The slump caused in the Congress prestige by this do nothing, policy of Mr. Gandhi has been disastrous to Mr. Gandhi and to the Congress and this desperate game of Mr. Gandhi is intended to retrieve his position and to die covered with glory.

'This move may be the best way to serve the best interests of the Congress party. But it certainly is not the way to serve the country. At this juncture such a move is fraught with the greatest mischief and is sure to result in the greatest harm to the country.

'There are two ways open to the Congress party to further the political advancement of this country; direct action by the Congress and united demand by all parties representing the different elements in the national life of the country. Mr. Gandhi and the Congress are very keen about the first. It is a stock plan. Except Mr. Gandhi, everyone knows that beyond a certain limit it is worse than useless and even when it succeeds because the British Government, unlike the Nazi Government are not addicted to the use of brute force and do not use unmoral means to suppress a moral cause. Mr. Gandhi will not admit it. That is only because he fortunately has no experience as to how the Nazis will deal with his mass Civil Disobedience. No doubt the Nazis will give Mr. Gandhi a very short shrift and prove that his plan of direct action can be put out of action at the very start.

Unity Among Parties

'The question that agitates my mind is this: Why does Mr. Gandhi resort to his method of direct action carried on single-handed by the Congress when it is proved to be so inefficacious? Why does he not try the other method, namely bringing about unity among all parties? Why does Mr. Gandhi not call a conference of all leaders of the different parties to find out their demands and to settle if there is any dispute about them. This is a way worth trying. It is also a way of statesmanship and a way which will bring enduring peace among the communities. But Mr. Gandhi has never made such an attempt and I have never been able to understand his reasons for avoiding this way of solving the problem. To say that no settlement can take place while the British are there can, to my mind, mean only two things: that the leaders of the minority communities are tools in the hands of the British or that the Congress thinks it would be better to talk of communal settlement after the British Government have withdrawn because the Congress than in charge of law and order will be in a better position to dictate to the minorities and force a settlement on its own terms. If it means the first, then it is a vile and wanton aspersion on the character of, the leaders of the minority communities. The Congress must drop this selfrighteous attitude and admit that even those who differ from it are as good patriots, if not better, Settlement of the communal problem, is, I am sure, rendered more difficult by such stupid and baseless allegations which the Congress and its Press have persistently indulging in against the leaders of the minority communities. If it means the second, then there is no doubt that the move is a deceitful one. In either case, it proclaims the bankruptcy of statesmanship on the part of Mr. Gandhi.

'Mr. Gandhi has not realised one thing which the sooner he realizes the better. His most advertised political virtues were to bring about-Hindu-Muslim unity and to serve the Untouchables.

After 20 years, neither the Muslims nor the Untouchables trust Mr. Gandhi. This is the greatest tragedy in his life.

The sooner he realises this, the better. Even now Mr. Gandhi can call the leaders of the minorities for consultation. There is no use saying that they are making impossible demands: for, it is always open to Mr. Gandhi to call upon them to agree to refer the matter to international arbitration.

'The general public has no cause to support Mr. Gandhi in this move which is quite uncalled for. The minorities have no reason to join

Mr. Gandhi for, he refuses to give them an assurance as to their safety and security under the new constitution in terms which are explicit and in a spirit which has all the hallmark of sincerity.

'We are living in such perilous times that our duty cannot end in merely expressing our disagreement with Mr. Gandhi. Duty requires that those who do not believe in his movement must take steps to prevent it from taking shape. In the C. D. movement of 1930, the Muslims and the Depressed Classes, although they did not participate in it, had observed a kind of benevolent neutrality towards it. The situation in 1930 was very different from what it is now. In the 1930 movement, there were only two possibilities. Either political power would have remained with the British or it would have devolved upon Indians. There was no possibility of Japan or Germany stepping in and making itself the master of India. The possibility is now staring us in the face. It would be madness to weaken law and order at a time when the barbarians are at our gates, intending not merely to defeat the British but to enslave us forever. There, in my mind, lies the great difference between the C. D. Movement of 1930 and the mass movement now threatened by Mr. Gandhi.

False Claim

'The Congress and Mr. Gandhi have been arrogating to themselves the right to speak in the name of the country. It is a false claim but nobody has cared to challenge it. That is because of the feeling that so long as the Congress was doing no harm to the interests of the country it was a matter of small moment whether it claimed to speak in the name of the nation or in the name of the party which it is. But when the Congress, being only a party, proposes to launch upon a policy which puts the safety, security and even the possibility of the independence of the country in jeopardy, it becomes the duty to other parties to drop the attitude of benevolent neutrality and oppose the Congress when it is throwing the country in chaos and inviting certain frustration of the realization of the political destiny of this country which is so near at hand. I wish Indians to realize two things: first, that their destiny is bound up with the victory of democracy against Nazism and second, that once democracy wins nothing in the world can stop India to gain her freedom if Indians take care to unite themselves. I am sure Mr. Gandhi's move is quite uncalled for.

If democracy wins, no one can stand in the way of India's freedom. The supreme task of Indians at the moment is to see that democracy wins. It is not out of love for principle that they should do so. It is our country's future that requires us to do it as our duty. Mr. Gandhi is an old man in a hurry. Indians should be careful not to do anything in a hurry which they will have to regret in leisure.

Dr Ambedkar left Bombay on Monday night for New Delhi by the Frontier Mail. At Bombay Central, he was given a hearty send-off by nearly 400 persons, representing the Scheduled Classes, the Independent Labour Party, the Municipal Kamgar Sangh and various other organisations, and several personal friends and admirers.'

8   Separate Settlements (1 September 1943)

A BRIEF SKETCH ABOUT THE DOCUMENT

The following excerpt is part of the paper written for Pacific Relations Conference held in December 1942. After the proceedings were made public by the Secretary of the conference, Ambedkar published it in 1943 (BAWS, Volume 9, 1991; pp. 419–22). It was for the first time that he raised the question of Separate Settlements for the Scheduled Castes and that is why it was required in the light of the continuing discrimination and exploitation of them by the larger rural society.

Resolution no. IV referred to in the foregoing part of this paper is to my mind quite self-explanatory and not much detailed comment is necessary to explain its purport. Nor is it possible in the compass of this short paper to deal with it in more than general terms. The demand for separate settlements is the result of what might be called 'The New Life Movement' among the Untouchables. The object of the movement is to free the Untouchables from the thralldom of the Hindus. So long as the present arrangement continues it is impossible for the Untouchables either to free themselves from the yoke of the Hindus or to get rid of their Untouchability. It is the close-knit association of the Untouchables with the Hindus living in the same villages which marks them out as Untouchables and which enables the Hindus to identify them as being Untouchables. India is admittedly a land of villages and so long as the village system provides an easy method of marking out and identifying the Untouchable, the Untouchable has no escape from Untouchability. It is the village system which perpetuates Untouchability and the Untouchables therefore demand that it should be broken and the Untouchables who are as a matter of fact socially separate should be made separate geographically and territorially also, and be grouped into separate villages exclusively of Untouchables in which the distinction of the high and the low and of Touchable and Untouchable will find no place.

The second reason for demanding separate settlements arises out of the economic position of the Untouchables in the village. That their condition is most pitiable no one will deny. They are a body of landless labourers who are entirely dependent upon such employment as the Hindus may choose to give them and on such wages as the Hindus may find it profitable to pay. In the villages in which they live they cannot engage in any trade or occupation, for owing to untouchability no Hindu will deal with them. It is therefore obvious that there is no way of earning a living which is open to the Untouchables so long as they live as a dependent part of the Hindu village. This economic dependence has also other consequences besides the condition of poverty and degradation which proceeds from it. The Hindu has a code of life, which is part of his religion. This code of life gives him many privileges and heaps upon the Untouchable many indignities which are incompatible with the sanctity of human life. By the New Life Movement which has taken hold of the Untouchables, the Untouchables all over India are fighting against the indignities and injustices which the Hindus in the name of their religion have heaped upon them. A perpetual war is going on every day in every village between the Hindus and the Untouchables. It does not see the light of the day. The Hindu Press is not prepared to advertise it lest it should injure the cause of their freedom in the eyes of the world. The silent struggle is however a fact. Under the village system the Untouchable has found himself greatly handicapped in his struggle for free and honourable life. It is a contest between the economically and socially strong Hindus and an economically poor and socially small group of Untouchables. That the Hindus most often succeed in pulling down Untouchables is largely due to many causes. The Hindu has the Police and the Magistracy on his side. In a quarrel between the Untouchables and the Hindus the Untouchables will never get protection from the Police or justice from the Magistrate. The Police and the Magistracy are Hindus, and they love their class more than their duty. But the chief weapon in the armoury of the Hindus is economic power which they possess over the poor Untouchables living in the village. The economic processes by which the Hindus can hold down the Untouchables in their struggle for equality are well described in the Report made by a Committee appointed by the Government of Bombay in 1928 to investigate into the grievances of the Depressed Classes* and from which the following extracts are made. It illuminates the situation in a manner so simple that even foreigners who do not know the mysteries of the Hindu social system may understand what tyranny the Hindus can practise upon the Untouchables. The committee said:

'Although we have recommended various remedies to secure to the Depressed Classes their rights to all public utilities we fear that there will be difficulties in the way of their exercising them for a long time to come. The first difficulty is the fear of open violence against them by the orthodox classes. It must be noted that the Depressed Classes form a small minority in every village, opposed to which is a great majority of the orthodox who are bent on protecting their interests and dignity from any supposed invasion by the Depressed Classes at any cost. The danger of prosecution by the Police has put a limitation upon the use of violence by the orthodox classes and consequently such cases are rare.

The second difficulty arises from the economic position in which the Depressed Classes are found today. The Depressed Classes have no economic independence in most parts of the Presidency. Some cultivate the lands of the orthodox classes as their tenants at will. Others live on their earnings as farm labourers employed by the orthodox classes and the rest subsist on the food or grain given to them by the orthodox classes in lieu of service rendered to them as village servants. We have heard of numerous instances where the orthodox classes have used their economic power as a weapon against those Depressed Classes in their villages, when the latter have dared to exercise their rights, and have evicted them from their land, and stopped their employment and discontinued their remuneration as village servants. This boycott is often planned on such an extensive scale as to include the prevention of the Depressed Classes from using the commonly used paths and the stoppage of sale of the necessaries of life by the village Bania. According to the evidence, sometimes small causes suffice for the proclamation of a social boycott against the Depressed Classes. Frequently it follows on the exercise by the Depressed Classes of their right to the use of the common well, but cases have been by no means rare where a stringent boycott has been proclaimed simply because a Depressed Class man has put on the sacred thread, has bought a piece of land, has put on good clothes or ornaments, or has carried a marriage procession with the bridegroom on the horse through the public street.

This demand for separate settlements is a new demand which has been put forth by the Untouchables for the first time. It is not possible to say as yet as to what attitude the Hindus will take to this demand. But there is no doubt that this is the most vital demand made by the Untouchables, and I am sure that whatever may happen with regard to the other demands they are not likely to yield on this. The Hindus are prone to think that they and the Untouchables are joined together by the will of God as the Bible says the husband is joined to his wife and they will say in the language of the Bible that those whom God is pleased to join let no man put asunder. The Untouchables are determined to repudiate any such view of their relations with the Hindus. They want the link to be broken and a complete divorce from the Hindus effected without delay.

The only questions that arise are those of the cost it will involve in and time it will take. As to cost, the Untouchables say it should be financed by Government. It will no doubt fall for the most part on the Hindus. But there is no reason why the Hindus should not bear the same. The Hindus own everything. They own the land in this country. They control trade, and they also own the State. Every source of revenue and profit is controlled by them. Other communities and particularly the Untouchables are just hewers of wood and drawers of water. The social system helps the Hindus to have a monopoly of everything. There is no reason why they should not be asked to pay the cost of this scheme when they practically own the country.

As to time, it matters very little even if the transplantation of the Untouchables to new settlements takes 20 years. Those who have been the bounden slaves of the Hindus for a thousand years may well be happy with the prospect of getting their freedom by the end of 20 years.

9 Labour and Parliamentary Democracy (17 September 1943)

A BRIEF SKETCH ABOUT THE DOCUMENT

This is the speech delivered by Ambedkar at the concluding session of the All India Trade Union Workers' Study Camp held in Delhi from 8 to 17 September 1943, under the auspices of the Indian Federation of Labour. Dr Ambedkar emphasized that the labour class gets exploited and it has to own this responsibility to break free, as parliamentary democracy in reality is a government of a hereditary subject class by a hereditary ruling class, and that needs to be understood. He enumerated various reasons for the failure of parliamentary democracy in its present form as the poor, labour class and the downtrodden could not be benefited out of it. Offering a solution, he opined that for the parliamentary democracy to be successful, labour should be in charge of the government and the labour needs to get itself dissociated from communal and capitalist parties. The extracts in this chapter are from BAWS, Volume 10, 1991 (pp. 106–12).

I appreciate very much the kind invitation of your Secretary to come and address you this evening. I was hesitating to accept this invitation and for two reasons. In the first place I can say very little which can bind the Government. Secondly I can say very little about Trade Unionism in which you are primarily interested. I accepted the invitation because your Secretary would not take a 'No' from me. I also felt that this was probably the best opportunity I can have to speak out my thoughts on Labour organization in India which have been uppermost in my mind and which I thought may even interest those who are primarily interested in Trade Unionism.

The Government of human society has undergone some very significant changes. There was a time when the government of human society had taken the form of autocracy by Despotic Sovereigns. This was replaced after a long and bloody struggle by a system of government known as Parliamentary Democracy. It was felt that this was the last word in the framework of government. It was believed to bring about the millennium in which every human being will have the right to liberty, property and pursuit of happiness. And there were good grounds for such high hopes. In Parliamentary Democracy there is the Legislature to express the voice of the people; there is the Executive which is subordinate to the Legislature and bound to obey the Legislature. Over and above the Legislature and the Executive there is the Judiciary to control both and keep them both within prescribed bounds. Parliamentary Democracy has all the marks of a popular Government, a government of the people, by the people and for the people. It is therefore a matter of some surprise that there has been a revolt against Parliamentary Democracy although not even a century has elapsed since its universal acceptance and inauguration. There is revolt against it in Italy, in Germany, in Russia, and in Spain, and there are very few countries in which there has not been discontent against Parliamentary Democracy. Why should there be this discontent and dissatisfaction against Parliamentary Democracy? It is a question worth considering. There is no country in which the urgency of considering this question is greater than it is in India. India is negotiating to have Parliamentary Democracy. There is a great need of some one with sufficient courage to tell Indians 'Beware of Parliamentary Democracy, it is not the best product, as it appeared to be.'

Why has Parliamentary Democracy failed? In the country of the dictators it has failed because it is a machine whose movements are very slow. It delays swift action. In a Parliamentary Democracy the Executive may be held up by the Legislature which may refuse to pass the laws which the Executive wants, and if it is not held up by the Legislature it may be held up by the Judiciary which may declare the laws as illegal. Parliamentary Democracy gives no free hand to Dictatorship, and that is why it is a discredited institution in countries like Italy, Spain and Germany which are ruled by Dictators. If Dictators alone were against

Parliamentary Democracy it would not have mattered at all. Their testimony against Parliamentary Democracy would be no testimony at all. Indeed Parliamentary Democracy would be welcomed for the reason that it can be an effective check upon Dictatorship. But unfortunately there is a great deal of discontent against Parliamentary Democracy even in countries where people are opposed to Dictatorship. That is the most regrettable fact about Parliamentary Democracy. This is all more regrettable because Parliamentary Democracy has not been at a standstill. It has progressed in three directions. It has progressed by expanding the notion of Equality of Political rights. There are very few countries having Parliamentary Democracy which have not adult suffrage. It has recognized the principle of Equality of Social and Economic opportunity.

And thirdly, it has recognized that the state cannot be held at bay by corporations which are anti-social in their purpose. With all this, there is immense discontent against Parliamentary Democracy even in countries pledged to Democracy. The reasons for discontent in such countries must obviously be different from those assigned by the dictator countries. There is no time to go into details. But it can be said in general terms that the discontent against Parliamentary Democracy is due to the realization that it has failed to assure to the masses the right to liberty, property or the pursuit of happiness. If this is true, it is important to know the causes which have brought about this failure. The causes for this failure may be found either in wrong ideology or wrong organization, or in both. I think the causes are to be found in both. As an illustration of wrong ideology which has vitiated Parliamentary Democracy I can only deal with only two. I have no doubt that what has ruined Parliamentary Democracy is the idea of freedom of contract. The idea became sanctified and was upheld in the name of liberty. Parliamentary Democracy took no notice of economic inequalities and did not care to examine the result of freedom of contract on the parties to the contract, should they happen to be unequal. It did not mind if the freedom of contract gave the strong the opportunity to defraud the weak. The result is that Parliamentary Democracy in standing out as protagonist of Liberty has continuously added to the economic wrongs of the poor, the downtrodden and the dis-inherited class. The second wrong ideology which has vitiated Parliamentary Democracy is the failure to realize that political democracy cannot succeed where there is no social and economic democracy. Some may question this proposition. To those who are disposed to question it, I will ask a counter question.

Why Parliamentary Democracy collapsed so easily in Italy, Germany, and Russia? Why did it not collapse so easily in England and the U.S.A.? To my mind there is only one answer—namely, there was a greater degree of economic and social democracy in the latter countries than it existed in the former. Social and economic democracy are the tissues and the fibre of a Political Democracy. The tougher the tissue and the fibre, the greater the strength of the body. Democracy is another name for equality. Parliamentary Democracy developed a passion for liberty. It never made even a nodding acquaintance with equality. It failed to realize the significance of equality, and did not even endeavour to strike a balance between Liberty and Equality, with the result that liberty swallowed equality and has left a progeny of inequities.

I have referred to the wrong ideologies which in my judgement have been responsible for the failure of Parliamentary Democracy. But I am equally certain that more than bad ideology it has bad organization which has been responsible for the failure of Democracy. All political societies get divided into two classes—the Rulers and the Ruled. This is an evil. If the evil stopped here it would not matter much. But the unfortunate part of it is that the division becomes stereotyped and stratified so much so that the Rulers are always drawn from the Ruling Class and the class of the Ruled never becomes the Ruling class. People do not govern themselves, they establish a government and leave it to govern them, forgetting that is not their government. That being the situation. Parliamentary Democracy has never been a government of the people or by the people, and that is why it has never been a government for the people. Parliamentary Democracy, notwithstanding the paraphernalia of a popular government, is in reality a government of a hereditary subject class by a hereditary ruling class. It is this vicious organization of political life which has made Parliamentary Democracy such a dismal failure. It is because of this that Parliamentary Democracy has not fulfilled the hope it held out the common man of ensuring to him liberty, property and pursuit of happiness.

The question is who is responsible for this? There is no doubt that if Parliamentary Democracy has failed to benefit the poor, the labouring and the downtrodden classes, it is these classes who are primarily responsible for it. In the first place, they have shown a most appalling indifference to the effect of the economic factor in the making of men's life. Someone very recently wrote a book called the *End of the Economic Man*. We cannot really talk of the *End of the Economic Man* for the simple reason that the

Economic Man was never born. The common retort to Marx that man does not live by bread alone is unfortunately a fact. I agree with Carlyle that the aim of civilization cannot be merely to fatten men as we do pigs. But we are far off from that stage. The labouring class far from being fat like pigs are starving, and one wishes that they thought of bread first and everything else afterwards.

Marx propounded the doctrine of the Economic interpretation of History. A great controversy has raged over its validity. To my mind Marx propounded it not so much as doctrine as a direction to Labour that if Labour cares to make its economic interests paramount, as the owning classes do, history will be a reflection of the economic facts of life more than it has been. If the doctrine of Economic interpretation of History is not wholly true it is because the labouring class as a whole has failed to give economic facts the imperative force they have in determining the terms of associated life. The Labouring classes have failed to acquaint itself with literature dealing with the government of mankind. Everyone from the Labouring Classes should be acquainted with Rousseau's Social contract, Marx's Communist Manifesto, Pope Leo XIII's Encyclical on the conditions of Labour and John Stuart Mill on Liberty, to mention only four of the basic programmatic documents on social and governmental organization of modern times. But the labouring classes will not give them the attention they deserve. Instead labour has taken delight reading false and fabulous stories of ancient kings and queens and has become addicted to it.

There is another and a bigger crime which they have committed against themselves. They have developed no ambition to capture government, and are not even convinced of the necessity of controlling government as a necessary means of safeguarding their interests. Indeed, they are not even interested in government. Of all the tragedies which have beset mankind, this is the biggest and the most lamentable one. Whatever organization there is, it has taken the form of Trade Unionism. I am not against Trade Unions. They serve a very useful purpose. But it would be a great mistake to suppose that Trade Unions are a panacea for all the ills of labour. Trade Unions, even if they are powerful, are not strong enough to compel capitalists to run capitalism better. Trade Unions would be much more effective if they had behind them a Labour Government to rely on. Control of Government must be the target for Labour to aim at. Unless Trade Unionism aims at controlling government, trade unions will do very little good to the workers and will be a source of perpetual squabbles among Trade Union Leaders.

The third besetting sin of the labouring classes is the easy way which they are lead away by an appeal to Nationalism. The working classes who are beggared in every way and who have very little to spare, often sacrifice their all to the so-called cause of Nationalism. They have never cared to enquire whether the nationalism for which they are to make their offerings will, when established, give them social and economic equality. More often than not, the free independent national state which emerges from a successful nationalism and which reared on their sacrifices, turns to be the enemy of the working class under the hegemony of their masters. This is the worst kind of exploitation that Labour has allowed itself to be subjected to.

If the working classes have to live under a system of Parliamentary Democracy then it must devise the best possible means to turn it to their benefit. As far as I can see, two things are necessary if this object is to be achieved. First thing to do is to discard mere establishment of Trade Unions as the final aim and object of Labour in India. It must declare that its aim is to put labour in charge of Government. For this it must organize a Labour Party as a political party. Such a party will no doubt cover Trade Unions in its organization. But it must be free from the narrow and cramping vision of Trade Unionism, with its stress on the immediate gain at the cost of ultimate benefit and with the vested right of Trade Union officials to represent Labour. It must equally dissociate itself from communal or capitalistic political parties such as the Hindu Mahasabha or the Congress. There is no necessity for Labour to submerge itself in the Congress or the Hindu Mahasabha or be the camp followers of either, simply because these bodies claim to be fighting for the freedom of India. Labour by a separate political organization of its ranks can serve both the purposes. It can fight the battle of India's freedom better by freeing itself from the clutches of the Congress and the Hindu Mahasabha. It can prevent itself from being defrauded in the name of nationalism. What is most important is that it will act as a powerful check on the irrationalism of Indian politics, Congress politics is claimed to be revolutionary. That is why it has secured a large number of followers. But it is also a fact that Congress politics has brought nothing but frustration. The reason is Congress politics is so irrational and it is irrational largely because Congress has no rival. A Labour Party in India would be most welcome corrective to this irrationalism which has dominated Indian politics for the last two decades. The second thing for Labour in India to realize is that without knowledge there is no power. When a Labour Party is formed in India and when such a party puts forth its claim to be installed on the Gadi before the electorate, the question, whether Labour is fit to govern, is sure to be asked. It would be no answer to say that Labour could not govern worse or display greater bankruptcy in home or foreign affairs than the other classes. Labour will have to prove positively that it can govern better. Let it not also be forgotten that the pattern of Labour Government is a very difficult one than that of the other classes. Labour government cannot be a government of *laissez faire*. It will be a government which must essentially be based on a system of control. A system of control needs a far greater degree of Knowledge and training than a *laissez faire* government does. Unfortunately, Labour in India has not realized the importance of study. All that Labour leaders in India have done, is to learn how best to abuse Industrialists. Abuse and more abuse has become the be-all and end-all of his role as a labour leader.

I am therefore very glad to find that the Indian Federation of Labour has recognized this defect and has come forward to open these study circles for the Labouring Classes. They are going to be the most effective means of making Labour fit to govern. I hope the Federation will not forget the other necessity namely to inaugurate a Labour Party. When this is done, the Federation will deserve the thanks of the Labouring Classes to have raised them to the status of a governing class.

10   Newspaper in a Modern Democratic System Is Fundamental Basis of Good Government (2 October 1944)

A BRIEF SKETCH ABOUT THE DOCUMENT

Ambedkar was invited to inaugurate 'People's Herald', which was the weekly organ of the All India Scheduled Castes Federation. He opined that the newspaper has come to occupy an important place in the modern day democracy. He suggested that the newspaper should devote space for reporting the conduct of the legislators: why they took a particular stand on an issue and why they have not taken a stand on some issue. 'The Hindu' newspaper reported this on 2 October 1944. These excerpts are from BAWS, Volume 17, part III, 2003 (pp. 346–50).

... . The Hon'ble Mr. J. N. Mondal, President, Bengal Provincial Scheduled Castes Federation in welcoming Dr Ambedkar said that his entire life was dedicated not only for the Scheduled Castes but also for other downtrodden masses of India. He was sure that the emancipation of the Scheduled Castes and of the downtrodden masses would come through the activities, leadership and guidance of Dr Ambedkar.

Earlier, Mr Rashik Lai Biswas in course of his speech said that the reason for the appearance of this weekly 'People's Herald' at this juncture was obvious. The new India which was to emerge shortly as the result of this war, the Hindu community would form the main ingredient, and of this Hindu clement, the Scheduled Castes formed no inconsiderable part. These castes he added, had some peculiarities, traditions, rights and customs which marked them out from the other sections of the Hindus. The Scheduled Castes held a right to demand that these peculiarities be respected and that they should get their due position in the matter of education, appointments and all the benefits which any State could provide to its citizens. 'This paper, therefore, comes into being as the All India organ of the Scheduled Castes which will voice their sentiments and legitimate aspirations, their grievances, and their demands, and also their views on the present day problems which India is facing and the composition of the future Indian State,' he added.

In course of his speech, Dr Ambedkar referred to the future of the Indian National Congress and stated that after Mahatma Gandhi's death it would be blown to pieces. Because, they could not conceive that a couple of hundreds of landlords and capitalists and a few misguided labour leaders could make a party. So far as fighting the British was concerned they could all unite but when the British would be going, when the vacuum would be created. When they would be seated in gaddi and would re-examine their social, and economic situation, would the landlords and peasants and capitalists and workers agree to live with each other in the Congress? The Congress would be blown to pieces the moment Swaraj was attained.

But affirmed he, the Scheduled Castes party would live forever, it was an eternal party and they lived on certain fundamental principles. It was utter nonsense to say that they were fighting for loaves and fishes, they were fighting for the principles of liberty, equality, and fraternity which were to abide in this country. Their principles transcended the limited cause which they had in view, namely the cause of the Scheduled Castes. Theirs was the principle that would regenerate not only India but the world as well.

'Personally I do not think' said he, 'there is any work in India which can be said to be nobler than the elevation of. Scheduled Castes. I have many many, friends in the Congress who although dislike my politics, like me. They tell me that if I serve the wider cause of the country from within the Congress. I might one day become President of the Congress. Those appeals never allured me. I have always felt that as I have been born among these classes, it is my duty that I should do something for them first. I have also felt and quite convincingly I think, that if I or others who have the capacity to take up the cause of the Scheduled Castes leave the cause for other service and for other cause, no others will come to take up this cause and it will remain in the same rotten condition in which it has remained for the last two thousand years. But, that is only a limited view. I have struck to this cause as I regard it as a noble cause. What is the cause of the Hindus? What is the cause of the Congress? What is the talk of national freedom? So far as the cause of Hindus is concerned it is the cause of the parasitic class, which has been living upon the blood, money and work of the toiling millions of this country. Would anybody, asked Dr Ambedkar who has understood political and moral philosophy and has come to believe that the salvation of world cannot be had unless the economic and social organization of the world in every society is based upon liberty, equality and fraternity, can ever consent to give up the cause of Scheduled Castes, but serve the cause of Hindus?

'Then, take the cause of freedom of the country', proceeded Dr Ambedkar. 'There is a world of difference between freedom by the powerful to oppress the weak and freedom of the weak to have an opportunity to grow fully to manhood. I would like to ask our Hindu patriots, who talk about this nonsense of freedom, etc., what use are they going to make of this freedom? If the social freedom remains what it is, if the mentality is going to remain what it is, if the freedom that they will get from the Britishers is going to be used for suppressing the oppressed and suppressed classes, why should any one fight for it, I do not understand, if, on the other hand, you examine our cause, the principle we fight for, you will see it far transcends the limited class we have-in view.'

'A newspaper in a modern democratic system is the fundamental basis of good government. It is the one means of educating people. Therefore, we in India belonging to the Scheduled Castes whose misfortunes are the-worst, for which there is no comparison and for which we are also anxious to get rid of, can never succeed unless the 8 crores of Untouchables, are politically educated.'

Continuing he said: 'If this paper can devote some part of its space for reporting the conduct of our M. L. A.'s in the various legislature telling the people, why they have done this and why they have not done that, I have no hesitation in my mind that there will be a great reform in the conduct of our M.L. A.'s and the present chaos, which is enough to bring disgrace to our community, will stop. I, therefore, look upon this paper as a great instrument for purifying those who have gone wrong in their political life.'

Dr Ambedkar then referred to a Marathi paper that did his election campaign in 1937 and he advised the newspaper not only to educate their voters but also to see that men who were elected by the voters, stood by the voters and functioned their duties properly and did not 'misbehave.'

While presiding over the ceremony amidst a large gathering of Scheduled Castes leaders and workers, he said that, the occasion provided for him an opportunity to unburden his soul fully, because it was such an occasion which he had the best desire to attend. While wishing the successful advance of 'People's Herald' to the cause of Scheduled Castes people of India and speaking of the great role this paper is destined to play in the service of their people, he said that the importance of a political organ of this nature can never be underrated. He revealed on this occasion that perhaps it was not so much known that he himself edited a weekly organ at Bombay for a continuous period of more than 16 years. The tremendous influence that paper created was seen in the next elections to the Assembly from Bombay proper wherein in a general constituency he was elected with votes from all communities and defeated the rival Congress candidate with a large majority of votes. The political influence that paper created went much towards his success. So he wished a speedy success of 'People's Herald' and hoped that every member of the Scheduled Castes would make this paper as his own.

Congratulating the editor of the newspaper, Mr P.C. De for his taking up this responsible task of serving the cause of the Scheduled Castes, Dr Ambedkar said that he had noticed that many people in the country looked upon the work of the alleviation of the Scheduled Castes as nothing but 'Scavenging' and a 'dirty' piece of work.

Criticizing the Hindu Mahasabha, Dr Ambedkar said that, he had no hesitation in saying that their cause was the cause of a 'parasitic' which had been living upon the laboured money and work of the toiling millions of this country. The salvation of the world could not be had unless the economic, and the social organisation of the world and of other societies were based upon the principles of liberty, equality and fraternity.

11 Communal Deadlock and a Way to Solve It (6 May 1945)

A BRIEF SKETCH ABOUT THE DOCUMENT

This is an excerpt from the speech delivered by Ambedkar at the All India Scheduled Castes Federation held in Bombay on May 6, 1945. Here he argued for an alternative approach to solve the communal question. He emphasised that the communal question was being discussed around methods and not with concrete principles and that is why it was not getting resolved. Therefore there was a need to discuss major challenges and adopt a new approach to solve the communal question.

The excerpts in chapter have been taken from BAWS, Volume 1, 1979 (pp. 355-80).

Mr President,

....Ordinarily, at a gathering such as this I would have spoken—and our people would expect me to speak—on any one of the social and political problems of the Scheduled Castes. But I do not propose to engage myself in a discourse on so sectarian a subject. Instead, I propose to speak on a topic, which is general and has a wider appeal, namely the shape and form of the future Constitution of India.....

Necessity of a New Approach

I shall be asked that if the Constituent Assembly is not the correct approach, what is the alternative? I know I shall be confronted with such a question. But I am confident in my view that if the Communal Question has become difficult of solution it is not because it is insoluble, nor because we had not yet employed the machinery of Constituent Assembly. It has become insoluble because the approach to it is fundamentally wrong. The defect in the present approach is that it proceeds by methods instead of by principles. The principle is that there is no principle. There is only a series of methods. If one method fails another is tried. It is this swing from one method to another which has made the Communal Problem a jigsaw puzzle. There being no principle there is no guide to tell why a particular method has failed. There being no principle there is no assurance that the new method will succeed.

The attempts at the solution of the Communal Problem are either in the nature of a coward's plan to kowtow to the bully or of bully's plan to dictate to the weak. Whenever a community grows powerful and demands certain political advantages, concessions are made to it to win its goodwill. There is no judicial examination of its claim; no judgement on merits. The result is that there are no limits to demands and there are no limits to concessions. A start is made with a demand for separate electorate for a minority. It is granted. It is followed by a demand for a separate electorate for a community irrespective of the fact whether it is a minority or majority. That is granted. A demand is made for separate, representation on a population basis. That is conceded. Next, a claim is made for weightage in representation. That is granted. It is followed by a demand for statutory majority over other minorities with the right for the majority to retain separate electorates. This is granted. This is followed by a demand that the majority rule of another community is intolerable, and therefore without prejudice to its rights to maintain majority rule over other minorities, the majority of the offending community should be reduced to equality. Nothing can be more absurd than this policy of eternal appeasement. It is a policy of limitless demand followed by endless appeasement.

Frankly, I don't blame the community that indulges in this strategy. It indulges in it because it has found that it pays, it pursues it because there are no principles to fix the limits and it believes that more could be legitimately asked and would be easily given. On the other hand, there is a community economically poor, socially degraded, educationally backward and which is exploited, oppressed and tyrannized without shame and without remorse, disowned by society, unowned by Government and which has no security for protection and no guarantee for justice, fair play and equal opportunity. Such a community is told that it can have no safeguards, not because it has no case for safeguards but only because the bully on whom the bill of rights is presented thinks that because the community is not politically organized to have sanctions behind its demand he can successfully bluff.

All this differential treatment is due to the fact that there are no principles, which are accepted as authoritative and binding on those who are parties to the Communal Question. The absence of principles has another deleterious effect. It has made impossible for public opinion to play its part. The public only knows methods and notes that one method has failed another is being suggested. It does not know why one method has failed and why another is said to be likely to succeed. The result is that the public, instead of being mobilized to force obstinate and recalcitrant parties to see sense and reason, are only witnessing the discussions of Communal Questions whenever they take place as mere shows.

The approach I am making for the solution of the Communal Problem is therefore based upon two considerations:

(1) That in proceeding to solve the Communal Problem it is essential to define the governing principles which should be invoked for determining the final solution, and

(2) That whatever the governing principles they must be applied to all parties equally without fear or favour.

Proposals for Solution of the Communal Problem

Having made my position clear on certain preliminary points, I will now proceed to deal with the subject.

The Communal Problem raises three questions: (A) The question of representation, in the Legislature: (B) The question of representation in the Executive; and (C) The question of representation in the Services.

A. Representation in Public Services

To take the last question first. This can hardly be said to be a subject of controversy. The principle that all communities should be represented in the

Public Services in a prescribed proportion and no single community should be allowed to have a monopoly has been accepted by the Government of India. This principle has been embodied in the Government of India Resolutions of 1934 and 1943 and rules to carry it out have been laid down. It has even prescribed that any appointment made contrary to the rules shall be deemed to be null and void. All that is necessary is to convert administrative practice into statutory obligation. This can be done by adding a Schedule to the Government of India Act, which will include the provisions contained in these Resolutions and similar provisions for the different provinces and make the Schedule a part of the Law of the Constitution.

B. Representation in the Executive

This question raises three points:

(i) The quantum of representation in *the* Executive: (ii) The nature of the Executive; (iii) The method of filling the places in the Executive.

(i) Quantum of Representation

For the solution of this question, the principle which should be adopted is that the representation of the Hindus, the Muslims and the Scheduled Castes should be equal to the quantum of their representation in the Legislature.

With regard to the other minorities such as the Sikhs, Indian Christians and Anglo-Indians, it is difficult to give them representation in the Executive in strict proportion to their representation in the Legislature. This difficulty arises largely from the smallness of their numbers. If they are to get representation in the Executive in exact proportion to their numbers, the Executive would have to be enlarged to a fantastic degree. All that can be done, therefore, is to reserve a seat or two for them in the Cabinet for their representation and so establish a convention that they will get a fair portion of representation in the corps of Parliamentary Secretaries that will have to be raised, when the new Constitution comes into existence.

(ii) Nature of the Executive

In the Constitution of the Executive, I would propose the adoption, of following principles:

(1) It must be recognized that in a country like India where there is a perpetual antipathy between the majority and the minorities and on

which account the danger of communal discrimination by majority against minorities forms an ever-present menace to the minorities, the executive power assumes far greater importance than the legislative power.

(2) In view of (1) above, the system under which a party which has secured a majority at the poll is deemed entitled to form a Government on the presumption that it has the confidence of the majority is untenable in Indian conditions. The majority in India is a communal majority and not a political majority. That being the difference, the presumption that arises in England cannot be regarded as a valid presumption in the conditions of India.

(3) The Executive should cease to be a Committee of the majority party m the Legislature. It should be so constituted that it will have its mandate not only from the majority but also from the minorities in the Legislature.

(4) The Executive should be non-Parliamentary in the sense that it shall not be removable before the term of the Legislature.

(5) The Executive should be Parliamentary in the sense that the members of the Executive shall be chosen from the members of the Legislature and shall have the right to sit in the House, speak, vote and answer questions.

(iii) Method of Filling Places

In this connection, I would propose the adoption of the following principles:

(a) The Prime Minister as the executive head of the Government should have the confidence of the whole House.

(b) The person representing a particular minority in the Cabinet should have the confidence of the members of his community in the Legislature.

(c) A. member of the Cabinet shall not be liable to be removed except on impeachment by the House on the ground of corruption or treason.

Following these principles, my proposal is that the Prime Minister and the members of the Cabinet from the majority community should be elected by the whole House by a single transferable vote and that the representatives of the different Minorities in the Cabinet should be elected by a single transferable vote of the members of each minority community in the Legislature.

C. Representation in the Legislature

This is the most difficult question. All other questions depend upon the solution of this question, it raises two points: (i) The quantum of representation: and (ii) The nature of the electorate.

(i) Quantum of Representation

I would first, put forth my proposals and then explain the principles on which they are based. The proposals are worked out in the following tables which show the scale of representation for the different communities in British India in the Central Legislature as well as in the Provincial Legislature....

Principles Underlying the Proposals

I may now proceed to state the principles on which this distribution has been made. They are:

(1) Majority Rule is untenable in theory and unjustifiable in practice. A majority community may be conceded a relative majority of representation but it can never claim an absolute majority.

(2) The relative majority of representation given to a majority community in the legislature should not be so large as to enable the majority to establish its rule with the help of the smallest minorities.

(3) The distribution of seats should be so made that a combination of the majority and one of the major minorities should not give the combine such a majority as to make them impervious to the interest of the minorities.

(4) The distribution should be so made that if all the minorities combine they could, without depending on the majority, form a government of their own.

(5) The weightage taken from the majority should be distributed among the minorities in inverse proportion to their social standing, economic position and educational condition so that a minority which is large and which has a better social, educational and economic standing gets a lesser amount of weightage than a minority whose numbers are less and whose educational, economic and social position is inferior to that of the others.

If I may say so, the representation is a balanced representation. No one community is placed in a position to dominate others by reason of its numbers. The Muslim objection to the Hindu majority and the Hindu and Sikh objections to the Muslim majority are completely eliminated, both in the Central as well as in the Provinces.

Nature of the Electorate

With regard to the question of electorates the following propositions should be accepted:

(1) Joint electorate or separate electorate is a matter of machinery for achieving a given purpose. It is not a matter of principle.
(2) The purpose is to enable a minority to select candidates to the Legislature who will be real and not nominal representatives of the minority.
(3) While separate electorate gives an absolute guarantee to the minority, that its representatives will be no others except those who enjoy its confidence, a system of joint electorates which will give equal protection to the minorities should not be overlooked.
(4) A Four-member constituency, with a right to the minorities to have a double vote and requiring a minimum percentage of minority votes, may be considered as a possible substitute.

Matters Not Covered

(i) Question of Special Safeguards

There are other demands made on behalf of particular minorities such as:

(1) Provision of a Statutory Officer to report on the condition of minorities.
(2) Statutory provision of State aid for education, and
(3) Statutory provision for land settlement. But they are not of a communal character, I do not therefore wish to enlarge upon them here.

(ii) Aboriginal Tribes

It will be obvious that my proposals do not cover the Aboriginal Tribes although they are larger in number than the Sikhs, Anglo Indians, Indian

Christians and Parsees. I may state the reasons why I have omitted them from my scheme. The Aboriginal Tribes have not as yet developed any political sense to make the best use of their political opportunities and they may easily become mere instruments in the hands either of a majority or a minority and thereby disturb the balance without doing any good to themselves. In the present stage of their development it seems to me that the proper thing to do for these backward communities is to establish a Statutory Commission to administer what are now called the 'excluded areas' on the same basis as was done in the case of the South African Constitution. Every Province in which these excluded areas are situated should be compelled to *make* an annual contribution of a prescribed amount for the administration of these areas.

(iii) Indian States

It will also be noticed that my proposals do not include the Indian States. I am not opposed to the inclusion of the Indian States, provided the terms and conditions of inclusion are such—

(1) that the dichotomy of divided sovereignty between British India and Indian. States is completely done away with,

(2) that the judicial and political boundaries which separate British India from Indian States will disappear, that there will be no such entities as British India or Indian States and in their place there will be only one entity namely India, and

(3) that the terms and conditions of inclusion do not prevent India from having full and plenary powers of a Dominion. I have worked out a scheme for the fusion of the Indian States and British India, which will permit the realization of these objects. I do not wish to overburden this address with the details of the plan. For the moment, it is better if British India marches to her goal without complicating its progress by an entanglement with the Indian States......

A Word to Hindus

Much of the difficulty over the Communal Question is due to the insistence of the Hindus that the rule of majority is sacrosanct and that it, must be maintained at all costs. The Hindu does not seem to be aware of the fact that there is another rule, which is also operative in fields where important disputes between individual and nations arise and that rule is a rule of unanimity. If he will take the trouble to examine the position he will realize that such a rule is not a fiction, but it does exist. Let him take the Jury System. In the jury trial the principle is unanimity. The decision is binding upon the judge, only if the verdict of the jury is unanimous. Let him take another illustration that of the League of Nations. What was the rule for decisions in the League of Nations? The rule was a rule of unanimity. It is obvious that if the principle of unanimity was accepted by the Hindus as a rule of decision in the Legislature and in the Executive there would be no such thing as a Communal Problem in India.

One may well ask the Hindu that if he is not prepared to concede constitutional safeguards to the minorities, is he prepared to agree to the rule of unanimity? Unfortunately he is not prepared to accept either.

About the rule of majority the Hindu is not prepared to admit any limitations. The majority he wants is an absolute majority. He will not be satisfied with relative majority. He should consider whether his insistence on absolute majority is fair proposition, which political philosophers can accept. He is not aware that even the constitution of the United States does not lend support to the absolutistic rule of majority rule- on which the Hindu has been insisting upon.

Let me illustrate the point from the constitution of the United States. Take the clause embodying Fundamental Rights. What does that clause mean? It means that matters included in Fundamental Rights are of such supreme concern that a mere majority rule is not enough to interfere with them. Take another illustration also from the Constitution of the United States. The Constitution says that no part of the Constitution shall be altered unless the proposition is carried by three-fourths majority and ratified by the States. What does this show? It shows that the United States Constitution recognizes for certain purposes mere majority rule is not competent.

All these cases are of course familiar to many a Hindu. The pity of it is, he does not read from them the correct lesson. If he did, he would realize that the rule of the majority rule is not as sacrosanct a principle as he thinks it is. The majority rule *is* not accepted as a principle but is tolerated as a rule. I *might* also state why it is tolerated. It is tolerated for two reasons; (1) because the majority is always a political majority and (2) because the decision of a political majority accepts and absorbs so much of the point of view of the minority that the minority does not care to rebel against the decision.

In India, the majority is not a political majority. In India the majority is born; it is not made. That is the difference between a communal majority and a political majority. A political majority is not a fixed or a permanent majority. It is a majority which is always made, unmade and. remade. A communal majority is a permanent majority fixed in its attitude. One can destroy it, but one cannot transform it. If there is so much objection to a political majority, how very fatal must be the objection to a communal majority?

It may be open to the Hindus to ask Mr. Jinnah, why in 1930 when he formulated his fourteen points he insisted upon the principle of majority rule to such an extent that one of the fourteen points stipulated that in granting weightage, limits should be placed whereby a majority shall not be reduced to a minority or equality. It may be open to the Hindus to ask Mr Jinnah, if he is in favour of a Muslim majority in Muslim Provinces, why he is opposed to a Hindu Majority in the Centre? The Hindu must however realize that these posers may lead to the conclusion that Mr Jinnah's position is inconsistent. They cannot lead to the affirmation of the principle of majority rule.

The abandonment of the principle of majority rule in politics cannot affect the Hindus very much in other walks of life. As an element in social life they will remain a majority. They will have the monopoly of trade and business which they enjoy. They will have the monopoly of the property which they have. My proposals do not ask the Hindus to accept the principle of unanimity. My proposals do not ask the Hindus to abandon the principle of majority rule. All I am asking them is to be satisfied with a relative majority. Is it too much for them to concede this?

Without marking any such sacrifice the Hindu majority is not justified in representing to the outside world that the minorities are holding up India's Freedom. This false propaganda will not pay. For the minorities are doing nothing of the kind. They are prepared to accept freedom and the dangers in which they likely to be involved; provided they granted satisfactory safeguards. This gesture of the minorities is not to be treated as a matter for which Hindus need not be grateful. It may well be contrasted with what happened in Ireland. Mr Redmond, the leader of the Irish Nationalists once told Carson, the leader of Ulster; 'Consent to United Ireland, Ask for any safeguard and they shall be granted to you'. He is reported to have turned round and said: 'Damn your safeguards; we don't want to be ruled by you'. The minorities in India have not said that. They are ready to be satisfied with safeguards. I ask the Hindus is this not worth a mass? I am sure it is.

Conclusion

These are some of the proposals I have had in mind for the solution of the Communal Problem. They do not commit the All-India Scheduled Castes Federation. They do not even commit me. In putting them forth, I am doing nothing more than exploring a new way. My emphasis is more on the principle, I have enunciated, than on the actual proposals. If the principles are accepted then I am sure the solution of the Communal Question will not be as baffling as it has been in the past.

The problem of solving the Indian deadlock is not easy. I remember reading a historian describing the condition of Germany before the Confederation of 1867 as one of 'Divinely Ordained Confusion'. Whether that was true of Germany or not, it seems to me that they form a very accurate description of the present conditions of India. Germany did get out of this confusion, if not at one stroke at least by successive stages until just before the war she became a unified people, unified in mind, unified in outlook and unified by belief in a common destiny. India has not so far succeeded in evolving order out of her confusion. It is not that she had no opportunities to do so. In fact, there have been quite a number. The first opportunity came in 1927, when Lord Birkenhead gave a challenge to Indians asking them to produce a constitution for India. That challenge was taken up. A committee was formed to frame a constitution. A constitution was produced and was known as 'The Nehru Constitution'. It was, however, not accepted by Indians and was buried without remorse. A second opportunity presented itself to Indians in 1930, when they assembled at the Round Table Conference. There again, Indians failed to play their part and write out their own Constitution. A third attempt is the one recently made by the Sapru Committee. The proposals of this committee too have fallen flat.

There is neither enthusiasm nor optimism left to indulge in another attempt. One is pursued by a sense of fatality, which suggests that as every attempt is doomed to failure, none need be made. At the same time I feel that no Indian ought to be so down hearted or so callous as to let the deadlock stink, as though it was a dead dog, and say that he is prepared to do nothing more than be a mere witness to the political dog-fight that is going on in this country. The failures of the past need not daunt anybody.

They do not daunt me. For, I have a feeling that though it is true that all attempts to reach an agreement on the communal question have failed, the failure have been due not so much to any inherent fault of the Indians as they have been due to a wrong approach. I feel confident that my proposals, if considered dispassionately, should be found acceptable. They constitute a new approach and as such I commend them to my countrymen.

Before I conclude, I must, however, warn my critics that they may be able to amend my proposals in some respects; but it will not be easy to reject them. If they do reject them, the first thing they shall have to do is to controvert the principles on which they are based.

12 Resolution Regarding Aims and Objects (7 December 1946)

A BRIEF SKETCH ABOUT THE DOCUMENT

India's freedom assumed priority after the end of the Second World War in 1945. The British Government, through Cabinet Mission, announced on 16 March 1946 that a Constituent Assembly be set up to frame a Constitution for the future governance of India. Accordingly, elections to the Constituent Assembly were held. The Constituent Assembly started its work of framing free India's Constitution on 9th December 1946. The excerpts below form part of the response to the resolution moved by Jawaharlal Nehru. He argued for a united India in the light of the partition and how it will be beneficial for the Muslims as well. These extracts are from BAWS, Volume 13, 1994 (pp. 5–14).

..........On 13th December 1946, the Hon'ble Pandit Jawaharlal Nehru moved the resolution regarding Aims and Objects as under:—

*(1) This Constituent Assembly declares its firm and solemn resolve to proclaim India as an Independent Sovereign Republic and to draw up for her future governance a Constitution;

2. WHEREIN the territories that now comprise British India, the territories that now form the Indian States, and such other parts of India as are outside British India and the States as well as such other territories as are willing

to be constituted into the Independent Sovereign India, shall be a Union of them all; and

3. WHEREIN the said territories, whether with their present boundaries or with such others as may be determined by the Constituent Assembly and thereafter according to the Law of the Constitution, shall possess and retain the status of autonomous Units, together with residuary powers, and exercise all powers and functions of government and administration, save and except such powers and functions as are vested in or assigned to the Union, or as are inherent or implied in the Union or resulting therefrom; and

4. WHEREIN all power and authority of the Sovereign Independent India, its constituent parts and organs of government, are derived from the people; and

5. WHEREIN shall be guaranteed and secured to all the people of India justice, social, economic and political; equality of status, of opportunity, and before the law; freedom of thought, expression, belief, faith, worship, vocation, association and action, subject to law and public morality; and

6. WHEREIN adequate safeguards shall be provided for minorities, backward and tribal areas, and depressed and other backward classes; and

7. WHEREBY shall be maintained the integrity of the territory of the Republic and its sovereign rights on land, sea, and air according to justice and the law of civilised nations, and

This ancient land attains its rightful and honoured place in the world and make its full and willing contribution to the promotion of world peace and the welfare of mankind.

[Dr. M. R. Jayakar, moved his amendment to the above resolution on 16th December 1946]

The Right Hon'ble Dr. M. R. Jayakar (Bombay General): Well, I will read the amendment. I wanted to save your time by a few minutes. This is the amendment:

This Assembly declares its firm and solemn resolve that the Constitution to be prepared by this Assembly for the future governance of India shall be for a free and democratic Sovereign State; but with a view to securing, in the shaping of such a constitution, the co-operation of the Muslim League and the Indian States, and thereby intensifying the firmness of this resolve, this Assembly postpones the further consideration of this question to a later date, to enable the representatives of these two bodies to participate, if they so choose, in the deliberations of this Assembly.

In substance, my amendment means that the further consideration of this Resolution should be postponed to a later stage, the stage of Union constitution-making at which, I take it, the Indian States and the Muslim League are expected to be present.

[Dr. M. R. Jayakar objected to the timing of the resolution. He moved an amendment, seeking postponement of the passing of the resolution, as he wanted the Muslim League to join the task of laying down the fundamentals of the Constitution. This resolution created a tense atmosphere in the House. Amidst this tense situation Dr. Ambedkar was invited by the President Dr. Rajendra Prasad unexpectedly to have his say on 17th December 1946. When Dr. Ambedkar started, the House was all attention].

Dr. Dhananjay Keer writes, 'Everybody thought that Dr. Ambedkar by playing such dangerous role would go under with the mover of the amendment to rise against the will and the objections of the Congress bosses, who were the nation's most powerful leaders, was to meet one's Waterloo. The Congress members were ready with their hands raised to cripple their avowed enemy and throw him down'. This historic speech changed the course of Dr. Ambedkar's political career. The speech drew the longest and the most vociferous applause. As Mr. N. V. Gadgil, an eye-witness to this event observed 'His speech was so statesmanlike, so devoid of bitterness and so earnestly challenging that the whole of Assembly listened to it in rapt silence. The speech was greeted with tremendous ovation and he was smothered with congratulations in the lobby'. The speech had its ultimate effect and the Constituent Assembly postponed the consideration of the objective resolution till the next session. The said speech of Dr. Ambedkar is as under.—Ed.]

*Mr. Chairman: Dr. Ambedkar.

Dr. B. R. Ambedkar: (Bengal: General): Mr. Chairman, I am indeed very grateful to you for having called me to speak on the Resolution. I must however confess that your invitation has come to me as a surprise. I thought that as there were some 20 or 22 people ahead of me, my turn, if it did come at all, would come tomorrow.

I would have preferred that as today I have come without any preparation whatsoever. I would have like to prepare myself as I had intended to make a full statement on an occasion of this sort. Besides you have fixed a time limit of 10 minutes. Placed under these limitations, I don't know how I could do justice to the Resolution before us. I shall however do my best to condense in as few words as possible what I think about the matter.

Mr. Chairman, the Resolution in the light of the discussion that has gone on since yesterday, obviously divides itself into two parts, one part which is controversial and another part which is non-controversial. The part which is non-controversial is the part which comprises paragraphs

(5) to (7) of this Resolution. These paragraphs set out the objectives of the future constitution of this country. I must confess that, coming as the Resolution does from Pandit Jawaharlal Nehru who is reputed to be a Socialist, this Resolution, although non-controversial, is to my mind very disappointing. I should have expected him to go much further than he has done in that part of the Resolution. As a student of history, I should have preferred this part of the Resolution not being embodied in it at all. When one reads that part of the Resolution, it reminds one of the Declaration of the Rights of Man which was pronounced by the French Constituent Assembly. I think I am right in suggesting that, after the lapse of practically 450 years, the Declaration of the Rights of Man and the principles which are embodied in it has become part and parcel of our mental makeup. I say they have become not only the part and parcel of the mental make-up of modern man in every civilized part of the world, but also in our own country which is so orthodox, so archaic in its thought and its social structure, hardly anyone can be found to deny its validity. To repeat it now as the Resolution does is, to say the least, pure pedantry. These principles have become the silent immaculate premise of our outlook. It is therefore unnecessary to proclaim as forming a part of our creed. The Resolution suffers from certain other lacuna. I find that this part of the Resolution, although it enunciates certain rights, does not speak of remedies. All of us are aware of the fact that rights are nothing unless remedies are provided whereby people can seek to obtain redress when rights are invaded. I find a complete absence of remedies. Even the usual formula that no man's life, liberty and property shall be taken without the due process of law, finds no place in the Resolution. These fundamental rights set out are made subject to law and morality. Obviously what is law, what is morality will be determined by the Executive of the day and when the Executive may take one view another Executive may take another view and we do not know what exactly would be the position with regard to fundamental rights, if this matter is left to the Executive of the day. Sir, there are here certain provisions which speak of justice, economic, social and political. If this Resolution has a reality behind it and a sincerity, of which I have not the least doubt, coming as it does from the Mover of the Resolution, I should have expected some provision whereby it would have been possible for the State to make economic, social and political justice a reality and I should have from that point of view expected the Resolution to state in most explicit terms that in order

that there may be social and economic justice in the country, that there would be nationalization of industry and nationalization of land, I do not understand how it could be possible for any future Government which believes in doing justice socially, economically and politically, unless its economy is a socialistic economy. Therefore, personally, although I have no objection to the enunciation of these propositions, the Resolution is, to my mind, somewhat disappointing. I am however prepared to leave this subject where it is with the observations I have made.

Now I come to the first part of the Resolution, which includes the first four paragraphs. As I said from the debate that has gone on in the House, this has become a matter of controversy. The controversy seems to be centered on the use of that word 'Republic'. It is centered on the sentence occurring in paragraph 4 'the sovereignty is derived from the people'. Thereby it arises from the point made by my friend Dr. Jayakar yesterday that in the absence of the Muslim League it would not be proper for this Assembly to proceed to deal with this Resolution. Now, Sir, I have got not the slightest doubt in my mind as to the future evolution and the ultimate shape of the social, political and economic structure of this great country. I know to-day we are divided politically, socially and economically. We are a group of warring camps and I may go even to the extent of confessing that I am probably one of the leaders of such a camp. But, Sir, with all this, I am quite convinced that given time and circumstances nothing in the world will prevent this country from becoming one. *(Applause):* With all our castes and creeds, I have not the slightest hesitation that we shall in some form be a united people *(Cheers).* I have no hesitation in saying that notwithstanding the agitation of the Muslim League for the partition of India someday enough light would dawn upon the Muslims themselves and they too will begin to think that a United India is better even for them. *(Loud cheers and applause).*

So far as the ultimate goal is concerned, I think none of us need have any apprehensions. None of us need have any doubt. Our difficulty is not about the ultimate future. Our difficulty is how to make the heterogeneous mass that we have to-day take a decision in common and march on the way which leads us to unity. Our difficulty is not with regard to the ultimate, our difficulty is with regard to the beginning. Mr. Chairman, therefore, I should have thought that in order to make us willing friends, in order to induce every party, every section in this country to take on to road it would be an act of greatest statesmanship for the majority party even to make a concession to the prejudices of people who are not prepared to march together and it is for that, that I propose to make this appeal. Let us leave aside slogans, let us leave aside words which frighten people. Let us even make a concession to the prejudices of our opponents, bring them in, so that they may willingly join with us on marching upon that road, which as I said, if we walk long enough, must necessarily lead us to unity. If I, therefore, from this place support Dr. Jayakar's amendment, it is because I want all of us to realize that whether we are right or wrong, whether the position that we take is in consonance with our legal rights, whether that agrees with the Statement of May the 16th or December 6th, leave all that aside. This is too big a question to be treated as a matter of legal rights. It is not a legal question at all. We should leave aside all legal considerations and make some attempt, whereby those who are not prepared to come, will come. Let us make it possible for them to come, that is my appeal.

In the course of the debate that took place, there were two questions which were raised, which struck me so well that I took the trouble of taking them down on a piece of paper. The one question was, I think, by my friend, the Prime Minister of Bihar who spoke yesterday in this Assembly. He said, how can this Resolution prevent the League from coming into the Constituent Assembly? Today my friend. Dr. Syama Prasad Mookherjee, asked another question. Is this Resolution inconsistent with the Cabinet Mission's Proposal? Sir, I think they are very important questions and they ought to be answered and answered categorically. I do maintain that this Resolution whether it is intended to bring about the result or not, whether it is a result of cold calculation or whether it is a mere matter of accident is bound to have the result of keeping the Muslim League out. In this connection I should like to invite your attention to Paragraph 3 of the Resolution, which I think is very significant and very important. Paragraph 3 envisages the future constitution of India. I do not know what is the intention of the mover of the Resolution. But I take it that after this Resolution is passed, it will act as a sort of a directive to the Constituent Assembly to frame a constitution in terms of para 3 of the Resolution. What does paragraph 3 say? Paragraph 3 says that in this country there shall be two different sets of polity, one at the bottom, autonomous Provinces or the States or such other areas as care to join a United India. These autonomous units will have full power. They will have also residuary powers. At the top, over the Provincial units, there will be a Union Government, having certain subjects for legislation, for execution and for administration. As I read this part of the Resolution, I do not find any reference to the idea of grouping, an intermediate structure between the Union on the one hand and the provinces on the other. Reading this para, in the light of the Cabinet Mission's Statement or reading it even in the light of the Resolution passed by the Congress at its Wardha session, I must confess that I am a great deal surprised at the absence of any reference to the idea of grouping of the provinces. So far as I am personally concerned, I do not like the idea of grouping *(hear, hear)* I like a strong united Centre, *(hear, hear)* much stronger than the Centre we had created under the Government of India Act of 1935. But, Sir, these opinions, these wishes have no bearing on the situation at all. We have travelled a long road. The Congress Party, for reasons best known to itself consented, if I may use that expression, to the dismantling of a strong Centre which had been created in this country as a result of 150 years of administration and which I must say, was to me a matter of great admiration and respect and refuge. But having given up that position, having said that we do not want a strong centre, and having accepted that there must be or should be an intermediate polity, a sub-federation between the Union Government and the Provinces I would like to know why there is no reference in para 3 to the idea of grouping. I quite understand that the Congress Party, the Muslim League and His Majesty's Government are not *ad idem* on the interpretation of the clause relating to grouping. But I always thought that, I am prepared to stand corrected if it is shown that I am wrong, at least it was agreed by the Congress Party that if the Provinces which are placed within different groups consent to form a Union or Sub-federation, the Congress would have no objection to that proposal. I believe I am correct in interpreting the mind of the Congress Party. The question I ask is this. Why did not the Mover of this Resolution make reference to the idea of a Union of Provinces or grouping of Provinces on the terms on which he and his party was prepared to accept it? Why is the idea of Union completely effaced from this Resolution? I find no answer. None whatever. I therefore say in answer to the two questions which have been posed here in this Assembly by the Prime Minister of Bihar and Dr. Syama Prasad Mookherjee as to how this Resolution is inconsistent with the Statement of May 16th or how this Resolution is going to prevent the Muslim League from entering this Constituent Assembly, that here is para 3 which the Muslim League is bound to take advantage of and justify its continued absentation. Sir, my friend Dr. Jayakar, yesterday, in arguing his case for postponing a decision on this issue put his case, if I may say so, without offence to him, somewhat in a legalistic manner. The basis of his argument was, have you the right to do so? He read out certain portions from the Statement of the Cabinet Mission which related to the procedural part of the Constituent Assembly and his contention was that the procedure that this Constituent Assembly was adopting in deciding upon this Resolution straightaway was inconsistent with the procedure that was laid down in that Paper. Sir, I like to put the matter in a somewhat different way. The way I like to put it is this, I am not asking you to consider whether you have the right to pass this Resolution straightaway or not. It may be that you have the right to do so. The question I am asking is this. Is it prudent for you to do so? Is it wise for you to do so? Power is one thing; wisdom is quite a different thing and I want this House to consider this matter from the point of view, namely, whether it would be wise, whether it would be statesmanlike, whether it would be prudent to do so at this stage. The answer that I give is that it would not be prudent, it would not be wise. I suggest that another attempt may be made to bring about a solution of the dispute between the Congress and the Muslim League. This subject is so vital, so important that I am sure it could never be decided on the mere basis of dignity of one party or the dignity of another party. When deciding the destinies of nations, dignities of people, dignities of leaders and dignities of parties ought to count for nothing. The destiny of the country ought to count for everything. It is because I feel that it would in the interest not only of this Constituent Assembly so that it may function as one whole, so that it may have the reaction of the Muslim League before it proceeds to decision that I support Dr. Jayakar's amendment—we must also consider what is going to happen with regard to the future, if we act precipitately. I do not know what plans the Congress Party, which holds this House in its possession, has in its mind? I have no power of divination to know what they are thinking about. What are their tactics, what is their strategy, I do not know. But applying my mind as an outsider to the issue that has arisen, it seems to me there are only three ways by which the future will be decided. Either there shall have to be surrender by the one party to the wishes of the other—that is one way. The other way would be what I call a negotiated peace and the third way would be open war. Sir, I have been hearing from certain members of the Constituent Assembly that they are prepared to go to war. I must confess that I am appalled at the idea that anybody in this country should think of solving the political problems of this country by the method of war. I do not know how many people in this country support that idea. A good many perhaps do and the reason why I think they do, is because most of them, at any rate a great many of them, believe that the war that they are thinking of, would be a war on the British. Well, Sir, if the war that is contemplated, that is in the minds of people, can be localized, circumscribed, so that it will not be more than a war on the British, I probably may not have much objection to that sort of strategy. But will it be a war on the British only? I have no hesitation and I do want to place before this House in the clearest terms possible that if war comes in this country and if that war has any relation to the issue with which we are confronted to-day, it will not be a war on the British. It will be a war on the Muslims. It will be a war on the Muslims or which is probably worse, it will be a war on a combination of the British and the Muslims. I cannot see how this contemplated war be of the sort different from what I fear it will be. Sir, I like to read to the House a passage from Burke's great speech on Conciliation with America. I believe this may have some effect upon the temper of this House. The British people as you know were trying to conquer the rebellious colonies of the United States, and bring them under their subjection contrary to their wishes. In repelling this idea of conquering the colonies this is what Burke said:

> First, Sir permit me to observe, that the use of force alone is but temporary. It may subdue for a moment; but it does not remove the necessity of subduing again; and a nation is not governed which is perpetually to be conquered. My next objection is its uncertainty. Terror is not always the effect of force and an armament is not a victory. If you do not succeed, you are without resource for, conciliation failing, force remains; but, force failing, no further hope of reconciliation is left. Power and authority are sometimes bought by kindness; but they can never be begged as alms by an impoverished and defeated violence.

> A further objection to force is, that you impair the object by your very endeavours to preserve it. The thing you fought for is not the thing which you recover; but depreciated, sunk, wasted and consumed in the contest.

These are weighty words which it would be perilous to ignore. If there is anybody who has in his mind the project of solving the Hindu-Muslim problem by force, which is another name of solving it by war, in order that the Muslims may be subjugated and made to surrender to the Constitution that might be prepared without their consent, this country would be involved in perpetually conquering them. The conquest would not be once and for ever. I do not wish to take more time than I have taken and I will conclude by again referring to Burke. Burke has said somewhere that it is easy to give power, it is difficult to give wisdom. Let us prove by our conduct that if this Assembly has arrogated to itself sovereign powers it is prepared to exercise them with wisdom. That is the only way by which we can carry with us all sections of the country. There is no other way that can lead us to unity. Let us have no doubt on that point.

13 States and Minorities (15 March 1947)

A BRIEF SKETCH ABOUT THE DOCUMENT

This work is considered to be most significant contribution of Ambedkar before the he contributed to the Constitution, as he drafted a mini Constitution on two broader themes: first, Admission of Indian States into the Union of India, United States of India and New Territory; and second, Fundamental Rights of the Citizens in General, Provisions for the Safeguard of Minorities, and Safeguards for the Schedules Castes. It was written in 1947 and is part of BAWS, Volume 1, 1979 (pp. 381–452). While discussing fundamental rights he proposed judicial protection, protection against unequal treatment, against discrimination, and against economic exploitation. Protection of minorities included protection against communal Executive, against social and official tyranny, against social boycott, and obligation of Union and State governments to spend for purposes beneficial for minorities. Safeguards for the Scheduled Castes included guarantees of representation in Legislatures and Local bodies, in the Executive, in Services; and, special responsibilities for higher education and separate settlements; Safeguards against amendments of Safeguards. In addition to the other provisions, this remains significant for two major reasons, one Representation of Minorities and Scheduled Castes in the Executive and two, separate settlements for the Scheduled Castes, though these issues also came up when he wrote for the Instiiute for Pacific Studies and 'Communal Deadlock and How to Solve it', but here he seems more clear as there are sections on each concern and then clauses, and finally interpretation and arguments for all the issues raised.

Preface

Soon after it became definite that the framing of the future Constitution of India was to be entrusted to a Constituent Assembly, the Working Committee of the All-India Scheduled Castes Federation asked me to prepare a Memorandum on the Safeguards for the Scheduled Castes for being submitted to the Constituent Assembly, on behalf of the Federation. I very gladly undertook the task. The results of my labour are contained in this brochure.

The Memorandum defines Fundamental Rights, Minority Rights and Safeguards for the Scheduled Castes. Those who hold the view that the Scheduled Castes are not a minority might say that in this matter I have gone beyond prescribed bounds. The view that the Scheduled Castes are not a minority is a new dispensation issued on behalf of the High and Mighty Hindu Majority which the Scheduled Castes are asked to submit to. The spokesmen of the Majority have not cared to define its scope and its meaning. Anyone with a fresh and free mind, reading it as a general proposition, would be justified in saying that it is capable of double interpretation. I interpret it to mean that the Scheduled Castes are more than a minority and that any protection given to the citizens and to the minorities will not be adequate for the Scheduled Castes. In other words it means that their social, economic, and educational condition is so much worse than that of the citizens and other minorities that in addition to protection they would get as citizens and as minorities the Scheduled Castes would require special safeguards against the tyranny and discrimination of the majority. The other interpretation is that the Scheduled Castes differ from a minority and therefore they are not entitled to the protection which can be claimed by a minority. This interpretation appears to be such unmitigated nonsense that no sane man need pay any attention to it. The Scheduled Castes must be excused if they ignore it. Those who accept my interpretation of the view that the Scheduled Castes are not a minority will, I am sure, agree with me that I am justified in demanding for the Scheduled Castes, all the benefit of the Fundamental Rights of citizens, all the benefit of the Provisions for the Protection of the minorities and in addition special Safeguards.

The memorandum was intended to be submitted to the Constituent Assembly. There was no intention to issue it to the public. But my caste Hindu friends who have had the opportunity to read the typescript have pressed me to give it a wider circulation. Although it is meant for members of the Constituent Assembly, I do not see any breach of decorum in making it available to the general public. I have therefore agreed to fall in line with their wishes.

Instead of setting out my ideas in general terms, I have drafted the Memorandum in the form of Articles of the Constitution. I am sure that for the sake of giving point and precision this method will be found to be more helpful. For the benefit of the Working Committee of the Scheduled Castes Federation, I had prepared certain explanatory notes and other statistical material. As the notes and the statistical material are likely to be useful to the general reader, I have thought it better to print them along with the Memorandum rather than keep them back.

Among the many problems the Constituent Assembly has to face, there are two which are admittedly most difficult. One is the problem of the Minorities and the other is the problem of the Indian States. I have been a student of the problem of the Indian States and I hold some very definite and distinct views on the subject. It was my hope that the Constituent Assembly would elect me to the States Committee Evidently, it has found men of superior caliber for the work. It may also be because I am one of those who are outside the tabernacle and therefore undesirable. I am not sorry to find myself left out. My only regret is that I have lost an opportunity to which I was looking forward for placing my views for the consideration of the Committee. I have therefore chosen to do the next best thing—namely, to incorporate them in this brochure along with the Rights of Citizens, of Minorities and of the Scheduled Castes so that a wider public may know what they are, may value them for what they are worth and may make such use of them as it may deem fit....

Proposed Article II

Detailed Analysis

Article II, Section I—*Fundamental Rights of Citizens.*
Article II, Section II—*Remedies against Invasion of Fundamental Rights:*
Clause 1. Judicial Protection.
Clause 2. Protection against Unequal Treatment.
Clause 3. Protection against Discrimination.
Clause 4. Protection against Economic Exploitation.

Article II, Section III—*Provisions for the Protection of Minorities:*
Clause 1. Protection against Communal Executive.
Clause 2. Protection against Social and Official Tyranny.
Clause 3. Protection against Social Boycott.
Clause 4. Authority and obligation of the Union and State Governments to spend money for public purposes including purposes beneficial to Minorities.

Article II, Section IV—*Safeguards for the Scheduled Castes.*
Part I—*Guarantees:*
Clause 1. Right to Representation in the Legislature and in the Local Bodies,
Clause 2. Right to Representation in the Executive.
Clause 3. Right to Representation in Services.

Part II—*Special Responsibilities;*
Clause 1. For Higher Education.
Clause 2. For Separate Settlements.

Part III—*Sanction for Safeguards and Amendment of Safeguards:*
Clause 1. Safeguards to be embodied in the Constitution.
Clause 2. Amendment of Safeguards.

Part IV—*Protection of Scheduled Castes in Indian States.*
Part V—*Interpretation.*

Article II—Section I

Fundamental Rights of Citizens

The Constitution of the United States of India shall recognize the following as Fundamental Rights of citizenship:

1. All persons born or naturalized within its territories are citizens of the United States of India and of the State wherein they reside. Any privilege or disability arising out of rank, birth, person, family, religion or religious usage and custom is abolished.
2. No State shall make or enforce any law or custom which shall abridge the privileges or immunities of citizens; nor shall any State deprive any person of life, liberty and property without due process of law; nor deny to any person within its jurisdiction equal protection of law.

3. All citizens are equal before the law and possess equal civic rights. Any existing enactment, regulation, order, custom or interpretation of law by which any penalty, disadvantage or disability is imposed upon or any discrimination is made against any citizen shall, as from the day on which this Constitution comes into operation, cease to have any effect.

4. Whoever denies to any person, except for reasons by law applicable to persons of all classes and regardless of their social status, the full enjoyment of any of the accommodations, advantages, facilities, privileges of inns, educational institutions, roads, paths, streets, tanks, wells and other watering places, public conveyances on land, air or water, theatres or other places of public amusement, resort or convenience, whether they are dedicated to or maintained or licensed for the use of the public, shall be guilty of an offence.

5. All citizens shall have equal access to all institutions, conveniences and amenities maintained by or for the public.

6. No citizen shall be disqualified to hold any public office or exercise any trade or calling by reason of his or her religion, caste, creed, sex or social status.

7. (i) Every citizen has the right to reside in any part of India. No law shall be made abridging the right of a citizen to reside except for consideration of public order and morality.

(ii) Every citizen has the right to settle in any part of India, subject to the production of a certificate of citizenship from the State of his origin. The permission to settle shall not be refused or withdrawn except on grounds specified in sub-clause (iv) of this clause.

(iii) The State in which a citizen wishes to settle may not impose any special charge upon him in respect of such settlement other than the charge imposed upon its own inhabitants. The maximum fees chargeable in respect of permits for settlement shall be determined by laws made by the Union Legislature.

(iv) The permission to settle may be refused or withdrawn by a State from persons—

(a) who have been habitual criminals;

(b) whose intention to settle is to alter the communal balance of the State;

(c) who cannot prove to the satisfaction of the State in which they wish to settle that they have an assured means of subsistence and who are likely to become or have become a permanent burden upon public charity;

(d) whose State of origin refuses to provide adequate assistance for them when requested to do so,

(v) Permission to settle may be made conditional upon the applicant being capable of work and not having been a permanent charge upon public charity in the place of his origin, and able to give security against unemployment.

(vi) Every expulsion must be confirmed by the Union Government.

(vii) Union Legislature shall define the difference between settlement and residence and at the same time, prescribe regulations governing the political and civil rights of persons during their residence.

8. The Union Government shall guarantee protection against persecution of a community as well as against internal disorder or violence arising in any part of India.

9. Subjecting a person to forced labour or to involuntary servitude shall be an offence.

10. The right of the people to be secure in their persons, houses, papers and effects against unreasonable searches and seizures, shall not be violated, and no warrants shall issue, but upon probable cause, supported by oath or affirmation, and particularly describing the place to be searched, and the persons or things to be seized.

11. The right of a citizen to vote shall not be denied or abridged on any account other than immaturity, imprisonment and insanity.

12. No law shall be made abridging the freedom of Speech, of the Press, of Association and of Assembly except for consideration of public order and morality.

13. No Bill of attainder or *ex post facto* law shall be passed.

14. The State shall guarantee to every Indian citizen liberty of conscience and the free exercise of his religion including the right to profess, to preach and to convert within limits compatible with public order and morality.

15. No person shall be compelled to become a member of any religious association, submit to any religious instruction or perform any act of religion. Subject to the foregoing provision, parents and guardians shall be entitled to determine the religious education of children up to the age of 16 years.

16. No person shall incur any penalties of any kind whatsoever by reason of his caste, creed or religion nor shall any person be permitted to refuse to fulfil any obligation of citizenship on the ground of caste, creed or religion.

17. The State shall not recognize any religion as State religion.

18. Persons following a religion shall be guaranteed freedom of association and shall have, if they so desire, the right to call upon the State to pass legislation in terms approved by them making them into a body corporate.
19. Every religious association shall be free to regulate and administer its affairs, within the limits of the laws applicable to all.
20. Religious associations shall be entitled to levy contributions on their members who are willing to pay them if their law of incorporation permits them to do so. No person may be compelled to pay taxes the proceeds of which are specifically appropriated for the use of any religious community of which he is not a member.
21. All offences under this section shall be deemed to be cognizable offences. The Union Legislature shall make laws to give effect to such provisions as require legislation for that purpose and to prescribe punishment for those acts which are declared to be offences.

Article II—Section II

Remedies against Invasion of Fundamental Rights

The United States of India shall provide:

Clause 1

(1) That the Judicial Power of India shall be vested in a Supreme Court.
(2) The Supreme Court shall have the power of superintendence over all other Courts or officers exercising the powers of a court, whether or not such Courts or officers are subject to its appellate or revisional jurisdiction.
(3) The Supreme Court shall have the power on the application of an aggrieved party to issue what are called prerogative writs such as *Habeas Corpus, Quo Warranto Prohibition, Certiorari* and *Mandamus,* etc. For purposes of such writs the Supreme Court shall be a Court of general jurisdiction throughout India.
(4) The right to apply for a writ shall not be abridged or suspended unless when in cases of rebellion or invasion the public safety may require it.

Clause 2

That the Authority of the Legislature and the Executive of the Union as well as of every state throughout India shall be subject to following limitations:

It shall not be competent for any Legislature or Executive in India to pass a law or issue an order, rule or regulation so as to violate the following rights of the subjects of the State:

(1) to make and enforce contracts, to sue, be parties, and give evidence, to inherit, purchase, lease, sell, hold and convey real and personal property.

(2) to be eligible for entry into the civil and military employ and to all educational institutions except for such conditions and limitations as may be necessary to provide for the due and adequate representation of all classes of the subjects of the State.

(3) to be entitled to the full and equal enjoyment of the accommodations, advantages, facilities, educational institutions, privileges of inns, rivers, streams, wells, tanks, roads, paths, streets, public conveyances on land, air and water, theatres and other places of public resort or amusement except for such conditions and limitations applicable alike to all subjects of every race, class, caste, colour *or* creed.

(4) to be deemed fit for and capable of sharing without distinction the benefits of any religious or charitable trust dedicated to or created, maintained or licensed for the general public or for persons of the same faith and religion.

(5) to claim full and equal benefit of all laws and proceedings for the security of persons and property as is enjoyed by other subjects regardless of any usage or custom or usage or custom based on religion and be subject to like punishment, pains and penalties and to none other.

Clause 3

(1) Discrimination against citizens by Government officers in Public Protection or by private employers in factories and commercial concerns on the ground of race or creed or social status shall be treated as an offence. The jurisdiction to try such cases shall be vested in a tribunal to be created for the purpose.

(2) The Union Legislature shall have the right as well as the obligation to give effect to this provision by appropriate legislation.

Clause 4

The United States of India shall declare as a part of the law of its constitution—

(1) That industries which are key industries or which may be declared be owned and run by the State;

(2) That industries which are not key industries but which are basic industries shall be owned by the State and shall be run by State or by Corporations established by the State;

(3) That Insurance shall be a monopoly of the State and that the State shall compel every adult citizen to take out a life insurance policy commensurate with his wages as may be prescribed by the Legislature;

(4) That agriculture shall be State Industry;

(5) That State shall acquire the subsisting rights in such industries, insurance and agricultural land held by private individuals, whether as owners, tenants or mortgagees and pay them compensation in the form of debenture equal to the value of his or her right in the land. Provided that in reckoning the value of land, plant or security no account shall be taken of any rise therein due to emergency, of any potential or unearned value or any value for compulsory acquisition;

(6) The State shall determine how and when the debenture holder shall been titled to claim cash payment;

(7) The debenture shall be transferable and inheritable property but neither the debenture holder nor the transferee from the original holder nor his heir shall be entitled to claim the return of the land or interest in any industrial concern acquired by the State or be entitled to deal with it in any way;

(8) The debenture-holder shall be entitled to interest on his debenture at such rate as may be defined by law, to be paid by the State in cash or in kind as the State may deem fit;

(9) Agricultural industry shall be organized on the following basis:

  (i) The State shall divide the land acquired into farms of standard size and let out the farms for cultivation to residents of the village as tenants (made up of group of families) to cultivate on the following conditions:

    (a) The farm shall be cultivated as a collective farm;

    (b) The farm shall be cultivated in accordance with rules and directions issued by Government;

    (c) The tenants shall share among themselves in the manner prescribed the produce of the farm left after the payment of charges properly leviable on the farm;

(ii) The land shall be let out to villagers without distinction of caste or creed and in such manner that there will be no landlord, no tenant and no landless labourer;

(iii) It shall be the obligation of the State to finance the cultivation of the collective farms by the supply of water, draft animals, implements, manure, seeds, etc.;

(iv) The State shall be entitled to—

    (a) to levy the following charges on the produce of the farm: (i) a portion for land revenue; (ii) a portion to pay the debenture-holders; and (iii) a portion to pay for the use of capital goods supplied; and

    (b) to prescribe penalties against tenants who break the conditions of tenancy or willfully neglect to make the best use of the means of cultivation offered by the State or otherwise act prejudicially to the scheme of collective farming;

(10) The scheme shall be brought into operation as early as possible but in no case shall the period extend beyond the tenth year from the date of the Constitution coming into operation.

Article II—Section III

Provisions for the Protection of Minorities

The Constitution of the United States of India shall provide:

Clause 1

(1) That the Executive—Union or State—shall be non-Parliamentary in the sense that it shall not be removable before the term of the Legislature.

(2) Members of the Executive if they are not members of the Legislature shall have the right to sit in the Legislature, speak, vote and answer questions.

(3) The Prime Minister shall be elected by the whole House by single transferable vote.

(4) The representatives of the different minorities in the Cabinet shall be elected by members of each minority community in the Legislature by single transferable vote.

(5) The representatives of the majority community in the Executive shall be elected by the whole House by single transferable vote.

(6) A member of the Cabinet may resign his post on a censure motion or otherwise but shall not be liable to be removed except on impeachment by the House on the ground of corruption or treason.

Clause 2

(1) That there shall be appointed an Officer to be called the Superintendent of Minority Affairs.

(2) His status shall be similar to that of the Auditor-General appointed under section 166 of the Government of India Act of 1935 and removable in like manner and on the like grounds as a Judge of the Supreme Court.

(3) It shall be the duty of the Superintendent to prepare an annual report on the treatment of minorities by the public, as well as by the Governments, Union and State and of any transgressions of safeguards or any miscarriage of justice due to communal bias by Governments or their Officers.

(4) The Annual Report of the Superintendent shall be placed on the Table of the Legislatures—Union and State, and the Governments—Union and State, shall be bound to provide time for the discussion of the Report.

Clause 3

That Social Boycott, Promoting or Instigating a Social Boycott or Threatening a Social Boycott as defined below shall be social boycott declared to be an offence:

(i) *Boycott Defined.*—A person shall be deemed to boycott another who—

 (a) refuses to let or use or occupy any house or land, or to deal with, work for hire, or do business with another person, or to render to him or receive from him any service, or refuses to do any of the said things on the terms on which such things should commonly be done in the ordinary course of business, or

 (b) abstains from such social, professional or business relations as he would, having regard to such existing customs in the community which are not inconsistent with any fundamental right or other rights of citizenship declared in the Constitution, ordinarily maintain with such person, or

 (c) in any way injures, annoys or interferes with such other person in the exercise of his lawful rights.

(ii) *Offence of Boycotting.*—Whoever, in consequence of any person having done any act which he was legally entitled to do or of his having omitted to do any act which he was legally entitled to omit to do, or with intent to cause any person to do any act which he is not legally bound to do or to omit to do any act which be is legally entitled to do, or with intent to cause harm to such person in body, mind, reputation or property, or in his business or means of living, boycotts such person or any person in whom such person is interested, shall be guilty of offence of boycotting. Provided that no offence shall be deemed to have been committed under this Section, if the Court is satisfied that the accused person has not acted at the instigation of or in collusion with any other person or in pursuance of any conspiracy or of any agreement or combination to boycott.

(iii) *Offence of Instigating or Promoting a Boycott*—Whoever—
  (a) publicly makes or publishes or circulates a proposal for, or
  (b) makes, publishes or circulates any statement, rumour or report with intent to, or which he has reason to believe to be likely to cause, or
  (c) in any other way instigates or promotes the boycotting of any person or class of persons, shall be guilty of the offence of instigating or promoting a boycott.
  Explanation—An offence under this clause shall be deemed to have been committed although the person affected or likely to be affected by any action of the nature referred to herein is not designated by name or class but only by his acting or abstaining from acting in some specified manner.

(iv) *Offence of Threatening a Boycott*—Whoever, in consequence of any person having done any act which he was legally entitled to do or of his having omitted to do any act which he was legally entitled to omit to do, or with intent to cause any person to do any act which he is not legally bound to do, or to omit to do any act which he is legally entitled to do, threatens to cause such person or any person in whom such person is interested, to be boycotted shall be guilty of the offence threatening a boycott.
  Exception.—It is not boycott—
  (i) to do any act in furtherance of a *bona fide* labour dispute; (ii) to do any act in the ordinary course of business competition.
  (2) All these offences shall be deemed to be cognizable offences. The Union Legislature shall make laws prescribing punishment for these offences.

Clause 4

That the Power of the Central and Provincial Governments to make grants for any purpose, notwithstanding that the purpose is not one for which the Union or State Legislature as the case may make laws, shall not be abridge or taken away.

Article II—Section IV

Safeguards for the Scheduled Castes Part I—Guarantees

The Constitution of the United States of India shall guarantee to the Scheduled Castes the following Rights:

Clause 1

Right to Representation in the Legislature

(1) *Quantum of Representation.*—(a)
   (i) The Scheduled Castes shall have minimum representation in the Legislature—Union and State—and if there be a group Constitution then in the group Legislature equal to the ratio of their population to the total population. Provided that no other minority is allowed to claim more representation than what is due to it on the basis of its population.
   (ii) The Scheduled Castes of Sind and N.W.F. Provinces shall be given their due share of representation.
   (iii) Weightage where it becomes necessary to reduce a huge communal majority to reasonable dimensions shall come out of the share of the majority. In no case shall it be at the cost of another minority community.
   (iv) Weightage carved out from the share of majority shall not be assigned to one community only. But the same shall be divided among all minority communities equally or in inverse proportion to their—(1) economic position, (2) social status, and (3) educational advance.
   (b) There should be no representation to special interests. But if the same is allowed it must be taken out of the share of representation given to that community to which the special interest belongs.

(2) *Method of Election—*

(A) For Legislative Bodies

(a) The system of election introduced by the Poona Pact shall be abolished.

(b) In its place, the system of *Separate Electorates* shall be substituted.

(c) Franchise shall be adult franchise.

(d) The system of voting shall be cumulative.

(B) For Local Bodies

The principles for determining the quantum of representation and the Method of election for Municipalities and Local Boards shall be the same as that adopted for the Union and State Legislatures.

Clause 2

(1) The Scheduled Castes shall have minimum representation in the Right to Executive—Union and State—and if there be a group Constitution then in the group Executive equal to the ratio of their population to the total population. Provided that no minority community is allowed to claim more than its population ratio.

(2) Weightage where it becomes necessary to reduce a huge majority to reasonable dimensions shall come out of the share of the majority community. In no case shall it be at the cost of another minority community.

(3) Weightage carved out from the share of the majority shall not be assigned to one community only But the same shall be divided among all minorities equally or in inverse proportion to:

(i) their economic position, (ii) social status, and (iii) educational advance.

Clause 3

Right to Representation in the Services

(a) The quantum of representation of the Scheduled Castes in the Services shall be as follows:

(i) *In the Union Services*—In proportion to the ratio of their population to the total population in India or British India as the case may be.

(ii) *In the State and Group Services*—In proportion to their population in the State or Union.

(iii) *In the Municipal and Local Board Services*—In proportion to their population in the Municipal and Local Boards areas:
Provided that no minority community is allowed to claim more than its population ratio of representation in the Services.

(b) Their right to representation in the Services shall not be curtailed except by conditions relating to minimum qualifications, education, age, etc.

(c) The conditions prescribed for entry in Services shall not abrogate any of the concessions given to the Scheduled Castes by the Government of India in their Resolutions of 1942 and 1945.

(d) The method of filling up the vacancies shall conform to the rules prescribed in the Government of India Resolutions of 1942 and 1946.

(e) On every Public Services Commission or a Committee constituted for filling vacancies, the Scheduled Castes shall have at least one representative.

Part II—Special Responsibilities

That the United States of India shall undertake the following special responsibilities for the betterment of the Scheduled Castes:

Clause 1

(1) Governments—Union and State—shall be required to assume financial responsibility for the higher education of the Scheduled Castes and shall be required to make adequate provisions in their budgets. Such Provisions shall form the first charge on the Education Budget of the Union and State Government.

(2) The responsibility for finding money for secondary and college education of the Scheduled Castes in India shall be upon the State Governments and the different States shall make a provision in their annual budgets for the said purpose in proportion to the population of the Scheduled Castes to the total budget of the States.

(3) The responsibility for finding money for foreign education of the Scheduled Castes shall be the responsibility of the Union Government and the Union Government shall make a provision of rupees 10 lakhs per year in its annual budget in that behalf.

(4) These special grants shall be without prejudice to the right of the Scheduled Castes to share in the expenditure incurred by the State Government for the advancement of primary education for the people of the State.

Clause 2

1. The following provision shall be made in the Constitution of the Union Government:
    (i)   There shall be a Settlement Commission under the new Constitution to hold uncultivated lands belonging to the State in trust for Settlement of the Scheduled Castes in separate villages.
    (ii) The Union Government shall set apart annually a fund of Rs. 5 crores for the purpose of promoting the scheme of settlement.
    (iii) That the Commission shall have the power to purchase any land offered for sale and use it for the said purpose.
2. The Union Government shall from time to time pass such legislation as may be necessary for the Commission to carry out its functions.

Part III—Sanction for Safeguards and Amendment of Safeguards

Clause 1

The Constitution of the United States shall provide that—

The United States of India undertakes to give the safeguards contained in Article II Section IV a place in the Constitution and make them a part of the Constitutional Law of India.

Clause 2

The provisions for the Scheduled Castes shall not be altered, amended or abrogated except in the following manner:

Any amendment or abrogation of Section IV of Article II or any part thereof relating to the Scheduled Castes shall only be made by a Resolution passed in the manner prescribed below by the more Popular Chamber of the Union Legislature:

(i) Any proposal for amendment or abrogation shall be initiated in the form of a Resolution in the more Popular Chamber of the Union Legislature.
(ii) No such Resolution shall be moved—
     (a) unless 25 years have elapsed after the Constitution has come into operation and has been worked; and
     (b) unless six months' notice has been given to the House by the mover of his intention to move such a Resolution.

(iii) On the passing of such a Resolution, the Legislature shall be dissolved and a new election held.

(iv) The original Resolution in the form in which it was passed by the previous Legislature shall be moved afresh in the same House of the newly elected Union Legislature.

(v) The Resolution shall not be deemed to have been carried unless it is passed by a majority of two-thirds of the members of the House and also two-thirds of members of the Scheduled Castes who have been returned through separate electorates.

Part IV—Protection of Scheduled Castes in the Indian States

The Constitution of the United States shall provide that the admission of the Indian States into the Union shall be subject to the following condition:

All provisions relating to the Scheduled Castes contained in Section IV of Article II of the Constitution of the United States of India shall be extended to the Scheduled Castes in the Indian States. Such a provision in the Constitution of an Indian States shall be a condition precedent for its admission into the Union.

Part V—Interpretation

I. For the purposes of Article II the Scheduled Castes, as defined in the Government Scheduled Castes of India Scheduled Caste Order, 1936, issued under the Government of India Act, 1935, shall be deemed to be a minority.

II. For the purposes of Article II a Caste which is a Scheduled Caste in one Scheduled Castes and state shall be treated as Scheduled Caste in one State shall be treated as Scheduled Caste in all States of Union.

Exploratory Notes

Article II—Section I

The inclusion of Fundamental Rights in the Constitution requires no justification. The necessity of Fundamental Rights is recognized in all Constitutions old and new. The Fundamental Rights included in the Article are borrowed from the Constitutions of various countries particularly from those wherein the conditions are more or less analogous to those existing in India.

Article II—Section II

Clause 1

Rights are real only if they are accompanied by remedies. It is no use giving rights if the aggrieved person has no legal remedy to which he can resort when his rights are invaded. Consequently when the Constitution guarantees rights it also becomes necessary to make provision to prevent the Legislature and the Executive from overriding them. This function has been usually assigned to the judiciary and the Courts have been made the special guardians of the rights guaranteed by the Constitution. The clause does no more than this. The clause proposes to give protection to the citizen against Executive tyranny by investing the Judiciary with certain powers of inquisition against the abuse of authority by the Executive. This power takes the form of issue of writs. The High Courts in India possess these powers under the Government of India and under their letters patent. These powers are however subject to two limitations. In the first place the powers given by the Letters Patent are available only to the High Courts in the Presidency Towns and not to all. Secondly these powers are subject to laws made by the Indian Legislature. Thirdly the powers given by the Government of India Act, 1935, are restricted and may prove insufficient for the protection of the aggrieved person. The clause achieves two objectives: (1) to give the fullest power to the Judiciary to issue what under the English Law are called Prerogative Writs and (2) to prevent the Legislature from curtailing these powers in any manner whatsoever.

Clause 2

It is difficult to expect that in a country like India where most persons are communally minded those in authority will give equal treatment to those who do not belong to their community. Unequal treatment has been the inescapable fate of the Untouchables in India. The following extract from the Proceedings of the Board of Revenue of the Government of Madras No. 723 dated 5th November, 1892, illustrates the sort of unequal treatment which is meted out to the Scheduled Castes by Hindu Officers. Says the report:

> There are forms of oppression only hitherto hinted at which must be at least cursorily mentioned. To punish disobedience of Pariahs, their masters—

(a) bring false cases in the village Court or in the criminal Courts;
(b) obtain, on application, from Government, waste lands lying all round the paracheri, so as to impound the Pariahs' cattle or obstruct the way to their temple;
(c) have mirasi names fraudulently entered in the Government account against the paracheri;
(d) pull down the huts and destroy the growth in the backyards;
(e) deny occupancy right in immemorial sub-tenancies;
(f) forcibly cut the Pariahs' crops, and on being resisted charge them with theft and rioting;
(g) under misrepresentations, get them to execute documents by which they are afterwards ruined;
(h) cut off the flow of water from their fields;
(i) without legal notice, have the property of sub-tenants attached for the landlords' arrears of revenue.

It will be said there are civil and criminal Courts for the redress of any of these injuries. There are the Courts indeed; but India does not breed village Hampdens. One must have courage to go to the Courts; money to employ legal knowledge, and meet legal expenses; and means to live during the case and the appeals. Further most cases depend upon the decision of the first Court; and these Courts are presided over by officials who are sometimes corrupt and who generally for other reasons, sympathize with the wealthy and landed classes to which they belong.

The influence of these classes with the official world can hardly be exaggerated. It is extreme with natives and great even with Europeans. Every office, from the highest to the lowest, is stocked with their representatives, and there is no proposal affecting their interests but they can bring a score of influence to bear upon it in its course from inception to execution.

The Punjab Land Alienation Act is another illustration of unequal treatment of the Untouchables by the Legislature.

Many other minority communities may be suffering from similar treatment at the hands of the majority community. It is therefore necessary to have such a provision to ensure that all citizens shall have equal benefit of Laws, Rules, and Regulations.

The provisions of Clause 2 are borrowed from Civil Rights Protection Act, 1866, and of March 1st, 1875 passed by the Congress of the United States of America to protect the Negroes against unequal treatment.

Clause 3

Discrimination is another menace which must be guarded against if the Fundamental Rights are to be real rights. In a country like India where it is possible for discrimination to be practised on a vast scale and in a relentless manner Fundamental Rights can have no meaning. The Remedy follows the lines adopted in the Bill which was recently introduced in the Congress of the U.S.A. the aim of which is to prevent discrimination being practised against the Negroes.

Clause 4

The main purpose behind the clause is to put an obligation on the State to plan the economic life of the people on lines which would lead to highest point of productivity without closing every avenue to private enterprise, and also provide for the equitable distribution of wealth. The plan set out in the clause proposes State ownership in agriculture with a collectivized method of cultivation and a modified form of State Socialism in the field of industry. It places squarely on the shoulders of the State the obligation to supply capital necessary for agriculture as well as for industry. Without the supply of capital by the State neither land nor industry can be made to yield better results. It also proposes to nationalize insurance with a double objective. Nationalized Insurance gives the individual greater security than a private Insurance Firm does inasmuch as it pledges the resources of the State as a security for the ultimate payment of his insurance money. It also gives the State the resources necessary for financing its economic planning in the absence of which it would have to resort to borrowing from the money market at a high rate of interest. State Socialism is essential for the rapid industrialization of India. Private enterprise cannot do it and if it did it would produce those inequalities of wealth which private capitalism has produced in Europe and which should be a warning to Indians. Consolidation of Holdings and Tenancy Legislation are worse than useless. They cannot bring about prosperity in agriculture. Neither Consolidation nor Tenancy Legislation can be of any help to the 60 millions of Untouchables who are just landless labourers. Neither Consolidation nor Tenancy Legislation can solve their problem. Only collective farms on the lines set out in the proposal can help them. There is no expropriation of the interests concerned. Consequently there ought to be no objection to the proposal on that account.

The plan has two special features. One is that it proposes State Socialism in important fields of economic life. The second special feature of the plan is that it does not leave the establishment of State Socialism to the will of the Legislature. It establishes State Socialism by the Law of the Constitution and thus makes it unalterable by any act of the Legislature and the Executive.

Students of Constitutional Law will at once raise a protest. They are sure to ask: Does not the proposal go beyond the scope of the usual type of Fundamental Rights? My answer is that it does not. If it appears to go beyond it is only because the conception of Fundamental Rights on which such criticism is based is a narrow conception. One may go further and say that even from the narrow conception of the scope of the Constitutional Law as comprising no more than Fundamental Rights the proposal can find ample justification. For what is the purpose of prescribing by law the shape and form of the economic structure of society? The purpose is to protect the liberty of the individual from invasion by other individuals which is the object of enacting Fundamental Rights. The connection between individual liberty and the shape and form of the economic structure of society may not be apparent to everyone. None the less the connection between the two is real. It will be apparent if the following considerations are borne in mind.

Political Democracy rests on four premises which may be set out in the following terms:

(i) The individual is an end in himself.
(ii) That the individual has certain inalienable rights which must be guaranteed to him by the Constitution.
(iii) That the individual shall not be required to relinquish any of his constitutional rights as a condition precedent to the receipt of a privilege.
(iv) That the State shall not delegate powers to private persons to govern others.

Anyone who studies the working of the system of social economy based on private enterprise and pursuit of personal gain will realize how it undermines, if it does not actually violate, the last two premises on which Democracy rests. How many have to relinquish their constitutional rights in order to gain their living? How many have to subject themselves to be governed by private employers?

Ask those who are unemployed whether what are called Fundamental Rights are of any value to them. If a person who is unemployed is offered a choice between a job of some sort, with some sort of wages, with no fixed hours of labour and with an interdict on joining a union and the exercise of his right to freedom of speech, association, religion, etc., can there be any doubt as to what his choice will be. How can it be otherwise? The fear of starvation, the fear of losing a house, the fear of losing savings if any, the fear of being compelled to take children away from school, the fear of having to be a burden on public charity, the fear of having to be burned or buried at public cost are factors too strong to permit a man to stand out for his Fundamental Rights. The unemployed are thus compelled to relinquish their Fundamental Rights for the sake of securing the privilege to work and to subsist.

What about those who are employed? Constitutional Lawyers assume that the enactment of Fundamental Rights is enough to safeguard their liberty and that nothing more is called for. They argue that where the State refrains from intervention in private affairs—economic and social—the residue is liberty. What is necessary is to make the residue as large as possible and State intervention as small as possible. It is true that where the State refrains from intervention what remains is liberty. But this does not dispose of the matter. One more question remains to be answered. To whom and for whom is this liberty? Obviously this liberty is liberty to the landlords to increase rents, for capitalists to increase hours of work and reduce rate of wages. This must be so. It cannot be otherwise. For in an economic system employing armies of workers, producing goods *en masse* at regular intervals someone must make rules so that workers will work and the wheels of industry run on. If the State does not do it the private employer will. Life otherwise will become impossible. In other words what is called liberty from the control of the State is another name for the dictatorship of the private employer.

How to prevent such a thing happening? How to protect the unemployed as well as the employed from being cheated out of their Fundamental Rights to life, liberty and pursuit of happiness? The useful remedy adopted by Democratic countries is to *limit* the power of Government to impose arbitrary restraints in political domain and to *invoke* the ordinary power of the Legislature to restrain the more powerful individual from imposing arbitrary restraints on the less powerful in the economic field. The inadequacy may the futility of the plan has been well-established. The successful invocation by the less powerful of the authority of the Legislature is a doubtful proposition. Having regard to the fact that even under adult suffrage all Legislatures and Governments are controlled by the more powerful an appeal to the Legislature to intervene is a very precarious safeguard against the invasion of the liberty of the less powerful. The plan follows quite a different method. It seeks to limit not only the power of Government to impose arbitrary restraints but also of the more powerful individuals or to be more precise to eliminate the possibility of the more powerful having the power to impose arbitrary restraints on the less powerful by withdrawing from the control he has over the economic life of people. There cannot be slightest doubt that of the two remedies against the invasion by the more powerful of the rights and liberties of the less powerful the one contained in the proposal is undoubtedly the more effective. Considered in the light of these observations the proposal is essentially a proposal for safeguarding the liberty of the individual. No Constitutional Lawyer can therefore object to it on the ground that it goes beyond the usual scope of Constitutional Law.

So far as the plan has been considered purely as a means of safeguarding individual liberty. But there is also another aspect of the plan which is worthy of note. It is an attempt to establish State Socialism without abrogating Parliamentary Democracy and without leaving its establishment to the will of a Parliamentary Democracy. Critics of State Socialism even its friends are bound to ask why make it a part of the Constitutional Law of the land? Why not leave it to the Legislature to bring it into being by the ordinary process of Law. The reason why it cannot be left to the ordinary Law is not difficult to understand. One essential condition for the success of a planned economy is that it must not be liable to suspension or abandonment. It must be permanent. The question is how this permanence can be secured. Obviously it cannot be secured under the form of Government called Parliamentary Democracy under the system of Parliamentary Democracy, the policy of the Legislature and of the Executive is the policy of the majority for the time being. Under the system of Parliamentary Democracy the majority in one election may be in favour of State Socialism in Industry and in Agriculture. At the next election the majority may be against it. The anti-State Socialism majority will use its Law-making power to undoing the work of the pro-State Socialism majority and the pro-State Socialism majority will use its Law-making power to doing over again what has been undone by their opponents. Those who want the economic structure of society to be modelled on State Socialism must realize that they cannot leave the fulfilment of so fundamental a purpose to the exigencies of ordinary Law which simple majorities—whose political fortunes are never determined by rational causes—have a right to make and unmake. For these reasons Political Democracy seems to be unsuited for the purpose.

What is the alternative? The alternative is Dictatorship. There is no doubt that Dictatorship can give the permanence which State Socialism requires as an essential condition for its fructification. There is however one fact against Dictatorship which must be faced. Those who believe in individual freedom strongly object to Dictatorship and insists upon Parliamentary Democracy as a proper form of Government for a Free Society. For they feel that freedom of the individual is possible only under Parliamentary Democracy and not under Dictatorship. Consequently those who want freedom are not prepared to give up Parliamentary Democracy as a form of Government. However, much they may be anxious to have State Socialism they will not be ready to exchange Parliamentary Democracy for Dictatorship even though the gain by such an exchange is the achievement of State Socialism. The problem therefore is to have State Socialism without Dictatorship, to have State Socialism with Parliamentary Democracy. The way out seems to be to retain Parliamentary Democracy and to prescribe State Socialism by the Law of the Constitution so that it will be beyond the reach of a Parliamentary majority to suspend, amend or abrogate it. It is only by this that one can achieve the triple object, namely, to establish socialism, retain Parliamentary Democracy and avoid Dictatorship.

The proposal marks a departure from the existing Constitutions whose aim is merely to prescribe the form of the political structure of society leaving the economic structure untouched. The result is that the political structure is completely set at naught by the forces which emerge from the economic structure which is at variance with the political structure. Those who want socialism with Parliamentary Democracy and without Dictatorship should welcome the proposal.

The soul of Democracy is the doctrine of one man, one value. Unfortunately, Democracy has attempted to give effect to this doctrine only so far as the political structure is concerned by adopting the rule of one man, one vote which is supposed to translate into fact the doctrine of one man, one value. It has left the economic structure to take the shape given to it by those who are in a position to mould it. This has happened because Constitutional Lawyers have been dominated by the antiquated conception that all that is necessary for a perfect Constitution for Democracy was to frame a Constitutional Law which would make Government responsible to the people and to prevent tyranny of the people by the Government. Consequently, almost all Laws of Constitution which relate to countries which are called Democratic stop with Adult Suffrage and Fundamental Right. They have never advanced to the conception that the Constitutional Law of Democracy must go beyond Adult Suffrage and Fundamental Rights. In other words, old time Constitutional Lawyers believed that the scope and function of Constitutional Law was to prescribe the shape and form of the political structure of society. They never realized that it was equally essential to prescribe the shape and form of the economic structure of society, if Democracy is to live up to its principle of one man, one value. Time has come to take a bold step and define both the economic structure as well as the political structure of society by the Law of the Constitution. All countries like India which are late-comers in the field of Constitution-making should not copy the faults of other countries. They should profit by the experience of their predecessors.

Article II—Section III

Clause 1

In the Government of India Acts of 1919 and 1935 the model that was adopted for framing the structure of the Executive in the Provinces and in the Centre was of the British type or what is called by Constitutional Lawyers Parliamentary Executive as opposed to the American type of Executive which in contradistinction of the British type is called Non-Parliamentary Executive. The question is whether the pattern for the Executive adopted in the two Acts should be retained or whether it should be abandoned and if so what model should be adopted in its place. Before giving final opinion on this issue it would be desirable to set out the special features of the British type of the Executive and the consequences that are likely to follow if it was applied to India.

The following may be taken to be the special features of British or the Parliamentary Executive:

1. It gives a party which has secured a majority in the Legislature the right to form a Government.
2. It gives the majority party the right to exclude from Government persons who do not belong to the Party.
3. The Government so formed continues in office only so long as it can command a majority in the Legislature. If it ceases to command a majority it is bound to resign either in favour of another Government formed out of the existing Legislature or in favour of a new Government formed out of a newly elected Legislature.

As to the consequences that would follow if the British System was applied to India the situation can be summed up in the following proposition:

1. The British System of Government by a Cabinet of the majority party rests on the premise that the majority is a political majority. In India the majority is a communal majority. No matter what social and political programme it may have the majority will retain its character of being a communal majority. Nothing can alter this fact. Given this fact it is clear that if the British System was copied it would result in permanently vesting Executive power in a Communal majority.
2. The British System of Government imposes no obligation upon the Majority Party to include in its cabinet the representatives of Minority Party. If applied to India the consequence will be obvious. It would make the majority community a governing class and the minority community a subject race. It would mean that a communal majority will be free to run the administration according to its own ideas of what is good for the minorities. Such a state of affairs could not be called democracy. It will have to be called imperialism.

In the light of these consequences it is obvious that the introduction of British type of the Executive will be full of menace to the life, liberty and pursuit of happiness of the minorities in general and of the Untouchables in particular.

The problem of the Untouchables is a formidable one for the Untouchables to face. The Untouchables are surrounded by a vast mass of Hindu population which is hostile to them and which is not ashamed of committing any inequity or atrocity against them. For a redress of these wrongs which are matters of daily occurrence, the Untouchables have to call in the aid of the administration. What is the character and composition of this administration? To be brief, the administration in India is completely in the bauds of the Hindus. It is their monopoly. From top to bottom it is controlled by them. There is no Department which is not dominated by them. They dominate the Police, the Magistracy and the Revenue Services, indeed any and every branch of the administration. The next point to remember is that the Hindus in the administration have the same positive anti-social and inimical attitude to the Untouchables which the Hindus outside the administration have. Their one aim is to discriminate against the Untouchables and to deny and deprive them not only of the benefits of Law, but also of the protection of the Law against tyranny and oppression. The result is that the Untouchables are placed between the Hindu population and the Hindu-ridden administration, the one committing wrong against them and the other protecting the wrong-doer, instead of helping the victims.

Against this background, what can Swaraj mean to the Untouchables? It can only mean one thing, namely, that while today it is only the administration that is in the hands of the Hindus, under Swaraj the Legislature and Executive will also be in the hands of the Hindus. It goes without, saying that such a Swaraj would aggravate the sufferings of the Untouchables. For, in addition to an hostile administration, there will be an indifferent Legislature and a callous Executive. The result will be that the administration unbridled in venom and in harshness, uncontrolled by the Legislature and the Executive, may pursue its policy of inequity towards the Untouchables without any curb. To put it differently, under Swaraj the Untouchables will have no way of escape from the destiny of degradation which Hindus and Hinduism have fixed for them.

These are special considerations against the introduction of the British System of Executive which have their origin in the interests of the minorities and the Scheduled Castes. But there is one general consideration which can be urged against the introduction of the British Cabinet System in India. The British Cabinet System has undoubtedly given the British people a very stable system of Government. Question is will it produce a stable Government in India? The chances are very slender. In view of the clashes of castes and creeds there is bound to be a plethora of parties and groups in the Legislature in India. If this happens it is possible, nay certain, that under the system of Parliamentary Executive like the one that prevails in England under which the Executive is bound to resign upon an adverse vote in the Legislature, India may suffer from instability of the Executive. For it is the easiest thing for groups to align and realign themselves at frequent intervals and for petty purposes and bring about the downfall of Government. The present solidarity of what are called the Major Parties cannot be expected to continue. Indeed as soon as the Problem of the British in India is solved the cement that holds these parties together will fall away. Constant overthrow of Government is nothing short of anarchy. The present Constitution has in it Section 93 which provides a remedy against it. But Section 93 would be out of place in the Constitution of a free India, Some substitute must therefore be found for Section 93.

Taking all these considerations together there is no doubt that the British type of the Executive is entirely unsuited to India.

The form of the Executive proposed in the clause is intended to serve the following purposes:

(i)   To prevent the majority from forming a Government without giving any opportunity to the minorities to have a say in the matter.
(ii) To prevent the majority from having exclusive control over administration and thereby make the tyranny of the minority by the majority possible.
(iii) To prevent the inclusion by the Majority Party in the Executive representatives of the minorities who have no confidence of the minorities.
(iv) To provide a stable Executive necessary for good and efficient administration.

The clause takes the American form of Executive as a model and adapts it to Indian conditions especially to the requirements of minorities. The form of the Executive suggested in the proposal cannot be objected to on the ground that it is against the principle of responsible government. Indians who are used to the English form of Executive forget that this is not the only form of democratic and responsible Government. The American form of Executive is an equally good type of democratic and responsible form of Government. There is also nothing objectionable in the proposal that a person should not be qualified to become a Minister merely because he is elected to the Legislature. The principle that a member of the Legislature before he is made a Minister should be chosen by his constituents was fully recognized by the British Constitution for over hundred years. A member of Parliament who was appointed a Minister had to submit himself for election before taking up his appointment. It was only lately given up. There ought therefore to be no objection to it on the ground that the proposals are not compatible with responsible Governments. The actual proposal is an improved edition of the American form of Government, for the reason that under it members of the Executive can sit in the Legislature and have a right to speak and answer questions.

Clause 2

The proposal cannot be controversial. The best remedy against tyranny and oppression by a majority against the minority is inquiry, publicity and discussion. This is what the safeguard provides for. A similar proposal was also recommended by the Sapru Committee.

Clause 3

Social boycott is always held over the heads of the Untouchables by the Caste Hindus as a sword of Damocles. Only the Untouchables know what a terrible weapon it is in the hands of the Hindus. Its effects and forms are well described in the Report made by a Committee appointed by the Government of Bombay in 1928 to investigate the grievances of the Depressed Classes and from which the following extracts are made. It illuminates the situation in a manner so simple that everybody can understand what tyranny the Hindus are able to practise upon the Untouchables. The Committee said:

> Although we have recommended various remedies to secure to the Depressed Classes their rights to all public utilities we fear that there will be difficulties in the way of their exercising them for a long time to come. The first difficulty is the fear of open violence against them by the orthodox classes. It must be noted that the Depressed Classes form a small minority in every village, oppose to which is a great majority of the orthodox who are bent on protecting their interests and dignity from any supposed invasion by the Depressed Classes at any cost. The danger of prosecution by the Police has put a limitation upon the use of violence by the orthodox classes and consequently such cases are rare.
>
> The second difficulty arises from the economic position in which the Depressed Classes are found today. The Depressed Classes have no economic independence in most parts of the Presidency. Some cultivate the lands of the orthodox classes as their tenants at will. Others live on their earnings as farm labourers employed by the orthodox classes and the rest subsist on the food or grain given to them by the orthodox classes in lieu of service rendered to them as village servants. We have heard of numerous instances where the

orthodox classes have used their economic power as a weapon against those Depressed Classes in their villages, when the latter have dared to exercise their rights, and have evicted them from their land, and stopped their employment and discontinued their remuneration as village servants. This boycott is often planned on such an extensive scale as to include the prevention of the Depressed Classes from using the commonly used paths and the stoppage of sale of the necessaries of life by the village Bania. According to the evidence, sometimes small causes suffice for the proclamation of a social boycott against the Depressed Classes. Frequently it follows on the exercise by the Depressed Classes of their right to use the common well, but cases have been by no mean rare where a stringent boycott has been proclaimed simply because a Depressed Class man has put on the sacred thread, has bought a piece of land, has put on good clothes or ornaments, or has carried a marriage procession with a bridegroom on the horse through the public street... ... .

Article II—Section IV

Part I—Clause I

There is nothing new in this clause. The right to representation in the Legislature is conceded by the Poona Pact. The only points that require to be reconsidered relate to (1) Quantum of Representation, (2) Weightage and (3) The System of Electorates.

(1) *Quantum*

The quantum of representation allowed to the Scheduled Castes by the Poona Pact is set out in Clause I of the Pact. The proportion set out in the Pact was fixed out of the balance of seats which remained after (i) the share of the other communities had been taken out; (ii) after weightage to other communities had been allotted, and (iii) after seats had been allocated to special interests. This allotment of seats to the Scheduled Castes has resulted in great injustice. The loss due to seats taken out as weightage and seats given to special interests ought not to have been thrown upon the Scheduled Castes. The allotment of those seats had already been made by the Communal Award long before the Poona Pact. It was therefore not possible then to rectify this injustice.

(2) *Weightage*

There is another injustice from which the Scheduled Castes have been suffering. It relates to their right to a share in weightage.

As one can see the right to weightage has become a matter of double controversy. One controversy is between the majority and the minorities, the other is a matter of controversy between the different minorities.

The first controversy relates to the principle of weightage. The majority insists that the minority has no right to representation in excess of the ratio of its population to the total population. Why this rule is insisted upon by the majority it is difficult to understand. Is it because the majority wants to establish its own claim to population ratio so that it may always remain as a majority and act as a majority? Or is it because of the fact that a minority no matter how much weightage was given to it must remain a minority and cannot alter the fact that the majority will always be able to impose its will upon it. The first ground leads to a complete negation of the basic conception of majority rule which if rightly understood means nothing more than a decision of the majority to which the minority has reconciled itself. This cannot be the intention of the majority. One must put a more charitable construction and assume that the argument on which the contention of the majority rests is the second and not the first. That a minority even with weightage will remain a minority has to be accepted in view of the insistence of a Communal Majority to remain a majority and to claim the privileges of a political majority which it is not. But surely there is a difference between a defeat which is a complete rout and a defeat which is almost victory though not a victory. Cricketers know what difference there is between the defeat of a team by a few runs, a defeat by a few wickets and a defeat by one whole innings. The defeat by one whole innings is a complete frustration which a defeat by a few runs is not. Such a frustration when it comes about in the political life of a minority depresses and demoralizes and crushes the spirit of the minority. This must be avoided at any price. Looked at from this point of view there is no doubt that the rule of population—ratio—representation insisted upon by the majority is wrong. What a minority needs is not more representation but effective representation.

And what is effective representation? Obviously the effectiveness of representation depends upon its being large enough to give the minority the sense of not being entirely overwhelmed by the majority. Representation according to population to a minority or to the minorities combined may be effective by reason of the fact that the population of a minority where there is only one or of the combined minorities where there are many is large enough to secure effective minority representation. But there may be cases where the population of a minority or of the minorities combined is too small to secure such effective representation if the population ratio of a minority is taken as an inflexible standard to determine its quantum of representation. To insist upon such a standard is to make mockery of the protection to the minority which is the purpose behind the right to representation which is accepted as the legitimate claim of a minority. In such cases weightage which is another name for deduction from the quantum of representation which is due to the majority on the basis of its population becomes essential and the majority if it wishes to be fair and honest must concede it. There can therefore be no quarrel over the principle of weightage. On this footing the controversy becomes restricted to the question, how is the magnitude of weightage to be determined? This obviously is a question of adjustment and not of principle.

There can therefore be no manner of objection to the principle of weightage. The demand for weightage is however a general demand of all the minorities and the Scheduled Castes must join them in it where the majority is too big. What is however wrong with the existing weightage is unequal distribution among the various minorities. At present, some minorities have secured a lion's share and some like the Untouchables have none. This wrong must be rectified by a distribution of the weightage on some intelligible principles.

(3) *Electorates*

1. The method of election to the seats allotted to the Scheduled Castes is set out in clauses (2) to (4) of the Poona Pact. It provides for two elections: (1) Primary election and (2) Final election. The Primary election is by a separate electorate of the Scheduled Castes. It is only a qualifying election and determines who is entitled to stand in the Final election on behalf of the Scheduled Castes for the seats reserved to them. The Final election is by a joint electorate in which both caste Hindus and the Scheduled Castes can vote and the final result is determined by their joint vote.

2. Clause 5 of the Poona Pact has limited the system of Primary election to ten years which means that any election taking place after 1947 will be by a system of joint electorates and reserved seats pure and simple.

3. Even if the Hindus agreed to extend the system of double election for a further period it will not satisfy the Scheduled Castes. There are two objections to the retention of the Primary election. Firstly, it does not help the Scheduled Castes to elect a man who is their best choice. As will be seen from Appendix III, the Scheduled Caste candidate who tops

the poll in the Primary election fails to succeed in the Final election and the Scheduled Caste candidate who fails in the Primary election tops the poll in the Final election. Secondly, the Primary election is for the most part a fiction and not a fact. In the last election, out of 151 seats reserved for the Scheduled Castes there were Primary elections only in 43. This is because it is impossible for the Scheduled Castes to bear the expenses of two elections—Primary and Final. To retain such a system is worse than useless.

4. Things will be much worse under the system of joint electorates and reserved seats which will hereafter become operative under the terms of the Poona Pact. This is no mere speculation. The last election has conclusively proved that the Scheduled Castes can be completely disfranchised in a joint electorate. As will be seen from the figures given in Appendix III, the Scheduled Caste candidates have not only been elected by Hindu votes when the intention was that they should be elected by Scheduled Caste votes but what is more the Hindus have elected those Scheduled Caste candidates who had failed in the Primary election. This is a complete disfranchisement of the Scheduled Castes. The main reason is to be found in the enormous disparity between the voting strength of the Scheduled Castes and the caste Hindus in most of the constituencies as may be seen from figures given in Appendix III. As the Simon Commission has observed, the device of the reserved seats ceases to be workable where the protected community constitutes an exceedingly small fraction of any manageable constituency. This is exactly the case of the Scheduled Castes. This disparity cannot be ignored. It will remain even under adult suffrage. That being the case, a fool-proof and a knave-proof method must be found to ensure real representation to the Scheduled Castes. Such a method must involve the abolition of—

   (i) the Primary election as a needless and heavy encumbrance; and
   (ii) the substitution of separate electorates.

5. One of the issues which has embittered the relations between the Hindu sand the Scheduled Castes in the political field is the issue of electorate. The Scheduled Castes are insisting upon separate electorates. The Hindus are equally insistent on opposing the demand. To arrive at a settlement on this issue—without which there can be no peace and amity between the Hindus and the Scheduled Castes—it is necessary to determine who is right and who is wrong and whether the opposition is based on rational grounds or is based on mere prejudice.

6. The grounds which are generally urged against the demand of the Scheduled Castes for separate electorates are:
   (i) that the Scheduled Castes are not a minority;
   (ii) that the Scheduled Castes are Hindus and therefore they cannot have separate electorates;
   (iii) that separate electorates will perpetuate untouchability;
   (iv) that separate electorates are anti-national; and
   (v) that separate electorates enables British Imperialism to influence the communities having separate electorates to act against the interests of the country.
7. Are these arguments valid?
   (i) To say that the Scheduled Castes are not a minority is to misunderstand the meaning of the word 'minority'. Separation in religion is not the only test of a minority. Nor is it a good and efficient test. Social discrimination constitutes the real test for determining whether a social group is or is not a minority. Even Mr. Gandhi thought it logical and practical to adopt this test in preference to that of religious separation. Following this test, Mr. Gandhi in an editorial under the heading 'The Fiction of Majority' in the *Harijan* dated 21st October 1939 has given his opinion that the Scheduled Castes are the only real minority in India.
   (ii) To argue that the Scheduled Castes are Hindus and therefore cannot demand separate electorates is to put the same argument in a different form. To make religious affiliation the determining factor for constitutional safeguards is to overlook the fact that the religious affiliation may be accompanied by an intense degree of social separation and discrimination. The belief that separate electorates go with separation in religion arises from the fact that those minorities who have been given separate electorates happen to be religious minorities. This, however, is not correct. Muslims are given separate electorates not because they are different from Hindus in point of religion. They are given separate electorates because—and this is the fundamental fact—the social relations between the Hindus and the Musalmans are marked by social discrimination. To put the point in a somewhat different manner, the nature of the electorates is determined not by reference to religion but by reference to social considerations. That it is social considerations and not religious affiliation or disaffiliation which is

accepted as the basis of determining the nature of the electorates is best illustrated by the arrangements made under the Government of India Act (1935) for the Christian community in India. The Christian community is divided into three sections—Europeans, Anglo-Indians and Indian Christians. In spite of the fact that they all belong to the same religion, each section has a separate electorate. This shows that what is decisive is not religious affiliation but social separation.

(iii) To urge that separate electorates prevent solidarity between the Untouchables and the Caste Hindus is the result of confused thinking. Elections take place once in five years. Assuming there were joint electorates, it is difficult to understand how social solidarity between the Hindus and the Untouchables can be promoted by their devoting one day for voting together when out of the rest of the five years they are leading severally separate lives? Similarly, assuming that there were separate electorates it is difficult to understand how one day devoted to separate voting in the course of five years can make for greater separation than what already exist? Or contrarywise, how can one day in five years devoted to separate voting prevent those who wish to work for their union from carrying out heir purposes. To make it concrete, how can separate electorate for the Untouchables prevent inter-marriage or inter-dining being introduced between them and the Hindus? It is therefore futile to say that separate electorates for the Untouchables will perpetuate separation between them and the Hindus.

(iv) To insist that separate electorates create anti-national spirit is contrary to experience. The Sikh have separate electorates. But no one can say that the Sikhs are anti-national. The Muslims have had separate electorates right from 1909. Mr. Jinnah had been elected by separate electorates. Yet, Mr. Jinnah was the apostle of Indian Nationalism up to 1935. The Indian Christians have separate electorates. Nonetheless a good lot of them have shown their partiality to the Congress if they have not been actually returned on the Congress ticket. Obviously, nationalism and anti-nationalism have nothing to do with the electoral system. They are the result of extra electoral forces.

(v) This argument has no force. It is nothing but escapism. Be that as it may, with free India any objection to separate electorates on such a ground must vanish.

8. The reason why the arguments advanced by the opponents of separate electorates do not stand the scrutiny of logic and experience is due entirely to the fact that their approach to the subject is fundamentally wrong. It is wrong in two respects:

   (i) They fail to realize that the system of electorates has nothing to do with the religious nexus or communal nexus. It is nothing but a mechanism to enable a minority to return its true representative to the Legislature. Being a mechanism for the protection of a minority it follows that whether the electorate should be joint or separate must be left to be determined by the minority.

   (ii) They fail to make any distinction between the demand for separate electorates by a majority community and a similar demand made by a minority community. A majority community has no right to demand separate electorates. The reason is simple. A right by a majority community to demand separate electorates is tantamount to a right to establish the Government of the majority community over the minority community without the consent of the minority. This is contrary to the well-established doctrine of democracy that government must be with the consent of the governed. No such evil consequence follows from the opposite principle namely that a minority community is entitled to determine the nature of the electorates suited to its interests, because there is no possibility of the minority being placed in a position to govern the majority.

9. A correct attitude towards the whole question rests on the following axioms:

   (i) The system of electorates being a device for the protection of the minority, the issue whether the electoral system should be the joint electorate or separate electorate must be left to the wishes of the minority. If it is large enough to influence the majority it will choose joint electorates. If it is too small for the purpose, it will prefer separate electorates for fear of being submerged.

   (ii) The majority, being in a position to rule can have no voice in the determination of the system of electorates. If the minority wants joint electorates, the majority must submit itself to joint electorates. If the minority decides to have separate electorates for itself the majority cannot refuse to grant them. In other words, the majority must look to the decision of the minority and abide by it.

Part I—Clause 2

This demand may appear to be outside the Poona Pact in as much as the Poona Pact made no provision for it. This would not be correct. As a matter of fact, if no provision was made, it was because there was no need to make such a provision. This was due to two reasons: *Firstly,* it was due to the fact that at the time when the Poona Pact was made no community was guaranteed by Law a specific quantum of representation in Executive, *Secondly,* the representation of the communities in the Executive was left to a convention which the Governor by his instrument of instructions was required to see observed. Experience has shown that the quantum of representation of the Scheduled Castes in the Executive should now be fixed.

Part I—Clause 3

This is not a new demand. Clause 8 of the Poona Pact guarantees to the Scheduled Castes fair representation in Public Services. It does not, however, define the quantum of representation. The demand has been admitted by the Government of India as legitimate and even the quantum of representation has been defined. All that remains is to give it a statutory basis.

Part II—Clause 1

This is not a new demand. Clause 9 of Poona Pact guarantees that an adequate sum shall be earmarked for the education of the Scheduled Castes. It does not define the quantum. All that the demand does is to define the quantum of liability the State should take. In this connection reference may be made to Section 83 of the Government of India Act, 1935, which relates to the education of the Anglo-Indians and Europeans and to the grants made to the Aligarh and Benaras Hindu Universities by the Central Government.

Part II—Clause 2

This a new demand but is justified by circumstances. At present, the Hindus live in the village and the Untouchables live in the Ghettoes. The object is to free the Untouchables from the thraldom of the Hindus. So long as the present arrangement continues it is impossible for the Untouchables either to free themselves from the yoke of the Hindus or to get rid of their Untouchability. It is the close knit association of the Untouchables with the Hindus living in the same villages which marks them out as Untouchables and which enables the Hindus to identify them as being Untouchables. India is admittedly a land of villages and so long as the village system provides an easy method of marking out and identifying the Untouchables, the Untouchable has no escape from Untouchability. It is the system of the Village plus the Ghetto which perpetuates Untouchability and the Untouchables therefore demand that the nexus should be broken and the Untouchables who are as a matter of fact socially separate should be made separate geographically and territorially also, and be settled into separate villages exclusively of Untouchables in which the distinction of the high and the low and of Touchable and Untouchable will find no place.

The second reason for demanding separate settlements arises out of the economic position of the Untouchables in the villages. That their condition is most pitiable no one will deny. They are a body of landless labourers who are entirely dependent upon such employment as the Hindus may choose to give them and on such wages as the Hindus may find it profitable to pay. In the villages in which they five they cannot engage in any trade or occupation, for owing to Untouchability no Hindu will deal with them. It is therefore obvious that there is no way of earning a living which is open to the Untouchables so long as they live in a Ghetto as a dependent part of the Hindu village.

This economic dependence has also other consequences besides the condition of poverty and degradation which proceeds from it. The Hindu has a Code of life, which is part of his religion. This Code of life gives him many privileges and heaps upon the Untouchable many indignities which are incompatible with the dignity and sanctity of human life. The Untouchables all over India are fighting against the indignities and injustices which the Hindus in the name of their religion have heaped upon them. A perpetual war is going on every day in every village between the Hindus and the Untouchables. It does not see the light of the day. The Hindu Press is not prepared to give it publicity lest it should injure the cause of their freedom in the eyes of the world. The existence of a grim struggle between the Touchables and the Untouchables is however a fact. Under the village system the Untouchable has found himself greatly handicapped in his struggle for free and honourable life. It is a contest between the Hindus who are economically and socially strong and the Untouchables who are economically poor and numerically small. That the Hindus most often succeed in suppressing the Untouchables is due to many causes. The Hindus have the Police and the Magistracy on their side. In a quarrel between the Untouchables and the Hindus the Untouchables will never get protection from the Police and justice from the Magistrate. The Police and the Magistracy naturally love their class more than their duty. But the chief weapon in the armoury of the Hindus is economic power which they possess over the poor Untouchables living in the village. The proposal may be dubbed escapism. But the only alternative is perpetual slavery.

Part III—Clause 1

No country which has the problem of Communal majority and Communal minority is without some kind of an arrangement whereby they agree to share political power. South Africa has such an understanding. So has Canada. The arrangement for sharing political power between the English and the French in Canada is carried to the minutes office. In referring to this fact Mr. Porritt (1918: 382–4) in his book on the *Evolution of the Dominion of Canada* says:

Conditions at Ottawa, partly due to race and language, and partly to long-prevailing ideas as to the distribution of all government patronage, have militated against the Westminster precedent of continuing a member in the chair for two or three parliaments, regardless of the fortunes of political parties at general elections. There is a new speaker at Ottawa for each new House of Commons; and it has long been a custom that when one political party continues in power for two or three parliaments, if the speaker in one parliament is of British extraction the next one shall be a French-Canadian. It is a rule also that the offices of speaker and of deputy speaker can at no time be held by men of the same race. If the speaker is a French-Canadian, the deputy speaker, who is also Chairman of committees, must be an English-speaking Canadian; for the rule of the House is that the member elected to serve as deputy speaker shall be required to possess the full and practical knowledge of the language which is not that of the speaker for the time being.

The clerkship and the assistant clerkship of the House, and the offices of sergeant-at-arms and deputy sergeant-at-arms—all appointive as distinct from elective offices—are, by usage, also similarly divided between the two races.

Nearly all the offices, important and unimportant, connected with parliament, with the Senate as well as with the House, are distributed in accordance with these rules or usages. A roll call of the staffs of the two Houses, including even the boys in knicker-bockers who act as pages, would contain the names of almost as many French-Canadians as Canadians of British ancestry.

The rules and usages by virtue of which this distribution of offices is made are older than Confederation. They date back to the early years of the United Provinces, when Quebec and Ontario elected exactly the same number of members to the Legislature, and when these were the only provinces in the union.

Quebec today elects only 65 of the 234 members of the House of Commons. Its population is not one-fourth of the population of the Dominion. Its contribution to Dominion revenues does not exceed one-sixth. But an equal division of the offices of the House of Commons is regarded by Quebec as necessary to the preservation of its rights and privileges; and so long as each political party, when it is in power, is dependent on support from French-Canada, it will be nearly as difficult to ignore the claim of Quebec to these parliamentary honours and offices as it would be to repeal the clause in the British North America Act that safeguards the separate schools system.

Unfortunately for the minorities in India, Indian Nationalism has developed a new doctrine which may be called the Divine Right of the Majority to rule the minorities according to the wishes of the majority. Any claim for the sharing of power by the minority is called communalism while the monopolizing of the whole power by the majority is called Nationalism. Guided by such a political philosophy the majority is not prepared to allow the minorities to share political power nor is it willing to respect any convention made in that behalf as is evident from their repudiation of the obligation (to include representatives of the minorities in the cabinet) contained in the Instrument of Instructions issued to the Governors in the Government of India Act of 1935. Under these circumstances there is no way left but to have the rights of the Scheduled Castes embodied in the Constitution.

Part III—Clause 2

This is not a new demand. It replaces Clause 6 of the Poona Pact which provides that the system of representation for the Scheduled Castes by reserved seats shall continue until determined by mutual consent between the communities concerned in the settlement. Since there is no safe method of ascertaining the will of the Scheduled Castes as to how to amend and alter the safeguards provided for them it is necessary to formulate a plan which will take the place of Clause 6 of the Pact. Provisions having similar objectives to those contained in the proposal exist in the Constitutions of Australia, America, and South Africa.

In dealing with a matter of this sort two considerations have to be borne in mind. One is that it is not desirable to rule out the possibility of a change in the safeguards being made in the future by the parties concerned. On the other hand it is by no means desirable to incessant struggle over their revision. If the new Union and State Legislatures are to address themselves successfully to their responsibilities set out in the preamble it is desirable that they should not be distracted by the acute contentions between religions and classes which questions of change in the safeguards are bound to raise. Hence a period of twenty-five years has been laid down before any change could be considered.

Part IV

The object of this provision is to see that whatever safeguards are provided for the Scheduled Castes in British India are also provided for the Scheduled Castes in the Indian States. The provision lays down that an Indian State seeking admission to the Union shall have to satisfy that its Constitution contains these safeguards.

Part V—Interpretation

Whether the Scheduled Castes are a minority or not has become a matter of controversy. The purpose of First Provision to set this controversy at rest. The Scheduled Castes are in a worst position as compared to any other minority in India. As such they required and deserve much more protection than any other minority does. The least one can do is to treat them as a minority.

The purpose of Second Provision is to remove the provincial bar. There is no reason why a person who belongs to Scheduled Castes in one Province should lose the benefit of political privileges given by the Constitution merely because he happens to change his domicile.

14 Draft Constitution— Discussion (4 November 1948– 25 November 1949)

A BRIEF SKETCH ABOUT THE DOCUMENT

While presenting the draft Constitution, Ambedkar accepted that this document is bulky compared with any other Constitution. He opined that there have to be criticisms but few are based on misunderstanding or inadequate understanding. However, he tried to respond to the maximum of those. Some of the points of criticism were: (1) Good part taken from the Government of India Act, 1935; (2) No part includes ancient Indian polity; (3) Safeguards for Minorities; (4) Fundamental rights not made absolute but have conditions; (5) Inclusion of Directive Principles of State Policy; (6) Few consider Centre too strong while others too weak; and, (7) Complex amendment procedure, etc. He responded to all these questions and asserted that the kind of democratic system that has been proposed by the drafting committee is not new to India but was prevalent in the Buddhist Bhikshu Sanghas including rule on Motions, Quorum, Whip, etc. Finally he accepted that with the Constitution coming into force we shall enter the life of contradictions, wherein there will be political values on the one hand and the social and economic values on the other. The excerpts in this chapter are taken from BAWS, Volume 12, 1993 (pp. 49–70, 351–3, 1206–18).

Mr. President: I think we shall now proceed with the discussion. I call upon the Honourable Dr. Ambedkar to move his motion.

The Honourable Dr. B. R. Ambedkar (Bombay: General): Mr. President, Sir, I introduce the Draft Constitution as settled by the Drafting Committee and move that it be taken into consideration.

The Drafting Committee was appointed by a Resolution passed by the Constituent Assembly on August 29, 1947.

The Drafting Committee was in effect charged with the duty of preparing a Constitution in accordance with the decisions of the Constituent Assembly on the reports made by the various Committees appointed by it such as the Union Powers Committee, the Union Constitution Committee, the Provincial Constitution Committee and the Advisory Committee on Fundamental Rights, Minorities, Tribal Areas, etc. The Constituent Assembly had also directed that in certain matters the provisions contained in the Government of India Act, 1935, should be followed. Except on points which are referred to in my letter of the 21st February 1948 in which I have referred to the departures made and alternatives suggested by the Drafting Committee, I hope the Drafting Committee will be found to have faithfully carried out the directions given to it.

The Draft Constitution as it has emerged from the Drafting Committee is a formidable document. It contains 315 Articles and 8 Schedules. It must be admitted that the Constitution of no country could be found to be so bulky as the Draft Constitution. It would be difficult for those who have not been through it to realize its salient and special features.

The Draft Constitution has been before the public for eight months. During this long time friends, critics and adversaries have had more than sufficient time to express their reactions to the provisions contained in it. I dare say that some of them are based on misunderstanding and inadequate understanding of the Articles. But there the criticisms are and they have to be answered.

For both these reasons it is necessary that on a motion for consideration I should draw your attention to the special features of the Constitution and also meet the criticism that has been leveled against it.

Before I proceed to do so I would like to place on the table of the House Reports of three Committees appointed by the Constituent Assembly (1) Report of the Committee on Chief Commissioners Provinces (2) Report of the Expert Committee on Financial Relations between the

Union and the States, and (3) Report of the Advisory Committee on Tribal Areas, which came too late to be considered by that Assembly though copies of them have been circulated to Members of the Assembly. As these reports and the recommendations made therein have been considered by the Drafting Committee it is only proper that the House should formally be placed in possession of them.

Turning to the main question. A student of Constitutional Law, if a copy of a Constitution is placed in his hands, is sure to ask two questions. Firstly, what is the form of Government that is envisaged in the Constitution; and secondly, what is the form of the Constitution? For these are the two crucial matters which every Constitution has to deal with. I will begin with the first of the two questions.

In the Draft Constitution there is placed at the head of the Indian Union a functionary who is called the President of the Union. The title of this functionary reminds one of the President of the United States. But beyond identity of names there is nothing in common between the forms of government prevalent in America and the form of Government proposed under the Draft Constitution. The American form of Government is called the Presidential system of Government. What the Draft Constitution proposes is the Parliamentary system. The two are fundamentally different.

Under the Presidential system of America, the President is the Chief Head of the Executive. The administration is vested in him. Under the Draft Constitution the President occupies the same position as the King under the English Constitution. He is the head of the State but not of the Executive. He represents the Nation but does not rule the Nation. He is the symbol of the nation. His place in the administration is that of a ceremonial device on a seal by which the nation's decisions are made known. Under the American Constitution the President has under him Secretaries in charge of different Departments. In like manner the President of the Indian Union will have under him Ministers in charge of different Departments of administration. Here again there is a fundamental difference between the two. The President of the United States is not bound to accept any advice tendered to him by any of his Secretaries. The President of the Indian Union will be generally bound by the advice of his Ministers. He can do nothing contrary to their advice nor can he do anything without their advice. The President of the United States can dismiss any Secretary at any time. The President of the Indian Union has no power to do so, so long as his Ministers command a majority in Parliament.

The Presidential system of America is based upon the separation of the Executive and the Legislature. So that the President and his Secretaries cannot be members of the Congress. The Draft Constitution does not recognize this doctrine. The Ministers under the Indian Union are members of Parliament. Only members of Parliament can become Ministers. Ministers have the same rights as other members of Parliament, namely, that they can sit in Parliament, take part in debates and vote in its proceedings. Both systems of Government are of course democratic and the choice between the two is not very easy. A democratic executive must satisfy two conditions—(1) It must be a stable executive and (2) it must be a responsible executive. Unfortunately it has not been possible so far to devise a system which can ensure both in equal degree. You can have a system which can give you more stability but less responsibility or you can have a system which gives you more responsibility but less stability. The American and the Swiss systems give more stability but less responsibility. The British system on the other hand gives you more responsibility but less stability. The reason for this is obvious. The American Executive is a non-Parliamentary Executive which means that it is not dependent for its existence upon a majority in the Congress, while the British system is a Parliamentary Executive which means that it is dependent upon a majority in Parliament. Being a non-Parliamentary Executive, the Congress of the United States cannot dismiss the Executive. A Parliamentary Government must resign the moment it loses the confidence of a majority of members of Parliament. Looking at it from the point of view of responsibility, a non-Parliamentary Executive being independent of Parliament tends to be less responsible to the Legislature, while a Parliamentary Executive being more dependent upon a majority in Parliament become more responsible. The Parliamentary system differs from a non-Parliamentary system in as much as the former is more responsible than the latter but they also differ as to the time and agency for assessment of their responsibility. Under the non-Parliamentary system, such as the one that exists in the U.S.A., the assessment of the responsibility of the Executive is periodic. It takes place once in two years. It is done by the Electorate. In England, where the Parliamentary system prevails, the assessment of responsibility of the executive is both daily and periodic. The daily assessment is done by members of Parliament, through Questions, Resolutions, No confidence motions, Adjournment motions and Debates on Addresses. Periodic assessment is done by the Electorate at the time of the election which may take place every five years or earlier. The daily assessment of responsibility which is not available under the American system is, it is felt, far more effective than the periodic assessment and far more necessary in a country like India. The Draft Constitution in recommending the Parliamentary system of Executive has preferred more responsibility to more stability... ... ...

As to the accusation that the Draft Constitution has produced a good part of the provisions of the Government of India Act, 1935, I make no apologies. There is nothing to be ashamed of in borrowing. It involves no plagiarism. Nobody holds any patent rights in the fundamental ideas of a Constitution. What I am sorry about is that the provisions taken from the Government of India Act, 1935, relate mostly to the details of administration. I agree that administrative details should have no place in the Constitution. I wish very much that the Drafting Committee could see its way to avoid their inclusion in the Constitution. But this is to be said on the necessity which justifies their inclusion. Grote, the historian of Greece, has said that:

> The diffusion of constitutional morality, not merely among the majority of any community but throughout the whole, is the indispensable condition of government at once free and peaceable; since even any powerful and obstinate minority may render the working of a free institution impracticable, without being strong enough to conquer ascendency for themselves.

By constitutional morality Grote meant 'a paramount reverence for the forms of the Constitution, enforcing obedience to authority acting under and within these forms yet combined with the habit of open speech, of action subject only to definite legal control, and unrestrained censure of those very authorities as to all their public acts combined too with a perfect confidence in the bosom of every citizen amidst the bitterness of party contest that the forms of the Constitution will not be less sacred in the eyes of his opponents than in his own.' (Hear, hear.)

While everybody recognizes the necessity of the diffusion of the Constitutional morality for the peaceful working of a democratic Constitution, there are two things interconnected with it which are not, unfortunately, generally recognized. One is that the form of administration has a close connection with the form of the Constitution. The form of the administration must be appropriate to and in the same sense as the form of the Constitution. The other is that it is perfectly possible to prevent the Constitution, without changing its form by merely changing the form of the administration and to make it inconsistent and opposed to the spirit of the Constitution. It follows that it is only where people are saturated with Constitutional morality such as the one described by Grote, the historian that one can take the risk of omitting from the Constitution details of administration and leaving it for the Legislature to prescribe them. The question is, can we presume such a diffusion of Constitutional morality? Constitutional morality is not a natural sentiment. It has to be cultivated. We must realize that our people have yet to learn it. Democracy in India is only a top-dressing on an Indian soil, which is essentially undemocratic.

In these circumstances it is wiser not to trust the Legislature to prescribe forms of administration. This is the justification for incorporating them in the Constitution.

Another criticism against the Draft Constitution is that no part of it represents the ancient polity of India. It is said that the new Constitution should have been drafted on the ancient Hindu model of a State and that instead of incorporating Western theories the new Constitution should have been raised and built upon village Panchayats and District Panchayats. There are others who have taken a more extreme view. They do not want any Central or Provincial Governments. They just want India to contain so many village Governments. The love of the intellectual Indians for the village community is of course infinite if not pathetic *(laughter)*. It is largely due to the fulsome praise bestowed upon it by Metcalfe who described them as little republics having nearly everything that they want within themselves, and almost independent of any foreign relations. The existence of these village communities each one forming a separate little State in itself has according to Metcalfe contributed more than any other cause to the preservation of the people of India, through all the revolutions and changes which they have suffered, and is in a high degree conducive to their happiness and to the enjoyment of a great portion of the freedom and independence. No doubt the village communities have lasted where nothing else lasts. But those who take pride in the village communities do not care to consider what little part they have played in the affairs and the destiny of the country; and why? Their part in the destiny of the country has been well described by Metcalfe himself who says:

Dynasty after dynasty tumbles down. Revolution succeeds to revolution. Hindoo, Pathan, Mogul, Maharatha, Sikh, English, are all masters in turn but the village communities remain the same. In times of trouble they arm and fortify themselves. A hostile army passes through the country. The village communities collect their little cattle within their walls and let the enemy pass unprovoked.

Such is the part the village communities have played in the history of their country. Knowing this, what pride can one feel in them? That they have survived through all vicissitudes may be tact. But mere survival has no value. The question is on what plane they have survived. Surely on a low, on a selfish level. I hold that these village republics have been the ruination of India. I am therefore surprised that those who condemn Provincialism and communalism should come forward as champions of the village. What is the village but a sink of localism, a den of ignorance, narrow-mindedness and communalism? I am glad that the Draft Constitution has discarded the village and adopted the individual as its unit.

The Draft Constitution is also criticized because of the safeguards it provides for minorities. In this, the Drafting Committee has no responsibility. It follows the decisions of the Constituent Assembly. Speaking for myself, I have no doubt that the Constituent Assembly has done wisely in providing such safeguards for minorities as it has done, in this country both the minorities and the majorities have followed a wrong path. It is wrong for the majority to deny the existence of minorities. It is equally wrong for the minorities to perpetuate themselves. A solution must be found which will serve a double purpose. It must recognize the existence of the minorities to start with. It must also be such that it will enable majorities and minorities to merge some day into one. The solution proposed by the Constituent Assembly is to be welcomed because it is a solution which serves this two-fold purpose. To diehards who have developed a kind of fanaticism against minority protection I would like to say two things. One is that minorities are an explosive force which, if it erupts, can blow up the whole fabric of the State. The history of Europe bears ample and appalling testimony to this fact. The other is that the minorities in India have agreed to place their existence in the hands of the majority. In the history of negotiations for preventing the partition of Ireland, Redmond said to Carson 'ask for any safeguard you like for the Protestant minority but let us have a United Ireland.' Carson's reply was 'Damn your safeguards, we don't want to be ruled by you.' No minority in India has taken this stand. They have loyally accepted the rule of the majority which is basically a communal majority and not a political majority. It is for the majority to realize its duty not to discriminate against minorities. Whether the minorities will continue or will vanish must depend upon this habit of the majority. The moment the majority loses the habit of discriminating against the minority, the minorities can have no ground to exist. They will vanish.

The most criticized part of the Draft Constitution is that which relates to Fundamental Rights. It is said that Article 13 which defines fundamental rights is riddled with so many exceptions that the exceptions have eaten up the rights altogether. It is condemned as a kind of deception. In the opinion of the critics Fundamental Rights are not Fundamental Rights unless they are also absolute rights. The critics rely on the Constitution of the United States and to the Bill of Rights embodied in the first ten Amendments to that Constitution in support of their contention. It is said that the Fundamental Rights in the American Bill of Rights are real because they are not subjected to limitations or exceptions.

I am sorry to say that the whole of the criticism about fundamental rights is based upon a misconception. In the first place, the criticism in so far as it seeks to distinguish fundamental rights from non-fundamental rights is not sound. It is incorrect to say that fundamental rights are absolute while non-fundamental rights are not absolute. The real distinction between the two is that non-fundamental rights are created by agreement between parties while fundamental rights are the gift of the law. Because fundamental rights are the gift of the State it does not follow that the State cannot qualify them.

In the second place, it is wrong to say that fundamental rights in America are absolute. The difference between the position under the American Constitution and the Draft Constitution is one of form and not of substance. That the fundamental rights in America are not absolute rights is beyond dispute. In support of every exception to the fundamental rights set out in the Draft Constitution one can refer to at least one judgment of the United States Supreme Court. It would be sufficient to quote one such judgment of the Supreme Court in justification of the limitation on the right of free speech contained in Article 13 of the Draft Constitution. In *Gitlow Vs. New York* in which the issue was the constitutionality of a New York 'criminal anarchy' law which purported to punish utterances calculated to bring about violent change, the Supreme Court said:

> It is a fundamental principle, long established, that the freedom of speech and of the press, which is secured by the Constitution, does not confer an absolute right to speak or publish, without responsibility, whatever one

may choose, or an unrestricted and unbridled license that gives immunity for every possible use of language and prevents the punishment of those who abuse this freedom.

It is therefore wrong to say that the fundamental rights in America are absolute, while those in the Draft Constitution are not.

It is agreed that if any fundamental rights require qualification, it is for the Constitution itself to qualify them as is done in the Constitution of the United States and where it does not do so, it should be left to be determined by the Judiciary upon a consideration of all the relevant considerations. All this, I am sorry to say, is a complete misrepresentation, if not a misunderstanding of the American Constitution. The American Constitution does nothing of the kind. Except in one matter, namely the right of assembly, the American Constitution does not itself impose any limitations upon the fundamental rights guaranteed to the American citizens. Nor is it correct to say that the American Constitution leaves it to the Judiciary to impose limitations on fundamental rights. The right to impose limitations belongs to the Congress. The real position is different from what is assumed by the critics. In America, the fundamental rights as enacted by the Constitution were no doubt absolute. Congress, however, soon found that it was absolutely essential to qualify these fundamental rights by limitations. When the question arose as to the constitutionality of these limitations before the Supreme Court, it was contended that the Constitution gave no power to the United States Congress to impose such limitation, the Supreme Court invented the doctrine of police power and refuted the advocates of absolute fundamental rights by the argument that every State has inherent in its police power which is not required to be conferred on it expressly by the Constitution. To use the language of the Supreme Court in the case I have already referred to, it said:

> That a State in the exercise of its police power may punish those who abuse this freedom by utterances inimical to the public welfare, tending to corrupt public morals, incite to crime or disturb the public peace, is not open to question.

What the Draft Constitution has done is that instead of formulating fundamental rights in absolute terms and depending upon our Supreme Court to come to the rescue of Parliament by inventing the doctrine of police power, it permits the State directly to impose limitations upon the fundamental rights. There is really no difference in the result. What one does directly the other does indirectly. In both cases, the fundamental rights are not absolute.

In the Draft Constitution the Fundamental Rights are followed by what are called 'Directive Principles'. It is a novel feature in a Constitution framed for Parliamentary Democracy. The only other constitution framed for Parliamentary Democracy which embodies such principles is that of the Irish Free State. These Directive Principles have also come up for criticism. It is said that they are only pious declarations. They have no binding force. This criticism is of course superfluous. The Constitution itself says so in so many words.

If it is said that the Directive Principles have no legal force behind them, I am prepared to admit it. But I am not prepared to admit that they have no sort of binding force at all. Nor am I prepared to concede that they are useless because they have no binding force in law.

The Directive Principles are like the Instrument of Instructions which were issued to the Governor-General and to the Governors of the Colonies and to those of India by the British Government under the 1935 Act. Under the Draft Constitution it is proposed to issue such instruments to the President and to the Governors. The texts of these Instruments of Instructions will be found in Schedule IV of the Constitution. What are called Directive Principles is merely another name for Instrument of Instructions. The only difference is that they are instructions to the Legislature and the Executive. Such a thing is to my mind to be welcomed. Wherever there is a grant of power in general terms for peace, order and good government, it is necessary that it should be accompanied by instructions regulating its exercise.

The inclusion of such instructions in a Constitution such as is proposed in the Draft becomes justifiable for another reason. The Draft Constitution as framed only provides a machinery for the government of the country. It is not a contrivance to install any particular party in power as has been done in some countries. Who should be in power is left to be determined by the people as it must be, if the system is to satisfy the tests of democracy. But whoever captures power will not be free to do what he likes with it. In the exercise of it, he will have to respect these instruments of instructions which are called Directive Principles. He cannot ignore them. He may not have to answer for their breach in a Court of Law. But he will certainly have to answer for them before the electorate at election time. What great value these directive principles possess will be realized better when the forces of right contrive to capture power.

Thus it has no binding force is no argument against their inclusion in the Constitution. There may be a difference of opinion as to the exact place they should be given in the Constitution. I agree that it is somewhat odd that provisions which do not carry positive obligations should be placed in the midst of provisions which do carry positive obligations. In my judgment their proper place is in Schedules III A & IV which contain Instrument of Instructions to the President and the Governors. For, as I have said, they are really Instruments of Instructions to the Executive and the Legislatures as to how they should exercise their powers. But that is only a matter of arrangement.

Some critics have said that the Centre is too strong. Others have said that it must be made stronger. The Draft Constitution has struck a balance. However much you may deny powers to the Centre, it is difficult to prevent the Centre from becoming strong. Conditions in modern world are such that centralization of powers is inevitable. One has only to consider the growth of the Federal Government in the U.S.A. which, notwithstanding the very limited powers given to it by the Constitution has outgrown its former self and has overshadowed and eclipsed the State Governments. This is due to modern conditions. The same conditions are sure to operate on the Government of India and nothing that one can do will help to prevent it from being strong. On the other hand, we must resist the tendency to make it stronger. It cannot chew more than it can digest. Its strength must be commensurate with its weight. It would be a folly to make it so strong that it may fall by its own weight.

The Draft Constitution is criticized for having one sort of constitutional relations between the Centre and the Provinces and another sort of constitutional relations between the Centre and the Indian States. The Indian States are not bound to accept the whole list of subjects included in the Union List but only those which come under Defence, Foreign Affairs and Communications. They are not bound to accept subjects included in the Concurrent List. They are not bound to accept the State List contained in the Draft Constitution. They are free to create their own Constituent Assemblies and to frame their own constitutions. All this, of course, is very unfortunate and I submit quite indefensible.

This disparity may even prove dangerous to the efficiency of the State. So long as the disparity exists, the Centre's authority over all-India matters may lose its efficacy. For, power is no power if it cannot be exercised in all cases and in all places. In a situation such as may be created by war, such limitations on the exercise of vital powers in some areas may bring the whole life of the State in complete jeopardy. What is worse is that the Indian States under the Draft Constitution are permitted to maintain their own armies. I regard this as a most retrograde and harmful provision which may lead to the break-up of the unity of India and the overthrow of the Central Government. The Drafting Committee, if I am not misrepresenting its mind, was not at all happy over this matter. They wished very much that there was uniformity between the Provinces; and the Indian States in their constitutional relationship with the Centre. Unfortunately, they could do nothing to improve matters. They were bound by the decisions of the Constituent Assembly, and the Constituent Assembly in its turn was bound by the agreement arrived at between the two negotiating Committees.

But we may take courage from what happened in Germany. The German Empire as founded by Bismark in 1870 was a composite State, consisting of 25 units. Of these 25 units, 22 were monarchical States and 3 were republican city States. This distinction, as we all know, disappeared in the course of time and Germany became one land with one people living under one Constitution. The process of the amalgamation of the Indian States is going to be much quicker than it has been in Germany. On the 15th August 1947 we had 600 Indian States in existence. Today by the integration of the Indian States with Indian Provinces or merger among themselves or by the Centre having taken them as Centrally Administered Areas there have remained some 20/30 States as viable States. This is a very rapid process and progress. I appeal to those States that remain to fall in line with the Indian Provinces and to become full units of the Indian Union on the same terms as the Indian Provinces. They will thereby give the Indian Union the strength it needs. They will save themselves the bother of starting their own Constituent Assemblies and drafting their own separate Constitution and they will lose nothing that is of value to them.

I feel hopeful that my appeal will not go in vain and that before the Constitution is passed, we will be able to wipe off the differences between the Provinces and the Indian States.

Some critics have taken objection to the description of India in Article 1 of the Draft Constitution as a Union of States. It is said that the correct phraseology should be a Federation of States. It is true that South Africa which is a unitary State is described as a Union. But Canada which is a Federation is also called a Union. Thus the description of India as a Union, though its constitution is Federal, does no violence to usage. But what is important is that the use of the word Union is deliberate. I do not know why the word 'Union' was used in the Canadian Constitution. But I can tell you why the Drafting Committee has used it. The Drafting Committee wanted to make it clear that though India was to be a Federation, the Federation was not the result of an agreement by the States to join in a Federation and that the Federation not being the result of an agreement no State has the right to secede from it. The Federation is a Union because it is indestructible. Though the country and the people may be divided into different States for convenience of administration the country is one integral whole, its people a single people living under a single *imperium* derived from a single source. The Americans had to wage a civil war to establish that the States have no right of secession and that their Federation was indestructible. The Drafting Committee thought that it was better to make it clear at the outset rather than to leave it to speculation or to dispute.

The provisions relating to amendment of the Constitution have come in for a virulent attack at the hands of the critics of the Draft Constitution. It is said that the provisions contained in the Draft make amendment difficult. It is proposed that the Constitution should be amendable by a simple majority at least for some years. The argument is subtle and ingenious. It is said that this Constituent Assembly is not elected on adult suffrage while the future Parliament will be elected on adult suffrage and yet the former has been given the right to pass the Constitution by a simple majority while the latter has been denied the same right. It is paraded as one of the absurdities of the Draft Constitution. I must repudiate the charge because it is without foundation. To know how simple are the provisions of the Draft Constitution in respect of amending the Constitution one has only to study the provisions for amendment contained in the American and Australian Constitutions. Compared to them, those contained in the Draft Constitution will be found to be the simplest. The Draft Constitution has eliminated the elaborate and difficult procedures such as a decision by a convention or a referendum. The Powers of amendment are left with the Legislatures, Central and Provincial. It is only for amendments of specific matters—and they are only few—that the ratification of the State legislatures is required. All other Articles of the Constitution are left to be amended by Parliament. The only limitation is that it shall be done by a majority of not less than two-thirds of the members of each House present and voting and a majority of the total membership of each House. It is difficult to conceive a simple method of amending the Constitution.

What is said to be the absurdity of the amending provisions is founded upon a misconception of the position of the Constituent Assembly and of the future Parliament elected under the Constitution. The Constituent Assembly in making a Constitution has no partisan motive. Beyond securing a good and workable constitution it has no axe to grind. In considering the Articles of the Constitution it has no eye on getting through a particular measure. The future Parliament, if it met as a Constituent Assembly, its members, will be acting as partisans seeking to carry amendments to the Constitution to facilitate to the passing of party measures which they have failed to get through Parliament by reason of some Article of the Constitution which has acted as an obstacle in their way. Parliament will have an axe to grind while the Constituent Assembly has none. That is the difference between the Constituent Assembly and the future Parliament. That explains why the Constituent Assembly though elected on limited franchise can be trusted to pass the Constitution by simple majority and why the Parliament though elected on adult suffrage cannot be trusted with the same power to amend it.

I believe I have dealt with all the adverse criticisms that have been leveled against the Draft Constitution as settled by the Drafting Committee. I don't think that I have left out any important comment or criticism that has been made during the last eight months during which the Constitution has been before the public. It is for the Constituent Assembly to decide whether they will accept the Constitution as settled by the Drafting Committee or whether they shall alter it before passing it.

But this I would like to say. The Constitution has been discussed in some of the Provincial Assemblies of India. It was discussed in Bombay, C.P., West Bengal, Bihar, Madras and East Punjab. It is true that in some Provincial Assemblies serious objections were taken to the financial provisions of the Constitution and in Madras to Article 226. But excepting this, in no Provincial Assembly was any serious objection taken to the Articles of the Constitution. No Constitution is perfect and the Drafting Committee itself is suggesting certain amendments to improve the Draft Constitution. But the debates in the Provincial Assemblies give me courage to say that the Constitution as settled by the Drafting Committee is good enough to make in this country a start with. I feel that it is workable, it is flexible and it is strong enough to hold the country together both in peace time and in war time. Indeed, if I may say so, if things go wrong under the new Constitution, the reason will not be that we had a bad Constitution. What we will have to say is, that Man was vile. Sir, I move.

.................I see that there is a great deal of misunderstanding as to the real provisions in the Constitution in the minds of those members of the House who are interested in this kind of directive principles. It is quite possible that the misunderstanding or rather inadequate understanding is due to the fact that I myself in my opening speech in support of the motion that I made, did not refer to this aspect of the question. That was because, not that I did not wish to place this matter before the House in a clear-cut fashion, but my speech had already become so large that I did not venture to make it more tiresome than I had already done; but I think it is desirable that I should take a few minutes of the House in order to explain what I regard as the fundamental position taken in the Constitution. As I stated, our Constitution as a piece of mechanism lays down what is called parliamentary democracy. By parliamentary democracy we mean 'one man, one vote'. We also mean that every Government shall be on the anvil, both in its daily affairs and also at the end of a certain period when the voters and the electorate will be given an opportunity to assess the work done by the Government. The reason why we have established in this Constitution a political democracy is because we do not want to install by any means whatsoever a perpetual dictatorship of any particular body of people. While we have established political democracy, it is also the desire that we should lay down as our ideal economic democracy. We do not want merely to lay down a mechanism to enable people to come and capture power. The Constitution also wishes to lay down an ideal before those who would be forming the Government. That ideal is economic democracy, whereby, so far as I am concerned, I understand to mean, 'one man, one vote'. The question is: Have we got any fixed idea as to how we should bring about economic democracy? There are various ways in which people believe that economic democracy can be brought about; there are those who believe in having a socialistic state as the best form of economic democracy; there are those who believe in having a socialistic state as the best form of economic democracy; there are those who believe in the communistic idea as the most perfect form of economic democracy.

Now, having regard to the fact that these various ways by which economic democracy may be brought about, we have deliberately introduced in language that we have used, in the directive principles, something which is not fixed or rigid. We have left enough room for people of different ways of thinking, with regard to the reaching of the ideal of economic democracy, to strive in their own way, to persuade the electorate that it is the best way of reaching economic democracy, the fullest opportunity to act in the way in which they want to act.

Sir, that is the reason why the language of the articles in Part IV is left in the manner in which this Drafting Committee thought it best to leave it. It is no use giving a fixed, rigid form to something which is not rigid, which is fundamentally changing and must, having regard to the circumstances and the times, keep on changing. It is, therefore, no use saying that the directive principles have no value. In my judgment, the directive principles have a great value, for they lay down that our ideal is economic democracy. Because we did not want merely a parliamentary form of Government to be instituted through the various mechanisms provided in the Constitution, without any direction as to what our economic ideal, as to what our social order ought to be, we deliberately included the Directive Principles in our Constitution. I think, if the friends who are agitated over this question bear in mind what I have said just now that our object-in framing this Constitution is really two-fold: (i) to lay down the form of political democracy, and (ii) to lay down that our ideal is economic democracy and also to prescribe that every Government whatever, it is in power, shall strive to bring about economic democracy, much of the misunderstanding under which most members are labouring will disappear.

My friend Mr. Tyagi made an appeal to me to remove the word 'strive', and phrases like that. I think he has misunderstood why we have used the word 'strive'. The word 'strive' which occurs in the Draft Constitution, in my judgment, is very important. We have used it because our intention is that even when there are circumstances which prevent the Government, or which stand in the way of the Government giving effect to these Directive Principles, they shall, even under hard and unpropitious circumstances, always strive in the fulfilment of these Directives. That is why we have used the word 'strive'. Otherwise, it would be open for any Government to say that the circumstances are so bad, that the finances are so inadequate that we cannot even make an effort in the direction in which the Constitution asks us to go. I think my friend Mr. Tyagi will see that the word[1] 'strive' in this context is of great importance and it would be very wrong to delete it.

As to the rest of the amendments, I am afraid I have to oppose them. ... ... Sir, looking back on the work of the Constituent Assembly it will now be two years, eleven months and seventeen days since it first met on the 9th of December 1946. During this period the Constituent Assembly has altogether held eleven sessions. Out of these eleven sessions the first six were spent in passing the Objectives Resolution and the consideration of the Reports of Committees on Fundamental Rights, on Union Constitution, on Union Powers, on Provincial Constitution, on Minorities and on the Scheduled Areas and Scheduled Tribes. The seventh, eighth, ninth, tenth and the eleventh sessions were devoted to the consideration of the Draft Constitution. These eleven sessions of the Constituent Assembly have consumed 165 days. Out of these, the Assembly spent 114 days for the consideration of the Draft Constitution.

Coming to the Drafting Committee, it was elected by the Constituent Assembly on 29th August 1947. It held its first meeting on 30th August. Since August 30th it sat for 141 days during which it was engaged in the preparation of the Draft Constitution. The Draft Constitution, as prepared by the Constitutional Adviser as a text for the Drafting Committee to work upon, consisted of 243 articles and 13 Schedules. The first Draft Constitution as presented by the Drafting Committee to the Constituent Assembly contained 315 articles and 8 Schedules. At the end of the consideration stage, the number of articles in the Draft Constitution increased to 386. In its final form, the Draft Constitution contains 395 articles and 8 Schedules. The total number of amendments to the Draft Constitution tabled was approximately 7,635. Of them, the total number of amendments actually moved in the house were 2,473....

Finally, I must thank you Mr. President for the way in which you have conducted the proceedings of this Assembly. The courtesy and the consideration which you have shown to the Members of the Assembly can never be forgotten by those who have taken part in the proceedings of this Assembly. There were occasions when the amendments of the Drafting Committee were sought to be barred on grounds purely technical in their nature. Those were very anxious moments for me. I am, therefore, specially grateful to you for not permitting legalism to defeat the work of Constitution-making.

As much defence as could be offered to the Constitution has been offered by my friends Sir Alladi Krishnaswami Ayyar and Mr. T. T. Krishnamachari. I shall not therefore enter into the merits of the Constitution. Because I feel, however good a Constitution may be, it is sure to turn out bad because those who are called to work it, happen to be a bad lot. However bad a Constitution may be, it may turn out to be good if those who are called to work it, happen to be a good lot. The working of a Constitution does not depend wholly upon the nature of the Constitution. The Constitution can provide only the organs of State such as the Legislature, the Executive and the Judiciary. The factors on which the working of those organs of the State depend are the people and the political parties they will set up as their instruments to carry out their wishes and their politics. Who can say how the people of India and their parties will behave? Will they uphold constitutional methods of achieving their purposes or will they prefer revolutionary methods of achieving them? If they adopt the revolutionary methods, however good the Constitution may be, it requires no prophet to say that it will fail. It is, therefore, futile to pass any judgment upon the Constitution without reference to the part which the people and their parties are likely to play.

The condemnation of the Constitution largely comes from two quarters, the Communist Party and the Socialist Party. Why do they condemn the Constitution? Is it because it is really a bad Constitution? I venture to say 'no.' The Communist Party wants a Constitution based upon the principle of the Dictatorship of the Proletariat. They condemn the Constitution because it is based upon parliamentary democracy. The Socialists want two things. The first thing they want is that if they come in power, the Constitution must give them the freedom to nationalize or socialize all private property without payment of compensation. The second thing that the Socialists want is that the Fundamental Rights mentioned in the Constitution must be absolute and without any limitations so that if their Party fails to come into power, they would have the unfettered freedom not merely to criticize, but also to overthrow the State.

These are the main grounds on which the Constitution is being condemned. I do not say that the principle of parliamentary democracy is the only ideal form of political democracy. I do not say that the principle of no acquisition of private property without compensation is so sacrosanct that there can be no departure from it. I do not say that Fundamental Rights can never be absolute and the limitations set upon them can never be lifted. What I do say is that the principles embodied in the Constitution are the views of the present generation or if you think this to be an overstatement, I say they are the views of the members of the Constituent Assembly. Why blame the Drafting Committee for embodying them in the Constitution? I say why blame even the Members of the Constituent Assembly? Jefferson, the great American statesman who played so great a part in the making of the American Constitution, has expressed some very weighty views which makers of Constitution, can never afford to ignore. In one place, he has said:—

We may consider each generation as a distinct nation, with a right, by the will of the majority, to bind themselves, but none to bind the succeeding generation, more than the inhabitants of another country.

In another place, he has said:

The idea that institutions established for the use of the nation cannot be touched or modified, even to make them answer their end, because of rights gratuitously supposed in those employed to manage them in the trust for the public, may perhaps be a salutary provision against the abuses of a monarch, but is most absurd against the nation itself. Yet our lawyers and priests generally inculcate this doctrine, and suppose that preceding generations held the earth more freely than we do; had a right to impose laws on us, unalterable by ourselves, and that we, in the like manner, can make laws and impose burdens on future generations, which they will have no right to alter; in fine, that the earth belongs to the dead and not the living.

I admit that what Jefferson has said is not merely true, but is absolutely true. There can be no question about it. Had the Constituent Assembly departed from this principle laid down by Jefferson it would certainly be liable to blame, even to condemnation. But I ask, has it? Quite the contrary. One has only to examine the provision relating to the amendment of the Constitution. The Assembly has not only refrained from putting a seal of finality and infallibility upon this Constitution by denying to the people the right to amend the Constitution as in Canada or by making the amendment of the Constitution subject to the fulfilment of extraordinary terms and conditions as in America or Australia, but has provided a most facile procedure for amending the Constitution. I challenge any of the critics of the Constitution to prove that any Constituent Assembly anywhere in the world has, in the circumstances in which this country finds itself, provided such a facile procedure for the amendment of the Constitution. If those who are dissatisfied with the Constitution have only to obtain a 2/3 majority and if they cannot obtain even a two-third majority in the parliament elected on adult franchise in their favour, their dissatisfaction with the Constitution cannot be deemed to be shared by the general public.

There is only one point of constitutional import to which I propose to make a reference. A serious complaint is made on the ground that there is too much of centralization and that the States have been reduced to Municipalities. It is clear that this view is not only an exaggeration, but is also founded on a misunderstanding of what exactly the Constitution contrives to do. As to the relation between the Centre and the States, it is necessary to bear in mind the fundamental principle on which it rests. The basic principle of Federalism is that the Legislative and Executive authority is partitioned between the Centre and the States not by any law to be made by the Centre but by the Constitution itself. This is what Constitution does. The States under our Constitution are in no way dependent upon the Centre for their legislative or executive authority. The Centre and the States are co-equal in this matter. It is difficult to see how such a Constitution can be called centralism. It may be that the Constitution assigns to the Centre too large a field for the operation of its legislative and executive authority than is to be found in any other federal Constitution. It may be that the residuary powers are given to the Centre and not to the States. But these features do not form the essence of federalism. The chief mark of federalism as I said lies in the partition of the legislative and executive authority between the Centre and the Units by the Constitution. This is the principle embodied in our Constitution. There can be no mistake about it. It is, therefore, wrong to say that the States have been placed under the Centre. Centre cannot by its own will alter the boundary of that partition. Nor can the Judiciary. For as has been well said:

> Courts may modify, they cannot replace. They can revise earlier inter-pretations as new arguments, new points of view are presented, they can shift the dividing line in marginal cases, but there are barriers they cannot pass, definite assignments of power they cannot reallocate. They can give a broadening construction of existing powers, but they cannot assign to one authority powers explicitly granted to another.

The first charge of centralization defeating federalism must therefore fall.

The second charge is that the Centre has been given the power to over-ride the States. This charge must be admitted. But before condemning the Constitution for containing such overriding powers, certain considerations must be borne in mind. The first is that these overriding powers do not form the normal feature of the Constitution. Their use and operation are expressly confined to emergencies only. The second consideration is: Could we avoid giving overriding powers to the Centre when an emergency has arisen? Those who do not admit the justification for such overriding powers to the Centre even in an emergency, do not seem to have a clear idea of the problem which lies at the root of the matter. The problem is so clearly set out by a writer in that well known magazine 'The Round Table' in its issue of December 1935 that I offer no apology for quoting the following extract from it. Says the writer:

> Political systems are a complex of rights and duties resting ultimately on the question, to whom, or to what authority, does the citizen owe allegiance. In normal affairs the question is not present, for the law works smoothly, and a man goes about his business obeying one authority in this set of matters and another authority in that. But in a moment of crisis, a conflict of claims may arise, and it is then apparent that ultimate allegiance cannot be divided. The issue of allegiance cannot be determined in the last resort by a juristic interpretation of statutes. The law must conform to the facts or so much the worse for the law. When all formalism is stripped away, the bare question is, what authority commands the residual loyalty of the citizen? Is it the Centre or the Constituent State?

The solution of this problem depends upon one's answer to this question which is the crux of the problem. There can be no doubt that in the opinion of the vast majority of the people, the residual loyalty of the citizen in an emergency must be to the Centre and not to the Constituent States. For it is only the Centre which can work for a common end and for the general interests of the country as a whole. Herein lies the justification for giving to the Centre certain overriding powers to be used in an emergency. And after all what is the obligation imposed upon the constituent States by these emergency powers? No more than this—that in an emergency, they should take into consideration alongside their own local interests, the opinions and interests of the nation as a whole. Only those who have not understood the problem, can complain against it.

Here I could have ended. But my mind is so full of the future of our country that I feel I ought to take this occasion to give expression to some of my reflections thereon. On 26th January 1950, India will be an independent country (*Cheers*). What would happen to her independence? Will she maintain her independence or will she lose it again? This is the first thought that comes to my mind. It is not that India was never an independent country. The point is that she once lost the independence she had. Will she lose it a second time? It is this thought which makes me most anxious for the future. What perturbs me greatly is the fact that not only India has once before lost her independence, but she lost it by the infidelity and treachery of some of her own people. In the invasion of Sind by Mahommed-Bin-Kasim, the military commanders of King Dahar accepted bribes from the agents of Mahommed-Bin-Kasim and refused to fight on the side of their King. It was Jaichand who invited Mahommed Ghori to invade India and fight against Prithvi Raj and promised him the help of himself and the Solanki kings. When Shivaji was fighting for the liberation of Hindus, the other Maratha noblemen and the Rajput Kings were fighting the battle on the side of Moghul Emperors. When the British were trying to destroy the Sikh Rulers, Gulab Singh, their principal commander sat silent and did not help to save the Sikh kingdom. In 1857, when a large part of India had declared a war of independence against the British, the Sikhs stood and watched the event as silent spectators.

Will history repeat itself? It is this thought which fills me with anxiety. This anxiety is deepened by the realization of the fact that in addition to our old enemies in the form of castes and creeds we are going to have many political parties with diverse and opposing political creeds. Will Indians place the country above their creed or will they place creed above country? I do not know. But this much is certain that if the parties place creed above country, our independence will be put in jeopardy a second time and probably be lost forever. This eventuality we must all resolutely guard against. We must be determined to defend our independence with the last drop of our blood. (*Cheers.*)

On the 26th of January 1950, India would be a democratic country in the sense that India from that day would have a government of the people, by the people and for the people. The same thought comes to my mind. What would happen to her democratic Constitution? Will she be able to maintain it or will she lose it again. This is the second thought that comes to my mind and makes me as anxious as the first.

It is not that India did not know what is Democracy. There was a time when India was studded with republics, and even where there were monarchies, they were either elected or limited. They were never absolute. It is not that India did not know Parliaments or Parliamentary Procedure. A study of the Buddhist Bhikshu Sanghas discloses that not only there were Parliaments—for the Sanghas were nothing but Parliaments—but the Sanghas knew and observed all the rules of Parliamentary Procedure known to modern times. They had rules regarding seating arrangements, rules regarding Motions, Resolutions, Quorum, Whip, Counting of Votes, Voting by Ballot, Censure Motion, Regularization, Res Judicata, etc. Although these rules of Parliamentary Procedure were applied by the Buddha to the meetings of the Sanghas, he must have borrowed them from the rules of the Political Assemblies functioning in the country in his time.

This democratic system India lost. Will she lose it a second time? I do not know, but it is quite possible in a country like India—where democracy from its long disuse must be regarded as something quite new—there is danger of democracy giving place to dictatorship. It is quite possible for this new born democracy to retain its form but give place to dictatorship in fact. If there is a landslide, the danger of the second possibility becoming actuality is much greater.

If we wish to maintain democracy not merely in form, but also in fact, what must we do? The first thing in my judgment we must do is to hold fast to constitutional methods of achieving our social and economic objectives. It means we must abandon the bloody methods of revolution. It means that we must abandon the method of civil disobedience, non-cooperation and satyagraha. When there was no way left for constitutional methods for achieving economic and social objectives, there was a great deal of justification for unconstitutional methods. But where constitutional methods are open, there can be no justification for these unconstitutional methods. These methods are nothing but the Grammar of Anarchy and the sooner they are abandoned, the better for us.

The second thing we must do is to observe the caution which John Stuart Mill has given to all who are interested in the maintenance of democracy, namely, not 'to lay their liberties at the feet of even a great man, or to trust him with powers which enable him to subvert their institutions.' There is nothing wrong in being grateful to great men who have rendered life-long services to the country. But there are limits to gratefulness. As has been well said by the Irish Patriot Daniel O'Connel, 'no man can be grateful at the cost of his honour, no woman can be grateful at the cost of her chastity and no nation can be grateful at the cost of its liberty.' This caution is far more necessary in the case of India than in the case of any other country, for in India, Bhakti or what may be called the path of devotion or hero-worship, plays a part in its politics unequalled in magnitude by the part it plays in the politics of any other country in the world. Bhakti in religion may be a road to the salvation of the soul. But in politics, Bhakti or hero-worship is a sure road to degradation and to eventual dictatorship.

The third thing we must do is not to be content with mere political democracy. We must make our political democracy a social democracy as well. Political democracy cannot last unless there lies at the base of it social democracy. What does social democracy mean? It means a way of life which recognizes liberty, equality and fraternity as the principles of life.

These principles of liberty, equality and fraternity are not to be treated as separate items in a trinity. They form a union of trinity in the sense that to divorce one from the other is to defeat the very purpose of democracy. Liberty cannot be divorced from equality, equality cannot be divorced from liberty. Nor can liberty and equality be divorced from fraternity. Without equality, liberty would produce the supremacy of the few over the many. Equality without liberty would kill individual initiative. Without fraternity, liberty and equality could not become a natural course of things. It would require a constable to enforce them. We must begin by acknowledging the fact that there is complete absence of two things in Indian Society. One of these is equality. On the social plane, we have in India a society based on the principle of graded inequality which means elevation for some and degradation for others. On the economic plane, we have a society in which there are some who have immense wealth as against many who live in abject poverty. On the 26th of January 1950, we are going to enter into a life of contradictions. In politics we will have equality and in social and economic life we will have inequality. In Politics we will be recognizing the principle of one man one vote and one vote one value. In our social and economic life, we shall, by reason of our social and economic structure, continue to deny the principle of one man one value. How long shall we continue to live this life of contradictions? How long shall we continue to deny equality in our social and economic life? If we continue to deny it for long, we will do so only by putting our political democracy in peril. We must remove this contradiction at the earliest possible moment or else those who suffer from inequality will blow up the structure of political democracy which this Assembly has so laboriously built up.

The second thing we are wanting in is recognition of the principle of fraternity. What does fraternity mean? Fraternity means a sense of common brotherhood of all Indians—if Indians being one people. It is the principle which gives unity and solidarity to social life. It is a difficult thing to achieve. How difficult it is, can be realized from the story related by James Bryce in his volume on American Commnowealth about the United States of America.

The story is—I propose to recount it in the words of Bryce himself—that—

Some years ago the American Protestant Episcopal Church was occupied at its triennial convention in revising its liturgy. It was thought desirable to introduce among the short sentence prayers a prayer for the whole people, and an eminent New England divine proposed the words 'O Lord, bless our nation'. Accepted one afternoon on the spur of the moment, the sentence was brought up next day for reconsideration, when so many objections were raised by the laity to the word 'nation' as importing too definite a recognition of national unity, that it was dropped, and instead there were adopted the words 'O Lord, bless these United States'.

There was so little solidarity in the U.S.A. at the time when this incident occurred that the people of America did not think that they were a nation. If the people of the United States could not feel that they were a nation, how difficult it is for Indians to think that they are a nation. I remember the days when politically-minded Indians resented the expression 'the people of India'. They preferred the expression 'the Indian nation'. I am of opinion that in believing that we are a nation, we are cherishing a great delusion. How can people divided into several thousands of castes be a nation? The sooner we realize that we are not as yet a nation in the social and psychological sense of the word, the better for us. For then only we shall realize the necessity of becoming a nation and seriously think of ways and means of realizing the goal. The realization of this goal is going to be very difficult—far more difficult than it has been in the United States. The United States has no caste problem. In India there are castes. The castes are anti-national. In the first place because they bring about separation in social life. They are anti-national also because they generate jealousy and antipathy between caste and caste. But we must overcome all these difficulties if we wish to become a nation in reality. For fraternity can be a fact only when there is a nation. Without fraternity, equality and liberty will be no deeper than coats of paint.

These are my reflections about the tasks that lie ahead of us. They may not be very pleasant to some. But there can be no gainsaying that political power in this country has too long been the monopoly of a few and the many are not only beasts of burden, but also beasts of prey. This monopoly has not merely deprived them of their chance of betterment, it has sapped them of what may be called the significance of life. These downtrodden classes are tired of being governed, they are impatient to govern themselves. This urge for self-realization in the downtrodden classes must not be allowed to develop into a class struggle or class war. It would lead to a division of the House. That would indeed be a day of disaster. For, as has been well said by Abraham Lincoln, a house divided against itself cannot stand very long. Therefore the sooner room is made for the realization of their aspiration, the better for the few, the better for the country, the better for the maintenance for its independence and the better for the continuance of its democratic structure. This can only be done by the establishment of equality and fraternity in all spheres of life. That is why I have laid so much stress on them.

I do not wish to weary the House any further. Independence is no doubt a matter of joy. But let us not forget that this independence has thrown on us great responsibilities. By independence, we have lost the excuse of blaming the British for anything going wrong. If hereafter things go wrong, we will have nobody to blame except ourselves. There is great danger of things going wrong. Times are fast changing. People including our own are being moved by new ideologies. They are getting tired of government by the people. They are prepared to have Government for the people and are indifferent whether it is Government of the people and by the people. If we wish to preserve the Constitution in which we have sought to enshrine the principle of Government of the people, for the people and by the people, let us resolve not to be tardy in the recognition of the evils that lie across our path and which induce people to prefer Government for the people to Government by the people, nor to be weak in our initiative to remove them. That is the only way to serve the country. I know of no better.

Mr. President: The House will adjourn till Ten of the clock tomorrow morning when we shall take up the voting on the motion which was moved by Dr. Ambedkar.

The Assembly then adjourned till ten of the Clock on Saturday, the 26th November, 1949.

15 Buddhism Paved Way for Democracy and Socialistic Pattern of Society (6 June 1950)

A BRIEF SKETCH ABOUT THE DOCUMENT

A Conference of the World Fellowship of Buddhists was held in Ceylon (Srilanka) from 25th May to 6th June 1950. Dr. B. R. Ambedkar attended the Conference and argued that Buddhism is the first philosophy that advocated for not only democracy as a political approach but also for a society based on socialistic principles. The excerpts in this chapter are from BAWS, Volume 17, part III, 2003 (pp. 406–09).

Addressing an International gathering at Colombo, on June 6th, 1950. Dr. Ambedkar said:

Most people who have studied rise and fall of Buddhism in India would admit that this subject had not been adequately, dealt with as it should have been. I have not been able to find any authentic material explaining why Buddhism rose to the height it achieved and why it disappeared in India.

To know a subject thoroughly, one must know its relevant traditions exactly and precisely. Similarly, the significance of Buddhism would not be understood unless the exact circumstances which gave birth to it are understood. I disagree with the view that Hinduism has all along been the religion of India. Hinduism is the latest development of social thought in India.

The religion of India has undergone three changes. Vedic religion which was practised first—gave way, in course of time, to Brahmanism and this in turn to Hinduism. It was during Brahminic period that Buddhism was born. This was because Buddhism opposed inequality, authority and division of society into various classes which Brahminism had introduced in India.

It is easy to practice the Vedic religion. In it, performance of *yagya* (*yajnas*) is the main *puja.* The Vedic Aryans used to worship innumerable Gods. They used to please them by performing *yagyas*. The *puja* to be performed for these Gods should necessarily be sacred and superb. In those Agrarian times, cows were the chief wealth of the Aryans. Therefore, they used to sacrifice cows to honour their deities. In this way, Vedic Dharma encouraged violence. Brahmins succeded in organizing the society only by adopting *Vedic yagyas.* The Brahmins also divided the society into four sections (Varnas)—*Brahmin, Kshatriya. Vaishya and Shudra.* The division of the society into four varnas (Castes) created great inequalities. They said that the Brahmins were born of the *Brahma's* mouth and *Shudras* from his feet. Can anybody believe that the basic principle of any religion could be to divide the society? Yet, this is what *Brahminism* has perpetuated. On the other hand, equality is the main feature of Buddhism. The religion of the Buddha gives freedom of thought and freedom of self-development to all. To abjure violence is another essential teaching of Buddhism. It has never taught to achieve salvation by sacrificing animals or any living being to propitiate Gods. I would say that the rise of Buddhism in India was as significant as the French Revolution. Prior to the advent of Buddhism, it was impossible to even think that a *Shudra* would get throne. History of India reveals that after the emergence of Buddhism, Shudras are seen getting thrones. Verily, Buddhism paved way for establishment of democracy and socialistic pattern of society in India.

It is a perplexing problem how Buddhism, which had acquired a highest place, disappeared from India. There is very little material to tell us about the condition of Buddhism up to 274 B.C. It is, however, seen that Buddhism was at its climax of popularity in the reign of Asoka. How such a great and popular religion lost ground in India is a painful phenomena.

Buddhism appears to have met strong opposition in 185 B.C. when the last Mauryan King was assassinated by his Chief Commander. This was one of the lawful actions of the Brahmins to save their religion. But it is a pity that the historians have not given sufficient importance, to this incident. While going through the Buddhist literature, I find that 90% followers of the Buddha were Brahmins. Brahmins used to come to the Buddha for discussion and argumentation, and when defeated, used to become faithful to the Buddha and ultimately accepted Buddhism. The Buddhist literature is full of such incidents. Therefore, how is it that Buddhism that had flourished amongst the majority of Brahmins was later on destroyed by the Brahmins themselves.

In my opinion the main reason for this was the family deity's (*kula deva*) worship. In India like the village deity and national deity, there were family deities also who were worshipped through the Brahmins. The priests who used to go for worshipping these deities started influencing the affairs of the State through the queens. Asoka after embracing Buddhism discontinued this practice and removed the idols of such deities. Asoka said, 'As I venerate the Buddha, the Enlightened One, there is no need to worship any other deity.' This action of Asoka disturbed the Brahmins very much as it ended their unfair means of livelihood and exploitation. They pledged to take revenge for this loss.

The Brahmins were of the view that after death, kings go to hell because of their errors and omissions. Therefore, they did not agree to be rulers but preferred to be the Chief Advisers to the Kings. In order to take revenge for the loss they suffered on account of stoppage of *Kulapuja* (family deity's worship). Brahmins gave up the approved motto of being advisers only and tried to grab power. With the help of their well-wisher *Kshatriyas*, they also organized an united Brahmin-Kshatriya axis against Buddhism. The ascendency of Brahminism again in Indian society, is one of the reasons for the downfall of Buddhism.

The foreign invasions are also responsible for the decline of Buddhism in India. The Greeks did no harm to Buddhism. There are positive proofs available that the Greeks gave liberal financial assistance for Buddhist activities. The Huns invaded India, and after being defeated by the Guptas, they settled in India. Prior to this, the Huns tried to destroy Buddhism. The religion of the Buddha got the severest blow from the Muslim invasion. They destroyed the Buddhist idols and killed the *Bhikkhus*. They mistook the great Nalanda University as the Fort of Buddhists and killed a large number of monks thinking that they were soldiers. The few *Bhikkhus* who escaped an onslaught fled away to the neighbouring countries like Nepal, Tibet, and China.

Some of my Hindu friends often ask why Hinduism, which has also idol-worship, survived in India and Buddhism died.

My answer is that whatsoever the religion may be it requires the priest community to preserve it. Due to the shortage of Buddhist monks, Buddhism declined. Efforts were subsequently made by some Buddhists to raise another priesthood in order to revive Buddhism but their efforts failed. Such is not case with Hinduism. A Brahmin's son is priest by birth. Therefore, no separate priest community is required to protect their religion. This is why Hinduism survived Muslim onslaught. Moreover, Buddhism as a religion is difficult to practise while Hinduism is not. Besides, the political climate in India had also been inhospitable to its advancement.

I do not agree with the suggestion made by many people in India that Buddhism was destroyed by the dialectics of Shankaracharya. This is contrary to the facts as Buddhism existed for many centuries after his death. In my opinion, Shankaracharya himself was a Buddhist. His Guru too was Buddhist. Of course, Buddhism declined in India because of the rise of *Vaisknavism* and *Saivism,* the two cults which adopted and absorbed many good points of Buddhism. Today, Hinduism is in a very much changed form. Hinduism which taught and practiced violence earlier has started teaching non-violence. This has been copied from Buddhism. Buddhism may have disappeared, in material form but as a spiritual force it still exists in India.

16 Failure of Parliamentary Democracy Will Result in Rebellion, Anarchy and Communism (28 October 1951)

A BRIEF SKETCH ABOUT THE DOCUMENT

For Ambedkar parliamentary democracy rests on an opposition and free and fair elections, as in 1951 the Congress was exclusively the dominant party and lacked an effective opposition. There were a lot of constraints in having free and fair elections. While delivering a speech at a Student's Parliament, Ambedkar argued that if parliamentary democracy fails then it will lead to rebellion, anarchy and not socialism but communism that is marked by violence. The excerpts in this chapter have been taken from BAWS, Volume 17, 2003 (pp. 422–37).

.....He said,

Principal, the Hon'ble President and Hon'ble Speaker,

I am, indeed, thankful to you for the great honour done to me of asking me to address the special session of your Parliament. During my whole life, I have been, so to say, a wanderer, from subject to subject, from profession to profession. I began my career as a Professor of Political Economies in the Government Commerce College, Bombay. In 1919, after my return from England. But I soon felt that the Government service was no good for a man who wishes to do public service. A government servant is bound by rules of discipline. He is hampered at every stage in his work of public service. I then went back to England and qualified for Bar. After my return I practised for a short period and then accepted the post of the Principal of the Government Law College at Bombay. I came back to the profession of teaching. I worked as the Principal of the Law College for five years. Then, the 1935 Government of India Act came into being, which brought the popular legislatures in existence for the first time. I then thought of taking a jump into the politics and I left the service and took to politics. Since then I have alternatively been doing legal practice and serving the public. Legal practice and public service are, thus, the alternating currents in my life; and I do not know on which current my life will end whether A.C. or D.C.

I am very fond of teaching profession. I am also very fond of students. I have dealt with them. I have lectured them in my life. This is the first opportunity I have got to address the students since my resignation from the Cabinet. I am very glad to talk to the students. A great lot of the future of this country must necessarily depend on the students of this country. Students is an intelligent part of the community and they can shape the public opinion. I, therefore, take special pleasure in addressing you, the members of the parliament, and I am really thankful for this opportunity given to me.

When your principal wrote to me requesting me to address you , he did not indicate any particular subject. I also had nothing in my mind about the topic on which I shall speak to you in the morning. But suddenly, as this usually happens in my case, at the flash of moment the subject become clear to me, and I have decided to speak a few words with you on the subject of parliamentary government. The time at my disposal is very short and I will, therefore, be able to give only a brief analysis of the subject.

During the discussion in the Constitution Assembly there was a variety of opinion as regards the nature of the constitution that we should have. Some preferred British system; some American system. There were others who did not want either of these two types of Government. But after a long discussion, a large majority of members come to a conclusion that the system of the parliamentary government as it is in Britain is best suited to our country.

There are some sections of people who do not like parliamentary government. Communists want the Russian type of Government. The socialists are also against the present constitution of India. They are agitating against it. They have declared that if they come to power, they will modify it. Personally speaking, I am very greatly attached to the parliamentary system of Government. We must understand what it means and we must preserve it in the Constitution.

What is meant by Parliamentary Government? There is a book on the English constitution by Walter Bagehot. It is, indeed, a classic treatise. It was later expanded by other authorities on Constitutional Government like Laski and others. He has put the conception of the Parliamentary Government in one sentence. He says Parliamentary Government by discussion and not by fisticuffs. You will always find in British system of Government that they hardly ever resort to fisticuffs while taking any decision. The decision is always taken after discussion. Nobody introduces element of disturbance in British Parliament. Looking at the French Politics. Decision are arrived at more than often by knocking out blows. You will find that this system is hardly adequate to those not born in the system. It is an alien institution to them. We must learn understand and make it a success.

Parliamentary democracy is unknown to us at present. But India, at one time had Parliamentary institutions. India was far more advanced in the ancient times. If you go through the *Suktas of Mahaparinibbana*, you will find apple evidence in support of my point. In these *suktas* it is stated that while Bhagwan Buddha was dying at kusinara (kusinagara) a message to the effect was sent to Mallas who were sitting in session at that time. They were devoted to Parliamentary institutions. When they received the message about Buddha, they decided that they shall not close the session, but would carry on with their work and will go to kusinara after finishing of the business of the parliament. There are innumerable reference in our literature to prove that parliamentary system of government was not unknown to us.

There are many rulers about Parliamentary procedure. May's Parliamentary practice is generally followed. One rule that is invariably followed everywhere is that there can be no discussion without a motion. That is why there is no discussion on the question. This ruler is also practiced in our land in ancient times. The system of secret ballot now in vogue is also not new to us. It was followed in Buddhist Sanghas. They had the ballot papers which they called, 'Salapatraka Grahakas'. Unfortunately, we have lost all this past heritage that was good. Historians of India must tackle this question as to why these Parliamentary Institutions disappeared from our land. But I find that they cannot or do not want to find out the reasons for it. Ancient India was the master of world. There was such intellectual freedom in the ancient India as was nowhere else to be found. Then why this ancient civilization want to dogs? Why was India subjected to autocratic monarchies? We were familiar with Parliamentary Institutions. We know about votes, voting, committees and other things related to the Parliamentary Institutions. Today, Parliamentary System of the Government is alien to us. If we go to village, we find that the villagers do not understand what is vote, what is party. They find it something strange, something alien. It is therefore, a great problems to haw to preserve this institution. We will have to educate public, we will have to tell them the benefits of Parliamentary Democracy and of Parliamentary System of Government.

We know what Bagehot means by Parliamentary Government. But today his definition is of no use, it is utterly inadequate. There are three main things inherent in the Parliamentary System of Government.

Parliamentary Government means negations of hereditary rule. No person can claim to be hereditary ruler. Whoever wants to rule must be elected by the people from time to time. He must obtain the approval of the people. Hereditary rule has no sanction in the Parliamentary System of Government.

Secondly, any law, any measure applicable to be public life of the people must be based on the advice of the people chosen by the people. No single individual can presume the authority that he knows everything, that he can make the laws and carry the government. The laws are to be made by representatives of the people in the Parliament. They are the people who can advise the man in whose name the law is proclaimed. That is the difference between the Monarchical System of Government and the Democratic System of Government. In monarchy the affairs of the people are carried on the name of a monarch and under the authority of a monarch. In democracy, the affairs of the public are carried on in the name of the head of the State: but the laws and the executive measures are the authority on which the government is carried. The head of the state is the titular head; he is merely a symbol. He is a consecrated 'Murti.' He can be worshipped but he is not allowed to carry out the Government of the Country. The Government of the Country is carried out, though in his name, by the elected representatives of the people.

Thirdly and lastly, Parliamentary System of the Government means that at a stated period those who wanted to advise the head of the state must have the confidence of the people in themselves renewed. In Britain, formerly, the elections to the Parliament were every seven years. The Chartists agitated against this. They wanted the annual elections. The motive behind this agitation was very praiseworthy, indeed. It would have seen best in the interests of the people if annual election were held, had it been possible, of course. But, parliamentary elections are very costly affairs. So some sort of compromise was arrived at and five years period was supposed to be a responsible period at which the Legislators and the Ministers were to go back to the People and obtain the fresh renewal of their confidence.

This is also not enough. Parliamentary System of Government is much more than government by discussion. There are two pillars on which the Parliamentary System of Government rests. These are the fulcrums on which the mechanism works. Those two pillars are (i) an opposition an (ii) free and fair elections.

For the last 20 or 30 years, we acclimatized to one single political party. We have nearly forgotten the necessity and importance of 'opposition' for the fair working of Parliamentary Democracy. We are continuously told that opposition is an evil. Here again we are forgetting what the past history has to teach us. You know that there were 'Nibandhkaras' to interpret the Vedas and Smrities. They used to begin their comments on 'Slokas' an? 'Sutras' by stating firstly the 'Purva Paksha' the one side of the questions. They used to follow up by giving the 'Uttar Pakshas'—the other side. By this they wanted to show us that the question raised was not an easy question: it is a question where there is dispute, discussion and doubt. Then they used to give what they termed as Adhikaran' where they used to criticize both the 'Pakshas'. Finally, they gave the 'Siddharnt', their own decisions. Here from we can find that all our ancient teachers believed in two party system of Government.

One important thing in the Parliamentary Democracy is that people should know the other side, if there are two sides to a question. Hence, a functional opposition is required. Opposition is the key to a free political life. No democracy can do without it. Britain and Canada, the two exponents of Parliamentary Systems of Governments recognize this important fact and in both countries the leader of 'opposition' is paid salary by the Government. They regard the 'opposition' as an essential, thing. People of these countries believe that the 'opposition' should be as much alive as the

Government. The Government may suppress the facts, the Government may have only one-sided propaganda. The people have provision against this eventuality in these two countries.

Now the question arises as to whether there is any desire on the part of the party in power to permit any opposition to be created. Congress does not want any 'opposition'. Congress is attempting to gather people of sundry views under one canopy. I ask you whether this is a desirable trend in the political life of this country?

Free and fair elections is the other pillar on which Parliamentary Democracy rests. Free and fair elections are necessary for the transfer of power from one section of the community to the other in a peaceful manner and without any bloodshed. In olden times, if a king died, there was at least one murder in the palace. Revolution used to take place in palace resulting in murders before the new king used to take the reins of his country into his authority. This has been the history of India. Elections must be completely free and fair. People must be left to themselves to choose those whom they want to send to the Legislatures.

What about free and fair elections? We must not lose sight of the fact that 'Big Business' is trying to play a great part in political life of this country. The amount that is being contributed to the Congress on behalf of the 'Big Business' is very dangerous thing. If moneyed people try to influence the elections by contributing to the election fund of any political party, what will be the result. If the party to which they have supported financially comes into power, they will naturally try to extract concessions for themselves either by modifying the present legislation or by influencing the party in power to legislate in such a manner as would be beneficial to their interests. I ask you gentlemen, whether under these circumstances there is any hope left for the Parliamentary System of Government to do any good to the country. I would like you to refer to the Mahabharata. During the battle between the Pandvas and the Kaurvas, Bhishma and Drona were on the side of Kaurvas. Pandvas were in the right and the Kaurvas were in the wrong. Bhishma admitted this. When somebody asked Bhishma as to why he was supporting the Kaurvas if he found the Pandvas to be in the right. Bhishma replied that memorable sentence:

I must be loyal to the salt: If I eat the food of the Kaurvas, I must take their side even if they might be in the wrong.

Today the same thing is happening. Congress is accepting the financial help of the Banias, the Marwaries and other multi-millionaires. Congress is eating their food and it follows, therefore, naturally the congress will have to take the side of these Big Business' at all crucial times.

We also find that the government servants are influencing the elections in favour of the party which is feeding them and their dependents. No less a personality then Dr Shyama Prasad. Mukherjee, at the inaugural session of the Bhartiya Jan Sangh at Delhi recently, openly charged the Government Servants of helping the Congress and hereby nullifying the elections from being free and fair. Under these Circumstances, do you gentleman, think that there is any hope for the Parliamentary Democracy to succeed.

If Parliamentary Democracy fails in this country and it is bound to fail for the reasons mentioned by me, the only result will be rebellion, anarchy and communism. If the people in power do not realize that people will not tolerate hereditary authority, then this country is doomed. Either Communism will come, Russia having the sovereignty over our country, destroying individual liberty and our independence or the section of the people who are disgruntled for the failure of the party in power will start rebellion and anarchy will prevail. Gentlemen, I want you to take note of these eventual certainties and if you wish that Parliamentary System of Government and Parliamentary Democracy prevail in this country, if you are satisfied that we will be assured of our liberty of thought, speech and action, if we should preserve our independence, if we cherish the inherent right of individual liberty, then it is your duty as students intelligent community of our country, to strive your utmost to cherish this Parliamentary System of Government in its true spirit and work for it.

Gentlemen, I have done. I think you for having given me this opportunity to address this August gathering.

17 If Our True Representatives Are Not Elected, Independence Will Be a Farce (28 October 1951)

A BRIEF SKETCH ABOUT THE DOCUMENT

Ambedkar's concern for election of effective representatives of the Scheduled Castes remained central. However, he was apprehensive about how much the elected representatives from dominant political parties would be effective. In an election campaign speech on 28 October 1951 at Ludhiana in Punjab, he opined that for realizing freedom, there was need of electing true and genuine representatives not only for the community but also for the success of democracy. The following speech is part of BAWS, Volume 17, 2003 (pp. 429–37).

.....He said,

Dear brothers and sisters,

This is the first time that I have visited Ludhiana to speak to our people. Many times before I proposed to visit this place but due to certain unavoidable circumstances, I could not do so. What an auspicious occasion if is that you all have gathered here.

You know in two three months elections are going to be held in which many parties are talking part. The Scheduled Castes Federation is also putting its candidates for the election. We will contest all the seats reserved for the Scheduled Castes in the State Assemblies and the Union Parliament and also some general seats where we have sufficient number of votes. I hope that our candidates will be successful. Our candidates 'success depends mostly upon our own people. If all our people voted for our candidates, I am sure of our success, I would therefore urge that all the Scheduled Castes Federation, which is the only organization of the Scheduled Castes and other Backward Classes... ...

After so many years of struggle, we have secured some political powers. Now we can send our own representatives to the State Assemblies and the Union Parliament against the seats reserved for the Scheduled Castes.

There are many parties which are anxious to snatch away these rights. They are anxious to get our votes and send their own henchmen to the seats reserved for our people. You can very well understand their motives. They want that the Scheduled Castes should remain where they are and should not come into power so that the menial jobs which our people are performing should not suffer. So you will have to be careful about your votes in the coming election. You should see that only our true representatives are elected with our votes and none else. Only then your rights which have been incorporated in the Constitution can be safeguarded.

If our true representatives are not elected to the State Assemblies and the Union Parliament, then we cannot enjoy freedom. Independence will be a farce for our people. This will be independence of the high caste people and not ours. But if our true representatives are in parliament and state assemblies, they can fight for our cause and get grievances and redressed. Only then our children can get proper education; only then our poverty can be removed and only then we will be given equal share in all the spheres of life. Although special privileges have been provided for the scheduled castes people in the Indian constitution, the other parties specially the congress are unnecessarily interfering with them. They are putting of their own henchmen for the election to the state reserves for the scheduled castes. How can the people elected on the congress tickets safeguard our interests when they will have to go according to the wishes of their masters? What can they do for us?

I want to tell you about the people who were elected to the parliament on the Congress tickets to the seats reserved for the scheduled castes.

They were about 30 in numbers in the parliament for the last four years. Not a single member out of the 30 raised any question in the parliament about the grievances of the scheduled castes. Even if a question was put in the parliament, the speaker did not allow it and matter ended there. If the speaker was generous and had allowed the question and it was included in the business then the chief whip of the congress would go to the, member concerned and asked him to withdraw the question before it is printed. Per chance, if the question had been printed, then the chief whip would ask the member concerned to leave the station for the day when the answer is required and thus there would be no discussion at all in the parliament on the matter raised as the member himself would not be there. For one month there is discussion on the budget in the parliament. At that time any person can speak on the budget and point out that such and such privileges should provided for his community or his party. He can point out that so much money is being spend on unnecessary projects where as the important proposals have been neglected. During these four years, I have not seen a single members moving any cut motion. This is all due to Congress party's discipline (Dunda), if the members wanted to move resolutions, they had to obtain the permissions of the chief whip long before it was actually moved. Neither these members put up any bill during there four years. How can the untouchables, the Christians, Anglo-Indians, etc. avail of the privileges provide for them in the constitutions, if the seats reserved for them are occupied by there enemies though the congress tickets?

I want to make the point clear that if you voted for the congress you will have to suffer forever. Our representatives on Congress ticket will keep silent in the state assemblies and the parliament. Our interest can be safe-guarded only if our true representatives are elected on federations ticket, which is the only organization of the scheduled castes . Had there been any possibilities of getting our grievances redressed in the Congress. I would not have let the organization. I know the congress has sufficient money and will try to buy the votes with that. But you should be careful about it. If I wanted I could remain in the Congress for ever an definitely have got a good place there. But would have done only if I had selfish motives and not any regard for my community. I would have remained there, if I was in need of any licence or permit for myself. The man seeking license and permits can do so at the expense of his community. He will do anything for his own shelf and nothing for his community. This is the experience I have gained during the period I remained in the Congress Government... ...

Every political party has put forward its Manifesto. Every party promises that if it comes into power it will do this and that. Scheduled Castes Federation has also published a very voluminous Manifesto but when they came to understand that ordinary people would not follow it, they amended it and compressed into a small one. I hope by and by their Manifesto will become smaller and smaller and a day will come when there will be no Manifesto of the Congress. I want to tell you what should be in the Manifesto and what should not be. I challenge all the political parties to constitute a committee to find out which Manifesto is the best and I have no doubt in mind that our Manifesto will be the best of all. All the parties have promised many things in their Manifestoes to the people. To promise is easy but difficult to put it into practice. If you promise one thing you can promise one hundred. Manifesto should not be a list of promises only. It should deal with the problems facing the country and also how to solve these problems. Is there anything of that sort in the Manifesto of the Congress? The only thing impressed in the Congress Manifesto is the Muslim problem. According to it, there is no other problem facing the country. Can anybody agree to this? Of course, Muslim problem was there when India was united and when there was no Pakistan. But then too, this was not the only problem. The Muslims have migrated to Pakistan, and only Hindus, Sikhs and other minorities are in India. Do you think that India is now facing Muslim problem? Do you agree that nothing should be done for the Depressed Classes, who are ten times poorer and backward than the Muslims? There are Scheduled Castes, Scheduled Tribes and Criminal Tribes, which need the best attention of the Government. But the Congressmen say that people should not be communal minded and should not demand some special privileges for these backward classes.

The other problem is that poverty in India. People in India are very poor so much so that 90 per cent people do not get proper meals. They don't get any clothes. They don't have any shelter. Food-stuffs worth crores of rupees are being imported every year. If we have to import even food-stuffs from outside and spend so much, how will we be able to pull on? But all these things have no place in the minds of Congressmen. They have only one problem to solve and that is Muslim problem.

I want to inform you that we are putting up candidates for the upcoming elections through the Scheduled caste federation. The Scheduled Caste federation is for all backward classes. Ever backward class will be given representation. Nobody should be afraid of it. Chamers and Bhangis are all equal. We should be united and no-body should think himself separate from other. I want to request all men and women that they should leave aside everything on the day of polling and go to the polling booth and cast their votes. Already our votes are not sufficient and if the votes do not cast their votes on that day, it would not be good for us. We will be unrepresented. The day of polling is the day of life and death the scheduled castes.

Every political party which is taken in the coming elections has been allotted a party symbol. Our federation's symbol is Elephant. I have selected this so that there may not be any confusion in the minds of our people. Some parties selected oxen, horses, donkeys as their symbols. But for distinction I have selected 'Elephants'.

This time we be not have the cumulative system of the voting so that we may cast our votes to a single candidate of our choice. But we have distributive system and will have to distribute our votes among different candidates. In a constituency where a seat has been reserved for scheduled castes, people will have two votes, one for general seat and other for the reserved seat. We cannot cast both of our votes to our party candidate who is standing for the reserved seat. We can cast in his favour only one vote and the other vote must be given to the other candidates standing on General seat. So we shall have to join some party which will give their second vote to our candidate and get our second vote in return. We have not decided as yet which party we will join hands with many. Parties have approached as for alliance but nothing has yet been finalized. Negotiations are going on, we have to think many times before we join hands with any party. But we must join with some party or the other.

In the end I want to tell you that thousands of people come to Delhi from Punjab and UP and other distant places to put their grievances before me. Some complain that they have been beaten by *Zamindars* and when they approached and authorities concerned, decision were taken against them as the people in power also belong to high castes. So there are so many complaints that it is not possible for me cope with these single handed. Many people return to their homes disappointed. So I have decided to construct a building in Delhi and to keep a pleader there who will scrutinize our people's complaints and advise them in the matter. We have already purchased a piece of land in New Delhi for the purpose and on that site we want to construct a building which shall be the head office of the federation. People from outside will be entertained their and their grievances heard. We do not have sufficient funds for the construction of the building, although it is absolute essential. So I request that you all should contribute something according to your means. In this way we shall be able to achieve our purpose. Bawa Tula Dass will tour the whole Punjab for the collection of building fund. I once again request you to contribute liberally for this noble cause.

18 Conditions Precedent for the Successful Working of Democracy (22 December 1952)

A BRIEF SKETCH ABOUT THE DOCUMENT

Dr Ambedkar was invited by the Members of the Poona District Law Library on 22nd December 1952, for unveiling the portrait of late Shri L. R. Gokhale and for declaring open the collections of books donated by Shri A. B. Sethna and Shri H. V. Tulpule, two senior members of the Bar. The collection of books would be preserved as separate sections in the Law Library. In this address he defined democracy in his own words and carved out conditions for the success of democracy in general and in India in particular. The excerpts in this chapter are taken from BAWS, Volume 17, part III, 2003 (pp. 472–86).

Dr Ambedkar's Address:

Mr. Chairman and Gentlemen,

When the invitation came, I wrote to your Secretary that I would very much like to know what are the subjects in which the members of this District Library are interested, because I may come here and speak on a subject in which they may have no interest. If so, the visit would be of no value either to you or to me. He was kind enough to send me a list of four subjects. He said 'You can select anyone of them.' I was in a hurry to reply to him and could not convey to him my actual decision as to what subject I would select. But I told him in a general way that I would select one of the four and if I did not select one of the four, I will not travel beyond the ambit of the four which he had prescribed. The one subject which attracted me which he had mentioned was Parliamentary Democracy, and I thought that that was a subject on which I might speak. The subject which I have selected is not Parliamentary Democracy, but something which is very closely associated with Parliamentary Democracy and which from my point of view, and I believe from the point of view of the country, is a very important subject. Now, the subject which I am going to speak to you this evening is according to my wording of the subject: 'Conditions Precedent for the Successful Working of Democracy.' What are the conditions precedent which must exist in order that the democratic form of Government may continue to work without any kind or hindrance. That is the subject on which I propose to make a few observations.

Setting for The Subject

Now, before I actually deal with the subject-matter I propose to make a few preliminary observations in Order to provide, what I call, a setting for the subject.

The first preliminary observation I propose to make is this that democracy is always changing its form. We speak of democracy, but democracy is not always the same. The Greeks spoke of Athenian Democracy. But as everyone knows, the Athenian Democracy was as different from our modem democracy as chalk is from cheese. The Athenian Democracy consisted of people, 50 per cent of whom were slaves. Only 50 per cent were free. The 59 per cent who formed slaves had no place in the Government at all. Surely our democracy is quite different from the Athenian Democracy.

The second thing to which I would like to draw your attention by a preliminary observation is that even in the same country democracy is not always the same. You take the history of England. Nobody can say that the English Democracy before the English Revolution of 1688 was the same as the English Democracy which come after the revolution of 1688. Nor can anyone say that the English Democracy as existed between 1688 and 1832 when the first Reform Bill was passed, is the same as the democracy that developed after the passing of the Act of 1832. Democracy keeps on changing its form.

The third thing that I would like to draw your attention is that democracy not only undergoes changes in form; democracy always undergoes changes in purposes. You take the ancient English democracy. What was the purpose of that democracy? It was to curb the King, to prevent the King from exercising what we now in law call his prerogative rights. The King even went to the extent of saying that although parliament may be there, as an enactment making body, 'I as a King have got the prerogative to make the law and my law shall prevail.' It was this kind of autocracy of the King which made democracy to come into being.

Today what is the purpose of the democracy? *The purpose of modern democracy is not so much to put a curb on an autocratic king but to bring about the welfare of the people.* That is a distinct change in the purpose of democracy. You will therefore see that in the title which I have given to my subject, I have deliberately used the words 'conditions precedent for the success of modem democracy.'

Democracy Defined

Again what do we mean by democracy? Let us have a clear understanding before I proceed to my subject. Democracy has been defined, as you know, by various people, writers of political science aand philosophers, sociologists and so on. I take only two for the purpose of illustrating my point. I do not know whether any of you is acquainted with that famous book by Walter Bagehot on the English Constitution, the first modern attempt to give a clear picture of democracy. If you refer to that book of Walter Bagehot, his definition of democracy is 'government by discussion.' That is, how he defines democracy. Take another illustration that is of Abraham Lincoln. In his famous Getisburg speech which he made after' the conquest of the Southern States, he defined democracy as 'A government of the people, by the people, and for the people.' Well, many other definitions could be added in order to give an idea what people mean by democracy. Personally for myself, I define democracy in a different way, in a much more concrete way, I think. My definition of democracy is '*a form and a method of government whereby revolutionary changes in the economic and the social life of the people are brought without a bloodshed.*' That is my definition of democracy. If democracy can enable those who *are* running it to bring about fundamental changes in the social and economic life of the people and the people accept those changes without resorting to bloodshed, then I say that there is democracy. That is the real test. It is perhaps the severest test. But when you are judging the quality of a material, you must put it to the severest test. And this is how I propose to define democracy at any rate so far as today's address is concerned. Now, how can such a democracy be successful? This is the main subject matter of my address. Now, unfortunately there are no dogmas laid down by any of the authors who have written about this subject of democracy which can give us any idea in concrete, as to what are the conditions precedent according to their judgement to make democracy a success. One has to read history and as a result of reading history to find out the break-down period in democracy's life in the different parts of the world where it had functioned and come to one's own conclusion.

Condition No. I

The first condition which I think is a condition precedent for the successful working of the democracy is that there must 'be no glaring inequalities in the society. There must not be an oppressed class. There must not be a suppressed class. There must not be a class which has got all the privileges and a class which has got all the burdens to carry. Such a thing, such a division, such an organization of a society has within itself the germs of a bloody revolution, and perhaps it would be impossible for the democracy to cure them. Lincoln once said, although people have not understood his meaning, in the same Gatisburg's speech that 'a house divided against itself cannot stand.' He was of course referring to the conflict between the Southern States and the Northern States. He said, 'If you of the Southern States and we of the Northern States are divided, we shall not be able to stand together when a foreign enemy comes.' That was probably the meaning that he wanted to convey when he said that the house divided cannot stand. But I think that phrase of his or sentence of his is pregnant with much deeper meaning and it means, as I understand it, that the deep cleavages between class and class are going to be one of the greatest hindrances in the success of democracy. Because in democracy what happens? In democracy, everybody, even the oppressed, the suppressed, those who are deprived of their rights and those who carry the burden, they have the right to vote in the same way as those who have all the privileges, and probably those who are privileged are fewer than those who are unprivileged and since we adopt a majority rule as the rule of decision, it is quite possible that if the privileged few will not willingly and voluntarily surrender their privileges, then the distance between them and the lower orders will destroy democracy and bring into existence something quite different. There is, therefore, no doubt in my mind that if you examine the history of democracy in various parts of the world, you will find that one of the causes for the break-down of democracy is the existence of these social cleavages.

Condition No. II

The second thing which a successful working of democracy requires is the existence of opposition. Now, I have seen many people not only in this country but in England condemning the party system. I was just recently reading, just before I came, a small little book published by the Hansard Society on the party system in England and here is one whole chapter devoted to this question whether the party system is a good system and should be tolerated. There is a variety of views. Now, it seems to me that all those who are against the party system and who must be taken also on that very account to be against opposition, seem completely to misunderstand what democracy means. What does democracy mean? I am not defining it. I am asking a functional question. It seems to me that democracy means a veto of power. Democracy is a contradiction of hereditary authority or autocratic authority. Democracy means that at some stage somewhere there must be a veto on the authority of those who are ruling the country. In autocracy there is no veto. The King once elected is there with his inherent or divine right to rule. He does not have to go before his subject at the end of every five years to ask them, 'Do you think I am a good man? Do you think I have done well during the last five years? If so, will you re-elect me?' There is no veto on the part of anybody on the power of the King. But in democracy we have provided, that at every five years those who are in authority must go to the people and ask whether in the opinion of the people they are well qualified to be entrusted with power and author- ity to look after their interest, to mould their destiny, to defend them. That is what I call veto. Now, a democracy is not satisfied with a veto that the Government should go at the end of five years only to the people and in the meantime there should be nobody to question the authority of the Government. Democracy requires that not only that the Government should be subject to the veto, long-term veto of five years, at the hands of the people, but there must be an immediate veto. There must be people in the parliament immediately ready there and then to challenge the Government. Now, if you understand what I am saying, democracy means that nobody has any perpetual authority to rule, but that rule is subject to sanction by the people and can be challenged in the house itself. You will see how important it is to have an opposition. The Government must justify every act that it does to those of the people who do not belong to its party. Unfortunately, in our country all our newspapers, for one reason or other, I believe, it is the revenue from advertisements, have given far more publicity to the Government than to the opposition, because you cannot get any revenue from the opposition. They get revenue from the Government and you find columns after columns of speeches reeled out by members of the ruling party in the daily newspapers and the speeches made by the opposition are probably put somewhere on the last page in the last column. I am not criticizing what is democracy. I am saying what is the condition precedent for a democracy. *The opposition is the condition precedent of the democracy.* But do you know that in England not only is the opposition recognized, but the leader of the opposition is paid a salary by the Government in order to run the opposition. He gets a secretary, he gets a small staff of stenographers and writers, he has a room in the House of Commons where he does his business. In the same way, you will find that in Canada the leader of the opposition gets a salary in the way as a Prime Minister does, because in both these countries democracy feels that there must be someone to show whether the Government is going wrong. And this must be done incessantly and perpetually and that is why they do not mind spending money on the leader of the opposition.

Condition No. III

I think there is a third condition which may also be called a condition precedent for the success of democracy and that is equally in law and administration. One did need not at this stage delight too much on equality before the law, although there might be cases here and there when there is no equality before the law. But what is important is equality of treatment in administration. It is quite possible for good many of you to imagine or to recall cases where a party government is carrying on the administration for the benefit of the members of the party. At any rate, I can recall a great many instance of the sort. Suppose there is law which says that nobody shall deal in in a particular commodity without a license. Nobody quarrels with that law because it is universal. There is no discrimination in that particular piece of legislation. But let us go further and see what happens when a man goes to a particular officer or to the minister with an application for license in treading in a particular commodity. I don't known, it quite possible again that probably the minister may first look at his hat. What sort of a coloured hat he is wearing? If he is wearing hat which applies to him and it assures him that he is a party man and another man goes with another sort of dress or belonging to another party and in making his decision the license is given to the first and refused to the second, though both of them on merits are equally qualified to have that license, then obviously this is a discrimination in administration and there is no equity. Of course the question of license, i.e. the granting of this privilege and that privilege is perhaps small thing and affects only a very small class of people. But let us go further and see what would happen if this kind of discrimination enters administration. Supposing a member of a certain party is being prosecuted for a certain offence for which there is abundant evidence, and suppose the head of the party in that particular area goes to the District Magistrate and tells him that it is not right for him to prosecute this man because he belongs to his party and says, 'well, if you don't do it, I shall refer the matter to the Minister and get you transferred from this place to some other place.' You can just imagine what chaos and injustice would result in administration. The sort of a thing which used to happen in the United States which is called a Spoil System, that is to say, when one party came in office, it removed all the employees that were employed by their predecessor including even the clerks and the peons and they filled their vacancies by those gentlemen who helped the new party to go in power. The United States as a matter of fact, had no administration worth speaking of for a number of years. Subsequently, they themselves realized that this was not helpful to democracy. They abolished this Spoil System. In England, in order than administration should be remained pure, impartial, away from politics and policy, they have made a distinction between what is called political offices and civil offices. The civil service is permanent. It serves all the parties whichever is in office and carries out the administration without any kind of interference from the Minister. Such a thing at one time did exist in our country when the British were here. I recall very clearly an incident in my own career as a member of the Government of India. You perhaps will recollect that every Viceroy has got in Delhi some street or club named after him. The only Governor General who does not get his name attached to some street or institution is Lord Linlithgow. His. Private Secretary was my friend. I was then in charge of P. W. D. and there were plenty of works I was in charge of. He came and quietly said to me 'My dear Dr could you do something for naming some institution or work after the name of Lord Linlithgow?' He said it is looking very glaring that everybody's name is there but not his. I said 'I will consider.' I was then discussing the construction of a barrage over Jamuna in order to provide water to the city of Delhi in summer, because it goes dry in summer, I told my Secretary who was a European by name Priar. And I said, 'Mr. Priar look here, this is what the Secretary to the Governor General has said to me. Do you think we can do something?' What do you think was his reply? His reply was 'Sir, we must not do any such thing at all.' Such a thing at any rate in this country to do would be quite impossible. For any officer to say something which is contrary to the wishes of the Minister is, to my mind, utterly impossible. But in those days it was quite possible, because we too in India like Great Britain had made that wise decision that administration must not be interfered with by the Government, and that the function of the government was to lay down policy but not to interfere and not to make any discrimination. This is very fundamental and I am afraid we had already departed from that and may completely abnegate and abolish the thing we have had so far.

Condition No. IV

The fourth condition precedent, in my judgment, for the successful working of democracy is the observance of Constitutional morality. Many people seem to be very enthusiastic about the Constitution. Well, I am afraid, I am not. I am quite prepared to join that body of people who want to abolish the Constitution, at any rate to redraft it. But what we forget is that we have a Constitution which contains legal provisions, only a skeleton. The flesh of that skeleton is to be found in what we call constitutional morality. However, in England it is called the conventions of the constitution and people must be 'ready to observe the rules of the game. Let me give you one or two illustrations which come to my mind at this moment. You remember when the 13 American colonies rebelled, their leader was Washington. It is really a very inadequate way of defining his position in the American life of that day merely to say that he was a leader. To the American people Washington was God. If you read his life and history, he was made the first President of the United States after the constitution was drafted. After his term was over, what happened? He refused to stand for the second time have not the least doubt in my mind that if Washington had stood ten times one after the other for the Presidentship, he would have been elected unanimously without a rival. But he stepped down the second time. When he was asked why, he said, 'My dear people you have forgotten the purpose for which we made this constitution. We made this constitution because we did not want a hereditary monarchy and we did not want a hereditary ruler or a dictator. If after abandoning and swerving away from the allegiance of the English King, you come to this country and stick to worship me year after year and term after term what happens to your principles? Can you say that you have rightly rebelled against the authority of the English king when you are substituting me in his place?' He said, 'Even if your royalty and fidelity to me compels you to plead that I should stand a second time, I as one who enunciated that principle that we should not have hereditary authority, must not fall a prey to your emotion.' Ultimately, they prevailed upon him to stand at least a second time. And he did. And the third time when they approached him, he spurned them away. Let me give you another illustration. You know Windsor Edward the VIII whose serial story has now been published in the *Times of India*. I had gone to the Round Table Conference and there was a great controversy going on there as to whether the King should be allowed to marry the woman whom he wanted to marry, especially when he was prepared to marry her in a morganatic marriage, so that she may not be a queen or whether the British people should deny him even that personal right and force him to abdicate. Mr Baldwin was of course against the King's marriage. He would not allow him, and said, "If you do not listen to me, you will have to go. 'Our friend Mr. Churchill was the friend of Edward the VIII and was encouraging him. At that time Labour party was in the opposition. They had no majority and I remember very well the Labour Party people considered whether they could not make capital out of this issue and defeat Mr. Baldwin; because there was a large number of conservatives who in their loyalty wanted to support the king; and I remember the late Prof. Laski writing a series of articles in the *Herald* condemning any such move on the part of the Labour party. He said, 'By our convention we have always agreed that the king must accept the advice of the Prime Minister and if he does not accept the advice of the Prime Minister, the Prime Minister shall force his ejection.' That being our convention, it would be wrong on our part to defeat Mr. Baldwin, on an issue which increases the authority of the King. And the Labour Party listened to his advice and did nothing of the kind. They said, they must observe the rules of the game. If you read English history, you will find many such illustrations where the party leaders have had before them many temptations to do wrong to their opponents in office or in opposition by clutching at an issue which gave them temporary power, but which they refused to fall a prey to, because they knew that they would damage the constitution and damage democracy.

There is one other thing which I think is very necessary in the working of democracy and it is this that in the name of democracy there must be no tyranny of the majority over the minority. The minority must always feel safe that although the majority is carrying on the Government, the minority is not being hurt, or the minority is not being hit below the belt. This is a thing which is very greatly respected in the House of Commons. Good many of you must be remembering the results of elections in England in 1931 when Mr. Ramsay Mac Donald left the Labour Party and formed the National Government. When the election came, the Labour Party which I think numbered somewhere about 150 or so, had only 50 members out of 650 with Mr. Baldwin as the Prime Minister. I was then there. But I have never heard of a single instance of this small minority of 50 members belonging to the Labour Party under the huge majority of the conservatives ever complaining that they were denied their due rights of speech, or opposition or making motions of any kind as you probably know. You take our own Parliament. I am not justifying what the members of the opposition are doing by constantly bringing in notions of censure or adjournment motions. It is not a very happy thing to work in parliament to be constantly dunning these adjournment motions. All the same, you must have noticed that there is hardly any motion, whether of adjournment or censure which has been admitted for the debate. It surprises me considerably. In my reading of the English parliamentary debates I have very seldom come across a case where a demand for adjournment has been refused either by the' Speaker, provided of course it is an order by the government. When I was a member of the Bombay Legislative assembly, there were a few of our friends Mr. Morarji. Mr. Munshi and Mr. Kher and others who were in office. They never allowed a single one of adjournment to be discussed. Either our friend Mr. Mavlankar who was then the Speaker helped them by ruling it out or as he admitted, the Minister objected to it. You know what happens when a Minister objects? When a Minister objects, the man who proposes the adjournment motion has to produce 30 'or 40 people, whatever the quota is. It may be that if Government were constantly to oppose adjournment motions of the small community which is represented in the house by a group of few members such as 4, 5, 6, such small minorities can never get a chance to ventilate their grievances. What happens is that these minorities develop a contempt for parliamentary people and develop a revolutionary spirit something unconstitutional. It is therefore necessary that when democracy is working, the majority on which it is based, must not act in a tyrannical manner.

One other point I will refer and then close. I think that democracy does require the functioning of moral order in society. Somehow, our political scientists have never considered this aspect of democracy. Ethics is something separate from politics. You may learn politics and you may know nothing about ethics as though politics can work without ethics. To my mind it is an astounding proposition. After all, in democracy what happens? Democracy is spoken of as a free Government. And what do we mean by free Government? Free Government means that in vast aspects of social life people are left free to carry on without interference of law, or if law has to be made, then the law maker expects that society will have enough morality in it to make the law a success. The only person who. I think, has referred to this aspect of democracy is Laski. In one of his books he has very categorically stated that the moral order is always taken for granted in democracy. If there is no moral order, democracy will go to pieces as it is going now probably in our own country.

The last thing that I refer to is that democracy requires 'public Conscience.' There is no doubt about it that although there is injustice in every country, the injustice is not equally spread. There are some where the impact of injustice is very small. There are some against some whom the impact is very great. And there are some who are absolutely crushed under the burden of injustice. One might very easily cite the case of Jews in England. They were the people who suffered certain injustice which is Christians never did. What happened was that the Jews alone had to struggle in order to get this injustice removed. But the English Christians never helped them. In fact they liked it. The only man who helped the Jews in England was the king. This may be extraordinary but the reason also is extraordinary and the reason is this: Under the old Christianity law the children of the Jews could not inherent the property of the father for no other reason except that he was a Jew and not a Christian, and the king being the residuary legatee of the state received the property of the dead Jew. Now the king liked the sort of thing. He was very happy. When the children of the dead Jew went to the king in application the king handed over to them a little bit of property of their dead father and kept the rest from himself. But as I said, no English man ever helped the Jews, and the Jews continued to struggle for their liberation. This is the result of what is called 'public conscience.' Public conscience means conscience which becomes agitated at every wrong, no matter who is the sufferer and it means that everybody whether he suffers that particular wrong or not, it is prepared to join him in order to get him relieved. You take South Africa, the most recent example. Well the people who are suffering there are Indians. Are not they? The white people are not suffering yet you find this reverend Scott who is a white man doing his level best and in order to get this injustice removed. Recently I have been reading that a large number of young boys and girls belonging to the white race are also joining the struggle of the Indian in South Africa. That is called public conscience." I do not want to shock you, but sometimes I feel how forgetful we are. We are talking about South Africa. I have been wondering within myself whether are talking so much against segregation and so on do not have South Africa in every village. There is: we have only to go and see. There is South Africa everywhere in the village and yet I have very seldom found anybody not belonging to the scheduled class taking up the cause of the scheduled class and fighting, and why? Because there is no 'public conscience.' Myself and my India is the only world within which I am bound. If sort of things happens, the minority which is suffering from injustice gets no helps from others for the purpose of getting rid of this injustice. It again develops a revolutionary mentality which puts democracy in danger. Now, as I said, what I have said is not a series of dogmas which has been worked out by any political scientists, but the result of what is impressed upon me a result of reading the political histories of various countries, and I believe that these are the most essential conditions for the purpose of preserving democracy.

Now, ladies and gentlemen, I have no idea what has been the underlying purpose or motive which led you to give me this invitation. It might be that you wanted to add something to your programme. I hope I discharged that function. But so far as I am concerned, I have no doubt about it that the subject about which I have spoken this evening, to my mind, is a subject of the greatest importance to this nation. We have somehow developed the idea that we have got independence. The British have gone. We have got the constitution which provides democracy. Well what more do we want? We can't rest as we say on our ears, and do nothing more. Let me warn you against this kind of smug feeling that with the making of the constitution our task is done. It is not done. It is only begun. You must remember this democracy is not a plant which grown everywhere. It has grown in America. It has grown in England. To some extent it has grown in France. Yes these are examples by which we take certain amount of courage to ourselves to see what has happened elsewhere. You must be remembering that as a result of the first European War and the break-up of the Austria-Hungarian empire, Wilson created, on the basis of self-determination, small nationalities independent of Austria. They all began with democratic constitution, democratic government and they had also fundamental rights provided in their constitutions which was made obligatory for them to have the peace Treaty of Versailles, my friends, what has happened to that democracy? Do you see any trace of it there now? It has all gone. It has all vanished. They are probably under the dominance or surveillance of other countries. There is no democracy left. Take some of the most recent examples. Syria got a democratic government. After a few years there was military rebellion and the commander- in- chief of Syria become the ruler of Syria and democracy vanished in air. Take another example. What happened in Egypt? There too, they had been a democratic government beginning right from 1922 for 30 years. In one night Faruk had to leave and Nagib become the director of Egypt and he abolished the constitution.

With all these examples before us, I think we ought to be very cautious and very considerate regarding our own feature. You ought to consider whether we ought not to take some very positive steps in order to remove some of the stones and the boulders which are lying in our path in order to make our democracy safe. If, as a result of these few observations I have made, I have effected in you a consciousness that this is a problem on which we cannot afford to sleep, I think I would thank myself for the work I have done. Now , ladies and gentlemen, I do not wish to detain you long and thank for the kind attention with which you have listened to what I have said.

19   My Philosophy of Life
(3 October 1954)

A BRIEF SKETCH ABOUT THE DOCUMENT

By 1950, Ambedkar was greatly influenced by the Buddhist philosophy. In the following excerpts from BAWS, Volume 17, part II, 2003 (p. 503), he unraveled that his philosophy of life has major influence from liberty, equality and fraternity but these do not come from the French Revolution but from the teachings of his master, the Buddha.

Every man should have a philosophy of life, for everyone must have a standard by which to measure his conduct. And philosophy is nothing but a standard by which to measure.

Negatively, I reject the Hindu Social Philosophy propounded in the Bhagvat Geeta based as it is, on the *Triguna* of the Sankhya philosophy which is in my judgement a cruel perversion of the philosophy of Kapila, and which had made the Caste System and the System of Graded Inequality the law of Hindu Social Life.

Positively, my Social Philosophy, may be said to be enshrined in three words: Liberty, Equality, and Fraternity. Let no one, however, say that I have borrowed my philosophy from the French-Revolution. I have not. My philosophy has roots in religion and not in political science. I have derived them from the teachings of my Master, the Buddha. In his philosophy, liberty and equality had a place; but he added that unlimited liberty destroyed equality, and absolute equality left no room for liberty. In His Philosophy, law had a place only as a safeguard against the breaches of liberty and equality; but He did not believe that law can be a guarantee for breaches of liberty or equality. He gave the highest place to fraternity as the only real safeguard against the denial of liberty or equality or fraternity which was another name for brotherhood or humanity, which was again another name for religion.

Law is secular, which anybody may break while fraternity or religion is sacred which everybody must respect. My philosophy has a mission. I have to do the work of conversion'; for, I have, to make the followers of *Triguna* theory to give it up and accept mine. Indians today are governed by two different ideologies. Their political ideal set out in the Preamble to the Constitution affirms a life of Liberty, Equality, and Fraternity. Their social ideal embodied in their religion denies them.

20 Constitution (Fourth Amendment) Bill, 1954 (19 March 1955)

A BRIEF SKETCH ABOUT THE DOCUMENT

This bill was introduced in the parliament for compensation after acquiring land from the citizens. While participating in the discussion as a Member on 19 March 1955, Ambedkar expressed himself on the functioning of the democracy in India and especially the parliamentary democracy. He warned against the emerging notion that said that the Prime Minister can do no wrong (on the line of 'King can do no wrong' in Britain). He also advocated complimentary laws between the laws passed by the parliament and the state assemblies to avoid any confrontation. The selected excerpts in this chapter are from BAWS, Volume 15, 1997 (pp. 944–61).

Dr B.R. Ambedkar (Bombay): Mr. Chairman, those who are familiar with the British Parliamentary system will know that there is a dogma in the working of the British Constitution that all parties in England accept. That dogma is that the King can do no wrong. If any wrong is done in the working of the Constitution, the person responsible for the wrong is the Prime Minister and his colleagues. But the King can never be wrong and can never do wrong. We too in this country have adopted practically, with slight modifications, the British Constitution. But unfortunately the working of our Constitution is governed by a dogma, which is just the opposite of the dogma adopted by the British people. In our country the dogma on which we proceed is that the Prime Minister can do no wrong and that he will do no wrong. Therefore, anything that the Prime Minister proposes to do must be accepted as correct and without question. This devotion in politics to a personality may be excusable in some cases, but it does not seem to me excusable where the fundamental rights are being invaded. The fundamental rights are the very basis of the preamble to the Constitution. The Preamble says that this Constitution will have as its basis liberty, equality and fraternity. These objectives of the Constitution are carried out by the fundamental rights. And it is, therefore, the duty, I should have thought, of every Member of Parliament, apart from personal loyalty, to be critical when any invasion is made of the fundamental rights. Unfortunately, one does not find this kind of critical attitude. The history of fundamental rights in this country is very interesting. In olden times under the Hindu kings there were fundamental rights only for two—the Brahmin and the cow— and the Puranas described the king as 'Go Brahmana Pratipalaka.' That was the duty of a king; whether the other sections of his subjects received any consideration at his hands or not, or whether animals other than the 'Go' had any consideration was a matter of no moment at all. So long as the Brahmin and the cow were protected, the king was destined to go to heaven.

When the Muslims came, they took away these fundamental rights which the Hindu kings had granted to the Brahmin and the cow. The cow unfortunately not only lost its rights to live, but became the victim of everybody. So was the case of the Brahmin. What the Muslims did was to give privileges to the Mussalman and no rights to the non-Muslims. After the Muslim rule ended in this country, there came upon us the rule of the British. Anyone who examines the various Government of India Acts passed from 1772 to 1935 will find that there were no such thing as fundamental rights in any of the Government of India Acts that were passed by Parliament for the administration of this country. It is in 1947 or so when Swaraj became a fact in this country that this idea of fundamental rights emerged. It is our Constitution which for the first time contains the embodiment of what are called fundamental rights. It is a very strange thing that although the foreigners were ruling in this country, namely the British, no one ever agitated for the enactment of the fundamental rights. The Congress was in existence from 1886. Let anyone examine the annual resolutions passed by the Congress. They never asked for any fundamental rights.

Babu Gopinath Singh (Uttar Pradesh): Did you read the Karachi Congress Resolution of 1931.

Dr B.R. Ambedkar: Well, I have no idea about that. They said that they would have fundamental rights when they enact a Constitution. I am coming to that now, it is as I say a very strange commentary that no Indian—and the Indians who ran the Congress in the earliest times were intellectual giants: they were not ordinary people, they were most learned, they were wide awake—not one of them to my knowledge asked for any fundamental rights. But as soon as Swaraj came, there was a demand for fundamental rights. It is a matter worth consideration why this happened? Various people would no doubt give various replies, but my reply is very simple. My reply is very simple. My reply is this—the reason why Indians did not demand fundamental rights when the British were here is this. Although the British had their imperialism as one aspect of their rule, there cannot be any doubt that the administration of this country was governed by what was called the rule of justice, equity and good conscience. Sir, I remember, at least speaking for my own province, how independent was the judiciary which wholly consisted of Europeans. How independent it was of the executive. I remember a case

Dewan Chaman Lall (Punjab): Is it Tilak's case?

Dr B.R. Ambedkar: It is a very famous one, the case of a Mr. Justice Knight who was the Chief Justice of the Bombay High Court during the time of the East India Company. He had issued a writ against the Government of Bombay and the Government of Bombay refused to obey. They said that the Chief Justice of the Bombay High Court had no right to issue a writ against the Executive. When they informed him that they were not going to carry out that particular writ, what did Mr. Knight do? He called the Chaprassi and said: 'Bring the keys of the High Court', and he asked him to lock up every room of the High Court, including his own, and next day booked a passage for himself and went back to London, saying: 'If you are not going to obey my orders as the Chief Justice of the Bombay High Court, you will have no High Court, at all.' Subsequently, of course, his order was reversed by the Privy Council. But that is no matter at all. The point is that the British administered this country in a manner in which everybody felt that there was some sense of security. That is the reason why, in my judgement, nobody in this country clamoured for fundamental rights. But as soon as Swaraj presented itself, everybody thought—at least many of the minorities thought—that there was the prospect of political authority passing into the hands of a majority, which did not possess what might constitutionally be called constitutional morality. Their official doctrine was inequality of classes. Though there is inequality in every community, or whatever be the word, that inequality is a matter of practice. It is not an official dogma. But with a majority in this country, inequality, as embodied in their *Chaturvarana* is an official doctrine. Secondly, their caste system is a sword of political and administrative discrimination. The result was that the fundamental rights became inevitable. What I found—and I know this thing more than probably many do, because I had something, to do with it—was that the Congress Party was so jubilant over the fundamental rights. They wanted fundamental rights, and they thought that fundamental rights were so necessary that if the Indian people had a constitution which did not embody fundamental rights, they would appear nude to the world. That was the reason why they clamoured for fundamental rights. In the proceedings of the Constituent Assembly, I do not find a single Member who stood up and said 'We do not want fundamental rights.' Fundamental rights were regarded as a kind of an ornament which the Indian people must have. Today, their attitude has undergone a complete change. Today, they look upon the fundamental rights as an iron chain which ought to be broken, whenever occasion arose for breaking it. This, I find, is a fundamental change. I am sorry to say that this attitude of treating the fundamental rights with contempt, as though they were of no consequence, that they could be trodden upon at any time with the convenience of the majority or the wishes of a Party chief, is an attitude that may easily lead to some dangerous consequences in the future. And I therefore feel very sorry that even a matter of this sort, namely, the infringement of, or the deviation from, fundamental rights, is being treated by the Party in power as though it was a matter of no moment at all.

It seems to be suggested that those who made the Constitution had no sense, that fundamental rights must be elastic, that they must leave enough room for progressive changes. I must, Sir, as the Chairman of the Drafting Committee, repudiate any such suggestion. Any one, who reads the fundamental rights as they are enacted in the Constitution, will find that every fundamental right has got an exception. It says: Notwithstanding anything contained, the State may impose reasonable restrictions on them. We were quite aware of the fact that fundamental rights could not be rigid, that there must be elasticity. And we had provided enough elasticity.

Article 31, with which we are dealing now in this amending Bill, is an article for which I, and the Drafting Committee, can take no responsibility whatsoever. We do not take any responsibility for that. That is not our draft. The result was that the Congress Party, at the time when Article 31 was being framed, was so divided within itself that we did not know what to do, what to put and what not to put. There were three sections in the Congress party. One section was led by Sardar Vallabhbhai Patel, who stood for full compensation, full compensation in the sense in which full compensation is enacted in our Land Acquisition Act, namely, market price plus 15 per cent, solatium. That was his point of view. Our Prime Minister was against compensation. Our friend, Mr. Pant, who is here now—and I am glad to see him here—had conceived his Zamindari Abolition Bill before the Constitution was being actually framed. He wanted a very safe delivery for his baby. So he had his own proposition. There was thus this tripartite struggle, and we left the matter to them to decide in any way they liked. And they merely embodied what their decision was in article 31. This Article 31, in my judgement, is a very ugly thing, something which I do not like to look at. If I may say so, and I say it with a certain amount of pride the Constitution which has been given to this country is a wonderful document. It has been said so not by myself, but by many people, many other students of the Constitution. It is the simplest and the easiest. Many, many publishers have written to me asking me to write a commentary on the Constitution, promising a good sum. But I have always told them that to write a commentary on this Constitution is to admit that the Constitution is a bad one and an un-understandable one. It is not so. Anyone who can follow English can understand the Constitution. No commentary is necessary.

Dr Anup Singh (Punjab): Last time when you spoke, you said that you would burn the Constitution.

Dr B. R. Ambedkar: Do you want a reply to that? I would give it to you right here.

My friend says that the last time when I spoke, I said that I wanted to burn the Constitution. Well, in a hurry I did not explain the reason. Now that my friend has given me the opportunity, I think I shall give the reason. The reason is this: We built a temple for a god to come in and reside, but before the god could be installed, if the devil had taken possession of it, what else could we do except destroy the temple? We did not intend that it should be occupied by the *Asuras*. We intended it to be occupied by the devas. That is the reason why I said I would rather like to burn it.

Shri B. K. P. Sinha (Bihar): Destroy the devil rather than the temple.

Dr B. R. Ambedkar: You cannot do it. We have not got the strength. If you will read the Brahmana, the Sathapatha Brahmana, you will see that the gods have always been defeated by the *Asuras,* and that the *Asuras* had the *Amrit* with them which the gods had to take away in order to survive in the battle. Now, Sir, I am being interrupted... ... ...

... ... Now, Sir, one word with regard to clause 5. It seems to me very obnoxious. What are we asked to do by clause 5? By clause 5 we are asked to give constitutional validity to laws passed by State Legislatures. We have not seen those laws; they have not been circulated; they have not been debated here. And yet we are asked here to exercise the constituent powers of Parliament not only to validate them but to give them constitutional immunity from the other clauses of the Act. Sir, I think it is very derogatory to the dignity of the House that it should be called upon to validate laws passed by some other State which laws it has not seen, it has not considered. The proper thing for the Government to do is to put these subjects in the concurrent field so that Parliament may at least give them validity by the powers vested in it. But it is a very wrong thing. Because we did it in the case of the first amendment where we added the Ninth Schedule to the Constitution, that is no reason why we should widen this anomaly and this ugliness in the Constitution.

That is all that I want to say.

21   Why I Like Buddhism (12 May 1956)

A BRIEF SKETCH ABOUT THE DOCUMENT

This speech by Ambedkar was delivered at the BBC on 12 May 1956. Here he developed a critique of Marxian communism and relevance of Buddhist communism that advocated bloodless mental revolution as an indirect preference for democracy. The excerpts in this chapter are from BAWS, Volume 17, part II, 2003 (pp. 515–16).

In the short time allotted to me. I am asked to answer two questions. First is 'Why I like Buddhism' and the second is 'How useful it is to the world in its present circumstances'.

I prefer Buddhism because it gives three principles in combination which no other religion does. All other religions are bothering themselves with God and Soul and life after death. Buddhism teaches *Prajna* (understanding as against superstition and supernaturalism). It teaches *Karuna* (love). It teaches *Samata* (equality). This is what man wants for a good and happy life on earth. These three principles of Buddhism make their appeal to me. These three principles should also make an appeal to the world. Neither God nor Soul can save society.

There is a third consideration which should make an appeal to the world and particularly the South East Asian part of it. The world has been faced with the onslaught of Karl Marx and the Communism of which he is made the father. The challenge is a very serious one. That Marxism and Communism relate to secular affairs. They have shaken the foundation of the religious system of all the countries. This is quite natural for the religious system although today is unrelated to the secular system, yet is the foundation on which everything secular rests when the secular system cannot last very long unless it has got the sanction of the religion, however, remote it may be.

I am greatly surprised at the turn of mind of the Buddhist countries in South East Asia towards communism. It means that they do not understand what Buddhism is. I claim that Buddhism is a complete answer to Marx and his Communism.

Communism of the Russian type aims to bring it about by a bloody revolution. The Buddhist Communism brings it about by a bloodless mental revolution. Those who are eager to embrace Communism may note that the *Sangh is* a Communist Organisation. There is no private property. This has not been brought about violence. It is the result of a change of mind and yet it has stood for 2500 years. It may have deteriorated but idea is still binding. The Russian Communism must answer this question. They must also answer two other questions. One is that why communistic system is necessary for all times. They have done the work which it may be admitted the Russians could never have been able to do, but when the work is done why the people should not have freedom accompanied by love as the Buddha preached. The South East Asian countries must, therefore, be beware of jumping into the Russian Net. They will never be able to get out of it. All that is necessary to them is to study the Buddha and what he taught, a right and to give political form to his teachings. Poverty there is and there will always be. Even in Russia there is poverty but poverty cannot be an excuse for sacrificing human freedom.

Unfortunately, the Buddha's teachings have not been property interpreted and understood. That his gospel was a collection of doctrines and social reforms have been completely misunderstood. Once it is realized that Buddhism is a social gospel, the revival of it would be everlasting event for the world will realize why Buddhism makes such a great appeal to every one.

22 Prospects of Democracy In India (20 May 1956)

A BRIEF SKETCH ABOUT THE DOCUMENT

This was the lecture given by Ambedkar for Voice of America, included in BAWS, Volume 17, part III, 2003 (pp. 519–23). In this interesting lecture, Ambedkar delineates the prospects of democracy in India. Mere existence of Republic and Parliamentary democracy is not sufficient for democracy to be made possible but it requires doing away with inequalities of various kinds in a society in which caste predominates. He went on to argue that education needs to be imparted to those who want to blow up the existing social system of inequalities than to those who want to keep the Caste System. This system will not improve the prospect of Democracy in India but put Democracy in greater jeopardy.

The subject assigned to me is, 'What are the prospects of democracy in India?' Most Indians speak with great pride as though their country was already a democracy. The foreigners also, when they sit at a dinner table to do diplomatic honour to India, speak of the Great Indian Prime Minister and the Great Indian Democracy.

From this, it is held without waiting to argue that where there is a Republic, there must be democracy. It is also supposed that where there is Parliament which is elected by the people on adult suffrage and the laws are made by the People's Representatives in Parliament elected after every few years, there is democracy. In other words, democracy is understood to be a political instrument and where this political instrument exists, there is democracy.

Is there democracy in India or is there no democracy in India? What is the truth? No positive answer can be given unless the confusion caused by equating democracy with Republic and by equating democracy with Parliamentary Government is removed.

Democracy is quite different from a Republic as well as from Parliamentary Government. The roots of democracy lie not in the form of Government, Parliamentary or otherwise. A democracy is more than a form of Government. It is primarily a mode of associated living. The roots of Democracy are to be searched in the social relationship, in the terms of associated' life between the people who form a society.

What does the word 'Society' connote? To put it briefly when we speak of 'Society,' we conceive of it as one by its very nature. The qualities which accompany this unity are praiseworthy community of purpose and desire for welfare, loyalty to public ends and mutuality of sympathy and co-operation.

Are these ideals to be found in Indian Society? The Indian Society does not consist of individuals. It consists of an innumerable collection of castes which are exclusive in their life and have no common experience to share and have no bond of sympathy. Given this fact it is not necessary to argue the point. The existence of the Caste System is a standing denial of the existence of those ideals of society and therefore of democracy.

Indian Society is so imbedded in the Caste System that every thing is organized on the basis of caste. Enter Indian Society and you can see caste in its glaring form. An Indian cannot eat or marry with an Indian simply because he or she does not belong to his or her caste. An Indian cannot touch an Indian because he or she does not belong to his or her caste. Go and enter politics and you can see caste reflected therein. How does an Indian vote in an election? He votes for a candidate who belongs to his own caste and no other. Even the Indian Congress exploits the Caste System for election purpose as no other political party in India does. Examine the lists of its candidates in relation to the social composition of the constituencies and it will be found that the candidate belongs to the caste which is the largest one in that constituency.

The Congress, as a matter of fact, is upholding the Caste System against which it is out wordily raising an outcry against the existence of caste.

Go into the field of industry. What will you find? You will find that all the topmost men drawing the highest salary belong to the caste of the particular industrialist who owns the industry. The rest hang on for life on the lowest rungs of the ladder on a pittance. Go into the field of commerce and you will see the same picture. The whole commercial house is one/camp of one caste, with no entry board on the door for others.

Go into the field of charity. With one or two exceptions all charity in India is communal. If a Parsi dies, he leaves his money for Parsis. If a Jain dies, he leaves his money for Jains. If a Marwadi dies, he leaves his money for Marwadis. If a Brahmin dies, he leaves his money for Brahmins. Thus, there is no room for the downtrodden and the outcastes in politics, in industry, in commerce, and in education.

There are other special features of the Caste System which have their evil effects and which militate against Democracy. One such special feature of the Caste System lies in its being accompanied by what is called 'Graded Inequality'. Castes are not equal in their status. They are standing one above another. They are jealous of one another. It is an ascending scale of hatred and descending scale of contempt. This feature of the Caste System has most pernicious consequences. It destroys willing and helpful co-operation.

Caste and class differ in the fact that in the Class System there is no complete isolation as there is in the Caste System. This is the second evil effect in the Caste System accompanied by inequality. This manifests itself in the fact that the stimulus and response between two castes is only one-sided. The higher caste act in one recognized way and the lower caste must respond in one established way. It means that when there is no equitable opportunity to receive the stimulus from and to return the response from different caste, the result is that the influences which educate some into masters, educate others into slaves. The experience of each party loses its meaning when the free interchange of varying modes of life experience is arrested. It results into a separation of society, into a privileged and a subject class. Such a separation prevents social endosmosis.

There is a third characteristic of the Caste System which depicts the evils thereof which cuts at the very roots of democracy. It is that one caste is bound to one occupation. Society is no doubt stably organized when each individual is doing that for which he has aptitude by nature in such a way as to be useful to others; and that it is the business of society to discover these aptitudes and progressively to train them for social use. But there is in a man an indefinite pluralities of capacities and activities which may characterize an individual. A society to be democratic should open a way to use all the capacities of the individual. Stratification is stunting of the growth of the individual and deliberate stunting is a deliberate denial of democracy.

How to put an end to the Caste System? The first obstacle lies in the system of graded inequality which is the soul of the Caste System. Where people are divided into two classes, higher and lower, it is easier for the lower to combine to fight the higher, for there is no single lower class. The class consists of lower and lowerer. The lower cannot combine with the lowerer. For the lower is afraid that if he succeeds in raising the lowerer, he may well himself lose the high position given to him and his caste.

The second obstacle is that, the Indian Society is disabled by unity in action by not being able to know what is its common good. Plato has said that the organization of society depends ultimately upon knowledge of the end of existence. If we do not know its end, if we do not know its good, we shall be at the mercy of accident and caprice. Unless we know the good of the end, we have no criterion for rationally deciding what the possibilities are which we should promote. Question is, can the Indian Society in its caste-bound state achieve what is the ultimate question? We come upon the most insuperable obstacle that such knowledge is not possible save in a just and harmonious social order. Can there be a harmonious Social Order under the Caste System? Everywhere the mind of the Indians is distracted and misled by false valuations and false perspectives. A disorganized and factional society sets up number of different models and standards. Under such conditions it is impossible for individual Indian to reach consistency of mind on the question of caste.

Can education destroy caste? The answer is 'Yes' as well as 'No'. If education is given as it is to-day, education can have no effect on caste. It will remain as it will be. The glaring example of it is the Brahmin Caste. Cent percent of it is educated, nay, majority of it is highly educated. Yet not one Brahmin has shown himself to be against caste. In fact an educated person belonging to the higher caste is more interested after his education to retain the Caste System than when he was not educated. For education gives him an additional interest in the retention of the Caste System namely by opening additional opportunity of getting a bigger job.

From this point of view, education is not helpful as means to dissolve caste. So far is the negative side of education. But education may be solvent if it is applied to the lower strata of the Indian Society. It would raise their spirit of rebellion. In their present state of ignorance they are the supporters of the Caste System. Once their eyes are opened they will be ready to fight the Caste System.

The fault of the present policy is that though education is being given on a larger scale, it is not given to the right strata of Indian Society. If you give education to that strata of Indian Society which has a vested interest in maintaining the Caste System for the advantages it gives them, then the Caste System will be strengthened. On the other hand, if you give education to the lowest strata of Indian Society which is interested in blowing up the Caste System, the Caste System will be blown up. At the moment the indiscriminate help given to education by the Indian Government and American Foundation is going to strengthen the Caste System. To make rich richer and poor poorer is not the way to abolish poverty. The same is true of using education as a means to end the Caste System. To give education to those who want to keep up the Caste System is not to improve the prospect of Democracy in India but to put our Democracy in India in greater jeopardy.

23 Brahma Is Not Dharma. What Good Is Brahma? (Undated)

A BRIEF SKETCH ABOUT THE DOCUMENT

Largely, there were some principles which defined democracy. However, Ambedkar opined that there was no consensus on what constitutes democracy. Invoking the Hindus' conception of Brahma, he proposed that to support Democracy just for the reason that we all are children of God remains a very weak foundation for Democracy. Nevertheless, to recognize and realize that you and I are parts of the same cosmic principle leaves space for no other theory of associated life except democracy, as it does not merely preach Democracy but makes democracy an obligation for each and everyone. The following chapter, in this regard, is from BAWS, Volume 4, 1987 (281–7).

There are various forms of Government known to history—Monarchy, Aristocracy and Democracy to which may be added Dictatorship.

The most prevalent form of Government at the present time is Democracy. There is however no unanimity as to what constitutes Democracy. When one examines the que one finds that there are two views about it. One view is that Democracy is a form of Government. According to this view where the Government is chosen by the people that is where Government is a representative Government there is Democracy. According to this view Democracy is just synonymous with Representative Government which means adult suffrage and periodical elections.

According to another view a democracy is more than a form of Government. It is a form of the organization of Society. There are two essential conditions which characterize a democratically constituted society. First is the absence of stratification of society into classes. The Second is a social habit on the part of individuals and groups which is ready for continuous readjustment or recognition of reciprocity of interests. As to the first there can be no doubt that it is the most essential condition of Democracy. As Prof. Dewey[1] has observed: "The second condition is equally necessary for a democratically constituted society". The results of this lack of reciprocity of interests among groups and individuals produce anti-democratic results which have been well described by Prof. Dewey[2] when he says:

Of the two views about democracy there is no doubt that the first one is very superficial if not erroneous. There cannot be democratic Government unless the society for which it functions is democratic in its form and structure. Those who hold that democracy need be no more than a mere matter of elections seem to make three mistakes.

One mistake they make is to believe that Government is something which is quite distinct and separate from society. As a matter of fact Government is not something which is distinct and separate from Society. Government is one of the many institutions which Society rears and to which it assigns the function of carrying out some of the duties which are necessary for collective social life.

The Second mistake they make lies in their failure to realize that a Government is to reflect the ultimate purposes, aims, objects and wishes of society and this can happen only where the society in which the Government is rooted is democratic. If society is not democratic, Government can never be. Where society is divided into two classes governing and the governed the Government is bound to be the Government of the governing class.

The third mistake they make is to forget that whether Government would be good or bad democratic or undemocratic depends to a large extent up on the instrumentalities particularly the Civil Service on which everywhere Government has to depend for administering the Law. It all depends upon the social milieu in which civil servants are nurtured. If the social milieu is undemocratic the Government is bound to be undemocratic.

There is one other mistake which is responsible for the view that for democracy to function it is enough to have a democratic form of

Government. To realize this mistake it is necessary to have some idea of what is meant by good Government.

Good Government means good laws and good administration. This is the essence of good Government. Nothing else can be. Now there cannot be good Government in this sense if those who are invested with ruling power seek the advantage of their own class instead of the advantage of the whole people or of those who are downtrodden.

Whether the Democratic form of Government will result in good will depend upon the disposition of the individuals composing society. If the mental disposition of the individuals is democratic then the democratic form of Government can be expected to result in good Government. If not, democratic form of Government may easily become a dangerous form of Government. If the individuals in a society are separated into classes and the classes are isolated from one another and each individual feels that his loyalty to his class must come before his loyalty to everything else and living in class compartments he becomes class conscious bound to place the interests of his class above the interests of others, uses his authority to pervert law and justice to promote the interests, of his class and for this purpose practices systematically discrimination against persons who do not belong to his caste in every sphere of life what can a democratic Government do. In a Society where classes clash and are charged with anti-social feelings and spirit of aggressiveness, the Government can hardly discharge its task of governing with justice and fairplay. In such a society, Government even though it may in form be a government of the people and by the people it can never be a Government for the people. It will be a Government by a class for a class. A Government for the people can be *had* only where the attitude of each individual is democratic which means that each individual is prepared to treat every other individual as his equal and is prepared to give him the same liberty which he claims for himself. This democratic attitude of mind is the result of socialization of the individual in a democratic society. Democratic society is therefore a prerequisite of a democratic Government. Democratic Governments have toppled down in largely due to the fact that the society for which they were set up was not democratic.

Unfortunately to what extent the task of good Government depends upon the mental and moral disposition of its subjects has seldom been realized. Democracy is more than a political machine. It is even more than a social system. It is an attitude of mind or a philosophy of life.

Some equate Democracy with equality and liberty. Equality and liberty are no doubt the deepest concern of Democracy. But the more important question is what sustains equality and liberty? Some would say that it is the law of the state which sustains equality and liberty. This is not a true answer. What sustains equality and liberty is fellow-felling. What the French Revolutionists called fraternity. The word fraternity is not an adequate expression. The proper term is what the Buddha called, Maitree. Without Fraternity Liberty would destroy equality and equality would destroy liberty. If in Democracy liberty does not destroy equality and equality does not destroy liberty, it is because at the basis of both there is fraternity. Fraternity is therefore the root of Democracy.

The foregoing discussion is merely a preliminary to the main question. That question is—wherein lie the roots of fraternity without which Democracy is not possible? Beyond dispute, it has its origin in Religion. In examining the possibilities of the origin of Democracy or its functioning successfully one must go to the Religion of the people and ask—does it teach fraternity or does it not? If it does, the chances for a democratic Government are great. If it does not, the chances are poor. Of course other factors may affect the possibilities. But if fraternity is not there, there is nothing to build democracy on. Why did Democracy not grow in India? That is the main question. The answer is quite simple. The Hindu Religion does not teach fraternity. Instead it teaches division of society into classes or varnas and the maintenance of separate class consciousness. In such a system where is the room for Democracy?

The Hindu social system is undemocratic not by accident. It is designed to be undemocratic. Its division of society into *varnas* and castes, and of castes and outcastes are not theories but are decrees. They are all barricades raised against democracy.

From this it would appear that the doctrine of fraternity was unknown to the Hindu Religious and Philosophic thought. But such a conclusion would not be warranted by the facts of history. The Hindu Religious and Philosophic thought gave rise to an idea which had greater potentialities for producing social democracy *than* the idea of fraternity. It is the doctrine of Brahmaism.

It would not be surprising if someone asked what is this Brahmaism? It is something new even to Hindus. The Hindus are familiar with Vedanta. They are familiar with Brahmanism. But they are certainly not familiar with Brahmaism. Before proceeding further a few words of explanation are necessary.

There are three strands in the philosophic and religious thought of the Hindus. They may be designated as (1) *Brahmaism* (2) *Vedanta* and (3) *Brahmanism*. Although they are correlated they stand for three different and distinct ideologies.

The essence of Brahmaism is summed up in a dogma which is stated in three different forms. They are—(i) *Sarvam Khalvidam Brahma*—All this is Brahma, (ii) *Aham Brahmasmi*—Atmana (Self) is the same as Brahma. Therefore I am Brahma, (iii) *Tattvamasi*—Atmana (Self) is the same as Brahma.Therefore thou art also Brahma. I have borrowed this word from Prof. Hopkin's—*The Epics of India*.

They are called Mahavakyas which means Great Sayings and they sum up the essence of Brahmaism.

The following are the dogmas which sum up the teachings of Vedant—I Brahma is the only reality. II The world is maya or unreal. III Jiva and Brahma are—

(i) according to one school identical;

(ii) according to another not identical but are elements of him and not separate from him;

(iii) according to the third school they are distinct and separate. The creed of *Bramhanism* may be summed up in the following dogmas—

    (i) Belief in the chaturvarna.

    (ii) Sanctity and infallibility of the Vedas.

    (iii) Sacrifices to Gods the only way to salvation.

Most people know the distinction between the Vedanta and Brahmanism and the points of controversy between them. But very few people know the distinction between Brahmaism and Vedanta. Even Hindus are not aware of the doctrine of Brahmaism and the distinction between it and Vedanta. But the distinction is obvious. While Brahmaism and Vedanta agree that Atman is the same as Brahma. But the two differ in that Brahmaism does not treat the world as unreal, Vedanta does. This is the fundamental difference between the two.

The essence of Brahmaism is that the world is real and the reality behind the world is Brahma. Everything therefore is of the essence of Brahma.

There are two criticisms which have been levelled against Brahmaism. It is said that Brahmaism is piece of impudence. For a man to say 'I am Brahma' is a kind of arrogance. The other criticism levelled against

Brahmaism is the inability of man to know Brahma. 'I am Brahma' may appear to be impudence. But it can also be an assertion of one's own worth. In a world where humanity suffers so much from an inferiority complex such an assertion on the part of man is to be welcomed. Democracy demands that each individual shall have every opportunity for realizing its worth. It also requires that each individual shall know that he is as good as everybody else. Those who sneer at *Aham Brahmasmi* (I am Brahma) as an impudent utterance forget the other part of the *Maha Vakya* namely *Tatvamasi* (Thou art also Brahma). If *Aham Brahmasmi* has stood alone without the conjunct of *Tatvamasi* it may not have been possible to sneer at it. But with the conjunct of *Tatvanmsi* the charge of selfish arrogance cannot stand against Brahmaism.

It may well be that Brahma is unknowable. But all the same this theory of Brahma has certain social implications which have a tremendous value as a foundation for Democracy. If all persons are parts of Brahma then all are equal and all must enjoy the same liberty which is what Democracy means. Looked at from this point of view Brahma may be unknowable. But there cannot be slightest doubt that no doctrine could furnish a stronger foundation for Democracy than the doctrine of Brahma.

To support Democracy because we are all children of God is a very weak foundation for Democracy to rest on. That is why Democracy is so shaky wherever it made to rest on such a foundation. But to recognize and realize that you and I are parts of the same cosmic principle leaves room for no other theory of associated life except democracy. It does not merely preach Democracy. It makes democracy an obligation of one and all.

Western students of Democracy have spread the belief that Democracy has stemmed either from Christianity or from Plato and that there is no other source of inspiration for democracy. If they had known that India too had developed the doctrine of Brahmaism which furnishes a better foundation for Democracy they would not have been so dogmatic. India too must be admitted to have a contribution towards a theoretical foundation for Democracy.

The question is what happened to this doctrine of Brahmaism? It is quite obvious that Brahmaism had no social effects. It was not made the basis of Dharma. When asked why this happened the answer is that Brahmaism is only philosophy, as though philosophy arises not out of social life but out of nothing and for nothing. Philosophy is no purely theoretic matter. It has practical potentialities. Philosophy has its roots in the problems of life and whatever theories philosophy propounds must return to society as instruments of re-constructing society. It is not enough to know. Those who know must endeavour to fulfill.

Why then Brahmaism failed to produce a new society? This is a great riddle. It is not that the Brahmins did not recognize the doctrine of Brahmaism. They did. But they did not ask how they could support inequality between the Brahmin and the Shudra, between man and woman, between casteman and outcaste? But they did not. The result is that we have on the one hand the most democratic principle of Brahmaism and on the other hand a society infested with castes, sub-outcastes, primitive tribes and criminal tribes. Can there be a greater dilemma than this? What is more ridiculous is the teaching of the Great Shankaracharya. For it was this Shankarcharya who taught that there is Brahma and this Brahma is real and that it pervades all and at the same time upheld all the inequities of the Brahmanic society. Only a lunatic could be happy with being the propounder of two such contradictions. Truly as the Brahmin is like a cow, he can eat anything and everything as the cow does and remain a Brahmin.

Notes

1. Quotation referred to by the author is not recorded in the original manuscript from 'Democracy and Education', by Dewey p. 98.
2. Quotation from 'Democracy and Education' of page 99 referred to by the author is not recorded in the original MS.

Index

About the Editors

Christophe Jaffrelot is senior research fellow at CERI-Sciences Po/CNRS, Paris, France. His books include *The Hindu Nationalist Movement* (1996), *Dr Ambedkar and Untouchability* (2004), and *Religion, Caste, and Politics in India* (2010).

Narender Kumar is professor, Centre for Political Studies, Jawaharlal Nehru University, New Delhi, India. His academic interests include public policy and political institutions, with special reference to inequalities and marginalization.